Philip Osment

The Dear ... **ays,**

The Dearly Beloved: '1 ... ...ows one of the classic patterns of the story-type. Local boy made good comes back to visit his mother in a small West Country town where his presence brings home to his old friends who stayed put there the various ways in which their lives have failed ... There should be a moratorium on the word "Chekhovian", but you can't but be reminded of Chekhov at times.' *Independent*

What I Did in the Holidays: 'Philip Osment's wonderfully dense and detailed study of fraught farm life in rurally non-swinging Britain ... Osment's characters are beautifully nuanced, neither demonised nor idolised ... The play charts a painfully funny path through the casual, everyday cruelties inflicted by the thoughtless young and selfish old ... Poignant, gently powerful and deftly, tragicomically funny, Osment's play is a delight.' *Evening Standard*
'Osment's poignant new work ... proves fresh. It is funny and delicate even as it delves painfully into suppressed attractions.' *The Times*

Flesh and Blood: 'Brilliant at evoking the nostalgia of Devon country life in a strange, recidivist family – the clock ticks, you can smell the antimacassars – and in the elision between outdoor lust and indoor stuffiness.' *Observer*
'A wry, observant, gripping piece.' *The Times*

Philip Osment was brought up on a farm in North Devon and read Modern Languages at Keble College, Oxford. He trained as an actor and acted with leading alternative theatre companies, including Gay Sweatshop, The Half Moon and Shared Experience. He has also worked as a director and until 1989 was one of the artistic directors of Gay Sweatshop. More recently he directed plays for two young people's theatre companies, Theatre Centre and Red Ladder. As a writer, his plays include *Telling Tales* (1982), *The Island's Mine* (1988) and *The Undertaking* (1996) for Gay Sweatshop; *Who's Breaking?* (1989) and *Sleeping Dogs* (1993) for Red Ladder; *Listen* (1990) for Theatre Centre. His trilogy of 'Devon Plays' was commissioned by Mike Alfreds and produced by Cambridge Theatre Company (Method and Madness): *The Dearly Beloved* (toured, then Hampstead The... ...callan Writers Guild Award for ... ...ys* (toured, then Drill Hall, Lond... ...1995); and *Flesh and Blood* (toure...

Methuen World Classics and
Methuen Contemporary Dramatists

Aeschylus (two volumes)
Jean Anouilh
John Arden (two volumes)
Arden & D'Arcy
Aristophanes (two volumes)
Aristophanes & Menander
Peter Barnes (three volumes)
Sebastian Barry
Brendan Behan
Aphra Behn
Edward Bond (five volumes)
Bertolt Brecht (six volumes)
Howard Brenton (two volumes)
Büchner
Bulgakov
Calderón
Jim Cartwright
Anton Chekhov
Caryl Churchill
   (two volumes)
Noël Coward (five volumes)
Sarah Daniels (two volumes)
Eduardo De Filippo
David Edgar (three volumes)
Euripides (three volumes)
Dario Fo (two volumes)
Michael Frayn (two volumes)
Max Frisch
Gorky
Harley Granville Barker
   (two volumes)
Peter Handke
Henrik Ibsen (six volumes)
Terry Johnson
Bernard-Marie Koltès
Lorca (three volumes)

David Mamet (three volumes)
Marivaux
Mustapha Matura
David Mercer (two volumes)
Arthur Miller (five volumes)
Anthony Minghella
   (two volumes)
Molière
Tom Murphy (four volumes)
Musset
Peter Nichols (two volumes)
Clifford Odets
Joe Orton
Philip Osment
Louise Page
A. W. Pinero
Luigi Pirandello
Stephen Poliakoff
   (two volumes)
Terence Rattigan
Christina Reid
Philip Ridley
Willy Russell
Ntozake Shange
Sam Shepard (two volumes)
Sophocles (two volumes)
Wole Soyinka
David Storey (two volumes)
August Strindberg
   (three volumes)
J. M. Synge
Sue Townsend
Ramón del Valle-Inclán
Frank Wedekind
Michael Wilcox
Oscar Wilde

PHILIP OSMENT

Plays: 1

The Dearly Beloved
What I Did in the Holidays
Flesh and Blood

introduced by the author
with a preface by Mike Alfreds

Methuen Drama

METHUEN CONTEMPORARY DRAMATISTS

This collection first published in Great Britain in 1997
by Methuen Drama
an imprint of Reed International Books Ltd
Michelin House, 81 Fulham Road, London SW3 6RB
and Auckland, Melbourne, Singapore and Toronto
and distributed in the United States of America
by Heinemann, a division of Reed Elsevier Inc.
361 Hanover Street, Portsmouth, New Hampshire NH 03801 3959

The Dearly Beloved was first published in Great Britain in 1993 by Samuel
French Ltd. Revised for this edition 1997. Copyright © 1993, 1997 by Philip
Osment

What I Did in the Holidays was first published in Great Britain in 1995 by
Samuel French Ltd. Revised for this edition 1997. Copyright © 1995, 1997
by Philip Osment

Flesh and Blood was first published in Great Britain in 1996 by Methuen
Drama in association with Method and Madness. Revised for this edition
1997. Copyright © 1996, 1997 by Philip Osment

Introduction and collection copyright © 1997 by Philip Osment
Preface copyright © 1997 by Mike Alfreds

The authors have asserted their moral rights

ISBN 0-413-71070-X

A CIP catalogue record for this book is available from the British Library

Typeset by Wilmaset Ltd, Birkenhead, Wirral
Printed in Great Britain by Cox & Wyman Ltd, Reading, Berks

The extract from 'The Highwayman' by Alfred Noyes is reproduced by kind
permission of John Murray (Publishers) Ltd.

'Summer Holiday' words and music by Bruce Welch and Brian Bennett ©
1963, reproduced by permission of EMI Music Publishing Ltd trading as
Elstree Music, London WC2H OEA.

Caution
All rights in these plays are strictly reserved and application for performance
etc. should be made to the author's agent: Michael Imison Playwrights Ltd,
28 Almeida Street, London N1 1TD. No performance may be given unless a
licence has been obtained.

With regard to the performance of part of the lyrics from 'Summer Holiday',
a PRS licence must be obtained from the Performing Right Society Ltd, 29–
33 Berners Street, London W1P 4AA; tel. 0171 580 5544.

Contents

Philip Osment:
A Chronology

1982 *Telling Tales* originally performed at the Oval House, London. Subsequently toured by Gay Sweatshop.

1988 *This Island's Mine* commissioned and toured by Gay Sweatshop.

1989 *Who's Breaking?* commissioned and toured by Red Ladder.

1990 *Listen* commissioned and toured by Theatre Centre.

1993 *Sleeping Dogs* commissioned and toured by Red Ladder.
The Dearly Beloved commissioned by Mike Alfreds and toured by Cambridge Theatre Company; won the 1993 Macallan Writers Guild Award for Best Regional Play.

1995 *What I Did in the Holidays* commissioned by Mike Alfreds, toured by Cambridge Theatre Company and produced at the Drill Hall, London; nominated for the 1995 Macallan Writers Guild Award for Best Regional Play.

1996 *The Undertaking* commissioned and toured by Gay Sweatshop.
Flesh and Blood commissioned by Mike Alfreds, toured by Method and Madness (Cambridge Theatre Company) and produced at the Lyric Theatre, Hammersmith.

Preface

In the early eighties, I went to Oval House to see Philip Osment perform a solo piece he had written for himself. At this time Philip was an actor and had performed in three productions of mine. The play, his first, was called *Telling Tales* and I was flattered to see that in it he had incorporated some story-telling and mask techniques from our work together. But the strongest qualities in the performance belonged entirely to him. All that I've come to recognise as the distinctive hallmarks of his talent were already securely in place. It is something of a shock to have your perception of a person radically changed within a few moments. I knew him as a fine actor. Here was someone who wrote masterfully.

Initially, the most striking thing was his autobiographical bravery. I had the sense of intimate personal events being portrayed with total honesty and I experienced what is a rarity for me, such confidence in the integrity of the performance that I unreservedly gave myself up to it. His truthfulness as an actor should have led me to expect no less. Of course, he had transmuted the biographical elements of place, family, and sexuality into fiction. The structure of the piece – the interweaving of a double narrative – and the form in which he had chosen to perform it were integrated into a richly satisfying unity. Everything I've subsequently read or seen of his has had this combination of innate honesty and meticulous craftsmanship. When eventually I came to commission what turned out to be this trilogy – incidentally, none of the commissions ended up being what we had initially talked about! – I felt utterly confident that whatever he gave me would be true and utterly performable. That confidence hasn't been betrayed. These three plays are clearly plays he had to write and in every sense they are courageously authentic.

I want to go into some detail about his craftsmanship, because I find myself being endlessly irritated by plays where conventions are arbitrarily established and then ignored, where matters of form and organisation seem to be decided by momentary whim. The laconic surface of Philip's texts provides the art that hides art; beneath the deceptive simplicity lies rigorous structure. The relative length of scenes, the balance of scenes in the different sections of a play, the interplay of locations (inside and outside), all have their purpose. The long scene in the second half of *Flesh and Blood*, for example, poignantly counterpoints the long Christmas scene of the first.

On first reading, some people who should know better declared that nothing much happens in these plays. They couldn't be more wrong. They teem with action and there is a vital subtext to be plumbed. The dialogue may at times appear mundane, but I warn anyone who decides to produce his work not to ignore investigating those 'oh's and 'mmm's and 'yeah's! ... The economy of means makes almost every phrase of dialogue serve more than one purpose. Objects and references established in early scenes frequently turn up later to dramatic and thematic purpose. Watch the journey of the engagement ring through *Flesh and Blood* or of the drawing in *The Dearly Beloved*. Mention of a trip to India early in this play expands into a slide-show in which reaction to the slides reveals festering resentments in all the characters. In *What I Did in the Holidays* an oil lamp and a generator do not merely tell us the socio-economic position of the characters, they also, literally and figuratively, fuel a network of relationships. A dog charts the decline of a relationship, a heifer, the decline of a farm, the building of a well, failed aspirations. Everything is *used*; nothing is there for its own effect. Everything is motivated by character and justified by convention. The proof of all this stringency is that each time we started rehearsing – always the third draft – there was rarely much to be re-written. I would also point you to his use of music and imagery, his humour (never imposed on but created through the characters – i.e. no cheap gags), his skill in orchestrating a stageful of characters over long periods of stage time ...

Craftsmanship alone does not make a good play. It provides the appropriate form for the expression of its content. In good work, as here, the two are indivisible and the technique invisible. The craftsmanship here supports a serious vision of life by a writer who is unhectoringly political. He presents us with people who find it hard to change. His stories offer them possibilities of freedom and growth. The action is how they respond to these opportunities. In the trilogy change is, actually and symbolically, connected with escape from the claustrophobia of country life. *The Dearly Beloved* is about someone who left home and returns, *What I Did in the Holidays* about someone who *will* leave home, *Flesh and Blood* about those who can't.

One of Philip's great abilities (after all, he's an actor) is to imagine his characters *deeply*. In far too many plays words and jokes are shoved into the mouths of supposedly different characters who all end up sounding like – well – the playwright! Subjectively he is able to live their thoughts and feelings, objectively he sees and hears them in the round. They are not judged but depicted for us with all their intelligence and banality, their many griefs and small pleasures, their clichés and aspirations. He creates 'ordinary' people who are given the right to be complex and contradictory, whose human variability can elicit our sympathy, dislike and amusement all in the same breath. The audience is also given the right – to think and decide for themselves.

Working with Philip on these plays over the last four years has been one of my happiest experiences. I believe our collaboration has been exemplary. Having acted with me, Philip wrote the plays bearing in mind how I rehearsed. That in itself has made them precious gifts a director rarely gets given. But more than this, what has been so nourishing for me and all the actors who vividly and caringly created his people is a basic concern for human beings which permeates his writing and extends into the atmosphere of the rehearsal room. I think it is hard for any of us to avoid recognising some aspect of ourselves in his world. His plays are rooted in the reality of family life but aspire to a sort of poetry.

Mike Alfreds
October 1996

Introduction

I came to writing through acting: my first play, *Telling Tales*, was a solo show, created after I had just performed in three plays which Mike Alfreds had directed for Shared Experience. It used techniques borrowed from two of the productions but the play that had the most profound effect on my writing was the third one, *The Seagull*. This is, I know, a dangerous admission because it would seem that I am saying that my plays are deliberately Chekhovian, an adjective which sometimes seems debased by over-use. And of course such an admission invites the critic to point out where my own work falls short. However, through watching *The Seagull* in rehearsal and seeing how Mike allowed the actors to find the play, I learnt something about what is dramatic in ordinary life which left a deep impression.

It was 1981 in a church hall in North London. I was Konstantin and I remember watching the scene in the last act where the other characters are playing lotto. Arkadina suddenly stops and looks at her elderly brother. 'Petroosha, are you bored?' she asks. There is a pause. Then she says, 'He's asleep.' A seemingly banal moment.

Mike allows the actors gradually to build up a picture of their characters. We are detectives looking for evidence in the script and every day can bring a new insight. He also asks you to allow your performance constantly to change in relation to what the other actors are giving you. No two performances can ever be exactly the same. He says that we're not reheating yesterday's leftovers but serving the audience a fresh meal every night. This means that the performances have the feel of an improvisation even though the words remain exactly the same.

So back to that banal moment; all the way through the play, Sorin (Petroosha), the elderly brother, has been complaining about his health and his fear of death. We were nearing the end of rehearsals and Gillian Barge, who was playing Arkadina, suddenly asked the question 'Petroosha, are you bored?' with a level of anxiety that she had not had before. The other actors, used to responding to any new impulse, picked up on her anxiety and looked at the old man in alarm. As the audience, we saw that during that pause, they were considering the fact that sometime soon the old man was going to die – maybe he had just died. It was a heightened moment that made your hair stand on end. And then they realised that he was just asleep and their relief was tangible. They even laughed in embarrassment. The effect was comic and tragic at the same time and the humanity and vulnerability of the characters was manifest. This banal moment was suddenly illuminated by the actors' imagination and as the audience we understood the subtext. (The irony is, of course, that it is not old Sorin but young Konstantin who is about to die.) Reading the play you would very likely miss the significance of the pause but under Mike's guidance the actors were able to reveal Chekhov's genius.

Inspiring stuff indeed. It made me realise how a play can pull you emotionally in two different directions at the same time; how a group of actors working together can create a magic that no director could plan; how a pause can reverberate in your soul.

It was almost ten years later, in 1990, when Mike asked me to write a play for Cambridge Theatre Company. Given my knowledge of his rehearsal techniques, I decided that I wanted to write an ensemble piece with group scenes. The world of *The Dearly Beloved* had been in my head for some time: a small town not unlike the small town near where I grew up; a husband and wife who compete for the attention of a spiritually inclined confidante (Elaine); an elderly mother; a school teacher and her 'friend'; their dog; a character who left and now feels rootless; a scene on the moors where a pretentious conversation is punctured by farts. I had myself just been to India – Alaric's aphorism about our awareness of an experience removing you from that experience is cribbed from Krishnamurti whose books

I had been reading. I suppose I was interested in writing about people who are looking for something more; they feel spiritually impoverished; they have been living in a time of relative peace ('Relative Peace' was an early title for the play) but feel that their lives have not been adventurous, have not engaged with Big Events. In their search for more they inevitably miss and destroy what they already have. When I started writing the play I had all these elements and characters in my head but I did not know what the story was – what was the inciting incident which would set the story going? Obviously it had to be the fact that Alaric returns. But was that enough?

I was tempted at this point to make Alaric gay in order to heighten his difference. The other company that had a profound effect on my work was Gay Sweatshop. Gay Sweatshop and Shared Experience were two strands of the alternative theatre movement of the seventies. Although coming from different starting points there was a consonance in their aims and aesthetic. Shared Experience was based on the idea that for theatre to happen you needed actors in a space with an audience and a story to tell – the shared experience came from that direct relationship with the audience. Gay Sweatshop's concern was to present an accurate reflection of gay people's lives and so stress was laid upon the fact that the actors were themselves gay and were talking about their own lives and about our shared experiences. Without Gay Sweatshop I would never have had the confidence to write about the world in which I grew up and my own perception of that world as a gay person. *Telling Tales* was a highly autobiographical piece which did just that.

But when I came to write *The Dearly Beloved* I had just left Gay Sweatshop and was feeling worn down by the perception of that work as being ghetto theatre and therefore somehow theatrically uninteresting. (The fact is that the company's plays looked out at the world from a gay perspective, were often theatrically innovative, and played to a wide audience but that's another story.) Rightly or wrongly I didn't want *The Dearly Beloved* to be labelled 'a gay play', so Alaric's sexuality was not an issue and the tension caused by his return centred around his perceived success in television, his sophisticated London life, his facility with trendy ideas.

As I write this, I am inevitably reminded of early criticisms of the play. The script was sent to several theatres who were possible bookers. Some readers felt that nothing seemed to happen. One wrote in a report: 'There is little plot, just a series of mundane conversations.' In writing the play I always had in my mind Mike's method of working with actors, so I refrained from stage directions that explained what was going on – for example with characters who were on stage but not speaking – and also from putting in speeches where the characters explained themselves. Perhaps if I hadn't been so restrained it might have made the play easier to read, but it would have given the actors less room to manoeuvre and less to discover.

Then there is the matter of the invisible dog which some saw as an anomaly in a realistic play. I enjoy watching actors making the audience see something which isn't there and so I had no problem with the concept. Maybe it's a matter of taste.

A thornier problem is posed by the car accident. Matt's death, and Alaric's culpability in it, crept up on me. Some people have been of the opinion that the death is melodramatic and a mistake. I don't know if that's right. All I can say is that I was concerned to show the characters having to deal with the reality of something that big – something which makes them come to their senses and recognise the folly of their behaviour, which offers them the possibility of change and growth. Matt's death and the appearance of the deer are linked for me – they are part of a daemonic element which liberates and destroys at the same time.

Once *The Dearly Beloved* had opened, Mike and I started talking about a second commission. I felt that I wanted to go deeper into the Devon countryside and out onto the land. While I was growing up there, one would hear of violent suicides and shootings which would be reported in the local newspaper or might even involve our neighbours. I was fascinated by the way people became trapped by their land and their family history to such an extent. I suppose my fascination arose from the claustrophobia which being brought up on a farm engendered. I knew that I would have to leave but feared that I might not manage it.

I had been aware of a particularly dramatic case which took place on a farm near Winkleigh in the seventies. Two brothers and a sister were found shot. They had farmed in isolation, refusing to modernise, and there was a story of an engagement which the younger brother had been forced by the other two to give up. When, many years later, they could no longer run the farm, they were unable to make the decision to sell.

For this second Cambridge Theatre Company commission I decided to try to write this story. But when I reached the point where the younger brother took the engagement ring back, I gave up. I just found it too depressing. I showed it to Mike in that half-written form. He was particularly interested in the way the sister behaved – her duplicity and unwillingness to commit herself to either brother.

But I abandoned the play and decided to write a story much closer to home, which was eventually to become *What I Did in the Holidays*. I wanted to return to my own childhood and write something inspired by that. Our farm was on the main road and people would often stop and ask to camp in our field. These people would offer a glimpse into another world. I was the youngest of a large family, there was a big gap between me and my next brother and so I was, in some ways, in a similar position to Morley – happy to have new companions and influences. There was always a sadness as well when they left. So the hitchhikers offer a hope which the other story of the trapped siblings couldn't have. At the same time I wanted my story to suggest the possibility of escape.

It is for this reason that *What I Did in the Holidays* and *Flesh and Blood* share some motifs. Having abandoned the latter I had no qualms about filching aspects of the character of Rose for Eileen or about using the engagement ring in a similar way.

There is much in *What I Did in the Holidays* that is autobiographical. But there is also much poetic licence. I have tailored characters to the needs of the story and presented only the facets that suited my purpose. There is perhaps a dubious morality to this. Many of the characters do or say things that actual people have said or done but their personality has been altered in order to make the story work. So this family is like my family and yet is not my family.

The play opened in Ipswich at the Wolsey Theatre who had co-commissioned it. What was interesting for me, watching it with that audience, was that they were unsure about which character they were supposed to like and trust. Morley seemed like a good bet until he started touching Andy in Scene Two. Eileen was sympathetic one moment and cruel the next. My intention was to show how the cruelty came out of hurt – the slap you receive makes you snap at the next person you come across. Some audiences found this quite disturbing and were shocked by the relationships in the play. The Wolsey Theatre received several letters on the subject. One man wrote: 'I am a senior police officer, quite used to obscenities in every form, and when I pay money to be entertained I prefer to escape from the cancer that afflicts this country in respect of foul language and blatant exhibitions of obscenity.' However the general response was very different and it was just that wavering of sympathies which interested the sixth-formers with whom I was working in Suffolk. A few people just didn't recognise the behaviour, whereas others found it totally 'familiar'.

The main problem that the play poses for a director is, of course, casting eleven-year-old Morley, who is in many ways the central character. For the Cambridge Theatre Company production we felt it was important to cast someone who could act the role with understanding and we were extremely lucky in finding a twenty-two-year-old actor who could do just that.

When Mike Alfreds changed the company's name to Method and Madness he also wanted to find a way of working with the same actors over a longer period instead of casting separately for each play. And so for my third commission I did not have the same freedom to allow my story to define the cast. I met the actors when they were already working on *Jude the Obscure*. I went away and decided to write a play about four Oxford University undergraduates based on my own student days.

Two months later that story was going nowhere. One night I happened to watch a Russian documentary about an elderly brother and sister working on a ramshackle farm in the Russian countryside. There was something about the texture of their lives that reminded me of my half-finished play about the trapped siblings. The documentary inspired me to write the second half of *Flesh and Blood* and I suddenly saw that Mike's cast would fit the bill. There were other characters in my original draft of the first half: Shirley's mother, a Polish farm worker, the women who pluck the chickens; but it was easy to concentrate on just those four characters: the three siblings and the fiancée – for the first half at least.

When it came to writing the second half of the play I felt that the actress playing Shirley needed to play a part in the story but was unsure how that would work. I thought I had solved the problem by having her daughter come from Australia to find her father after Shirley's death. However when Mike read it he felt quite strongly that the play would be more powerful if it was Shirley herself who returned. Many weeks later I found a way of allowing this to happen.

My starting point for *The Dearly Beloved* had been the world and the characters – I found out what happened to them by writing the play. With *Flesh and Blood* my starting point was the gunshots and my journey was towards that point. It took me aback when sometimes audiences expressed surprise that the play ends so violently or when a critic said the end was implausible. For me it was the only possible ending. Certainly the audiences at the Northcott Theatre in Exeter took it in their stride and accepted it.

Clearly the play demands a lot from actors in terms of the ageing. But I saw no problem in writing a play with that time span because I enjoy watching actors transform themselves and make audiences suspend their disbelief. (I have however wondered how the play would work with two actors to play each part – one young and one older – with the older actors somehow present in the first half and the younger ones hanging around during the second.) There are more scenes and locations in this play than in the previous two. Mike and Paul Dart, the designer, wisely chose to have a composite set, thus dispensing with the need for scene changes which would have slowed down the action. I was particularly impressed by way the set had both a realistic and a poetic dimension which allowed snow to fall in the parlour and trees made of string to rise out of the kitchen.

When the play opened in Exeter it was like coming home. The company had already performed *Jude the Obscure* and *Private Lives* at the theatre and those audiences returned to see the same actors in this third production. This meant full houses which for a new play on tour was quite remarkable. They seemed to recognise clearly the characters and the situations – it was as if I had written a community play – and many people talked about the characters' resemblance to members of their own families and wanted to tell me similar family stories. This felt like the greatest compliment because the play had stirred up memories and thoughts about their own lives and experiences which they wanted to share. It seems that it is quite unfashionable to write plays set in rural England – one London-based critic was unable to see beyond the Devon dialect which he found comic – but I suppose with these plays I have deliberately set out to show the complexity behind the cliché of the yokel.

For me, plays emerge slowly and it takes several drafts and much agonising before I arrive at a rehearsal text. Every writer needs good friends to talk to when absolutely stuck and despairing; when it seems that you've embarked on a project that is worthless and going nowhere. Mike was always there and the advice of writers Noel Greig and Lin Coghlan has been invaluable at these times. Other people who gave help and feedback were Jenny Topper, Tony McBride, Willie Elliott, Ian Rickson, Martin McCrudden, my sister Maxine Bracher and my mother Honor Osment. Finally, the support of my friend, Nina Ward, has been crucial; she has read each play as I wrote it and was always prepared to talk about the problems to the point that it was like having a collaborator. I feel very fortunate to have such help.

I don't know if I have any more Devon plays in me. For the moment I'm interested in exploring other worlds. But that world of my childhood still has quite a hold over me. And so I won't be too surprised if in trying to write in the future the characters start speaking in Devon dialect.

Philip Osment
October 1996

The Dearly Beloved

Characters

Dulcie Barker, *about seventy years old*
Terry Barker, *her son, in his forties*
Caroline, *late thirties/early forties, married to Barton*
Barton, *Dulcie's nephew, early forties. A veterinarian*
Matt, *mid/late teens, Caroline's and Barton's son*
Margaret, *early forties. Headmistress of a primary school*
Tufty, *in her forties. Margaret's friend. A driver for social services*
Elaine, *late thirties. A primary school teacher*
Alaric Barker, *early forties. Dulcie's son. A freelance television director*

There is also Tufty's dog, Bruno, whom the actors create by their behaviour and responses.

Act One	A Saturday in late August
Act Two	The next day
Act Three	The following Friday
Act Four	Two and a half years later. The Saturday before Christmas

Setting: a small town in the West Country

Time: the present

Note   In the Cambridge Theatre Company production the actors sang rounds during the scene changes between Acts One and Two and between Acts Three and Four. This suggested the life of the choir.

The Dearly Beloved was commissioned, under the sponsorship of IBM, for Cambridge Theatre Company and first performed at the Connaught Theatre, Worthing, on 2 March 1993, and on tour, with the following cast:

Dulcie	Marlene Sidaway
Terry	Sam Cox
Caroline	Sally Knyvette
Barton	John Gillett
Matt	Lucien Taylor
Margaret	Veronica Roberts
Tufty	Annie Hayes
Elaine	Pamela Moiseiwitsch
Alaric	Peter Wight

Directed by Mike Alfreds
Designed by Paul Dart

The first London performance was on 26 May 1993 at the Hampstead Theatre.

Act One

Dulcie's house in a small town in the West Country. A Saturday in late August.

A window leads on to a balcony overlooking the street. Amongst the usual furnishings are a table, chairs, and a telephone.

A low light comes up on **Terry**, *a man in his forties, who stands naked in the middle of the room. He has just had his bath. His hair is wet. He touches it and looks at the water on his hand.*

Dulcie, *his mother, enters with a towel and his clothes. She starts to dress him in a very private ritual, starting with his underpants. She speaks quietly when she needs to but it is as if we are eavesdropping, and not everything she says needs to be heard.* **Dulcie** *sings 'You Are My Sunshine' to herself as she works.*

Dulcie   Lift.

Terry *lifts one leg while* **Dulcie** *pulls the underpants over his foot.*

Dulcie   And the other one.

Terry *lifts the other leg and* **Dulcie** *pulls the underpants over that foot and all the way up.*

Dulcie   And again.

Terry *lifts one leg while* **Dulcie** *puts the trousers over his foot.*

Dulcie   And the other.

Dulcie *puts* **Terry**'s *trousers on for him as she did with his underpants.*

Dulcie   Sit. Arms out.

He sits. She puts on his vest.

And your shirt. Come on.

She puts on his shirt and buttons it up.

Tuck it in.

Terry *tucks in his shirt while* **Dulcie** *attends to his shoes and socks.*

Dulcie   Now your shoes and socks. Lift your foot, then.

She puts the sock and shoe on one foot.

And the other.

She puts on the other shoe and sock. She holds out his cardigan.

Come on. That's right.

He holds out his arms so that she can put on his cardigan. She rubs his hair with the towel, then gets a comb and combs his hair.

What do you want? Tea or pop?

Terry   Yes.

Dulcie   Terry.

Terry   Yes.

Dulcie   Tea or pop?

Terry   Biscuit.

Dulcie   Don't you want a drink?

Terry   Yes.

Dulcie   What do you want then?

Terry   Pop.

Dulcie *exits.*

Terry *brushes his hair into a different style with his hand.*

Dulcie *returns with a biscuit tin and the drink.*

Dulcie   There you are. Don't make a mess.

She gives him a biscuit and then combs his hair again. She goes to the telephone and dials. She listens.

It's that machine again. (*She listens.*) Hallo Alaric, it's your mother. I hate this blooming thing. We were just wondering how you were. Thought you might pop down now you've finished your film. It's carnival night tonight. Got people coming round to watch from the balcony as usual – Barton and Caroline and a few others from the choir. You did say you might come down this weekend so I thought I'd try you before they all arrive – see what you're up to.

Terry Al.

Dulcie Don't think I've got anything else to tell you. Barton's bought Caroline a new washing machine so he's bringing round their old one for me to have. Don't know if I'll use it. Nothing else happening I don't think. Margaret will be here tonight – headmistress now. She's still not married.

Terry *tries to listen to the telephone.*

Dulcie Stop it, Terry. (*Into the telephone.*) Just given him his bath and we've had our tea – nice chop. Remember the butcher's daughter, Elaine? She's a teacher at Margaret's school. Don't think you knew her. Younger than you. Married Harold Smale. He's a mechanic at the garage. Anyway she comes to choir, she'll be here tonight. Now, what was it I wanted to tell you?

Terry *tries to take the phone.*

Dulcie Terry wants to say hallo. (*To* **Terry**.) Quick, it's the answerphone so just say hallo.

Terry *holds the phone and listens.*

Dulcie Say hallo.

Terry Al.

Dulcie Say, 'Hallo, Alaric.'

Terry Al.

She takes the telephone from him.

Dulcie Well, I'd better not run up my bill. Don't know what sort of weather you've had up in London. It's been terrible down here. We're hoping it won't rain tonight. Oh, that's what I was going to tell you. This Elaine I told you about – who comes to choir – well, her daughter is carnival queen. She's a lovely girl. Well, that's it then. Don't think there's anything else. Give my love to Miranda when you see her. All right? Bye. We saw your film about Brazil with the forests and everything. Very good. Well, give us a ring. It's Mum. God bless. Mum. (*She hangs up.*) Blooming answerphone.

Pause.

Terry   Al coming?

Dulcie   No, he's not coming. He's a very busy man.

Terry   When's he coming?

Dulcie   He's busy.

Terry   Soon?

Dulcie   I don't know, Terry. Don't go on about it. Finish your drink.

Terry   Biscuit please.

Dulcie   No. You'll be sick. (*She goes and looks out of the window.*) Lot of people out in the street already.

Terry   Carnival.

Dulcie   That's right. Carnival night tonight. There's some of the town band going past. They'll be late for the start if they don't get up to the car park pretty quick.

Terry   Music.

Dulcie   Yes. The band will be playing. Now is that Barton's car? Looks like it.

Terry *blows an imaginary trumpet.*

Dulcie   That's right. Stop it, Terry, finish your drink. Your friend Tufty will be here before you finish your tea.

Terry   Tufty coming.

Dulcie   Yes, Tufty's coming.

Terry *starts to dance around the room.*

Dulcie   Come and sit down.

Terry   Carnival. (*He tries to go out on to the balcony.*)

Dulcie   No. The carnival's not here yet, Terry. Now come back and sit down. We'll go out on the balcony later.

She leads him back to his seat.

Terry   Later.

The doorbell rings. **Terry** *starts to dance around the room again.*

Tufty.

Dulcie   It's not Tufty. It's Barton. Now come and sit down.

She exits to the front door.

Terry *goes to the biscuit tin and takes a biscuit. The telephone rings. It startles him. He looks at it and takes it off the hook.*

Dulcie (*off*)   No, don't leave it in the hall, Barton. It'll be in the way. Bring it up and put it in the bathroom.

Caroline *enters.*

Caroline   Hallo, Terry.

Dulcie (*off*)   It'll have to stay there until I can get it plumbed in. Careful. Mind the wallpaper, Matt.

Dulcie *enters.*

Have to clear a space for it in the kitchen.

Caroline   I don't know how you've managed without a washing machine all these years.

Dulcie   I've always washed by hand.

Caroline   Living with a vet you need a washing machine.

Barton *enters.*

Caroline   Don't we?

Barton   What?

Caroline   Need a washing machine for your smelly clothes. He comes back from his rounds stinking of pigs and sheep and cows.

Barton   Are you sure you don't want it left on the landing, Aunty? It'll block up the bathroom.

Dulcie   No. It's better in there.

Barton *exits.*

Caroline   I get him to dump everything in the machine.

Dulcie   I used to use a tin bath on the stove.

Caroline   Thank goodness for modern technology.

Dulcie   I'll just put the kettle on.

Dulcie *exits.*

Caroline *takes out her compact and checks her appearance.* **Terry** *watches her. She notices him and pokes her tongue out at him.*

Barton *and* **Matt** *enter.*

Caroline   All right?

Barton   I suppose so. He nearly dropped it on my foot.

Terry   Matt, Matt, Matt.

Matt   'Lo, Terry.

Caroline   It's heavy, isn't it, darling?

Barton   He hasn't got a clue.

Pause.

Caroline   It will make things easier for her.

Barton   Mmm.

Caroline   Especially with all the sheets she has to wash.

Barton   He hasn't been wetting the bed lately.

Caroline   Not that we know of.

Barton   Why did you mention it then?

Caroline   He used to.

Barton   You haven't wet the bed lately, have you, Terry?

Caroline   Barton!

Barton   God! You're so squeamish. Anyway, you brought it up.

Pause.

Caroline You don't have to hang around here you know, darling.

Barton Aunty's making a cup of tea.

Caroline You meeting Jason?

Matt Yeah.

Barton Going to the carnival dance, are you?

Matt Dunno.

Barton All those farmers' daughters on the town looking for a good time, eh?

Matt Yeah.

Barton Why didn't they ask your band to play at the dance this year?

Matt Dunno.

Caroline They're not very imaginative, are they?

Barton I suppose you're too way out for them.

Caroline Better to be way out than dull, eh, Matt?

Dulcie *enters.*

Dulcie Kettle won't be a minute. Are you hungry?

Caroline I hope they're not.

Dulcie Want a sandwich, Matt?

Matt No thanks.

Dulcie You sure now?

Matt Yes, thanks.

Dulcie Won't take me a minute.

Matt Don't want one, thanks.

Dulcie Got some nice ham.

Barton Go on, Matt.

Caroline He doesn't want one.

Pause.

Dulcie   Been trying to phone Alaric. He said he might come down.

Caroline   That will be nice.

Terry   When's Al coming?

Dulcie   Be quiet, Terry.

Caroline   We haven't seen him for ages, have we?

Barton   No.

Caroline   Is he bringing Miranda with him?

Dulcie   I expect she's staying with her mother.

She exits.

Barton   Oh, very clever.

Caroline   What?

Barton   Reminding her how little she sees her only grandchild.

Caroline   I thought he might bring her.

Matt   I'm going out.

Barton   You haven't had your tea.

Matt   Don't want any.

Caroline   Have a lovely time. Do you want a lift to Jason's later?

Barton   I'm not driving him all the way to Jason's house tonight.

Matt *exits.*

Caroline   Be nice to see him.

Barton   Who?

Caroline   Alaric.

Barton   I'm surprised he's got the time to come down here. Important fellow like him.

Caroline Oh, Barton.

Barton What?

Caroline I wish you wouldn't be so ...

Barton So what?

Caroline He's your cousin.

Barton God, you annoy me sometimes. Just because you think he's so wonderful.

Dulcie *enters with a sandwich.*

Dulcie Here we are. Oh, where's Matt gone?

Caroline He had to meet Jason.

Dulcie Brought him a sandwich.

Caroline Is Elaine coming tonight?

Dulcie I think so.

Barton (*to* **Caroline**) You know very well she is.

Caroline She said she *might*.

Barton She told me she was definitely coming.

Caroline When did she say that?

Barton The other night, after choir practice.

Dulcie Her Gwen will make a lovely carnival queen.

Barton She could do with losing some weight.

Caroline Don't be horrible, Barton.

Barton She's fat.

Dulcie Elaine must be very proud.

Caroline I think she's a bit embarrassed.

Barton Don't talk rubbish. She told me she was delighted.

Caroline And she told me she was embarrassed.

The doorbell rings.

Dulcie   Answer that, will you, Barton? While I make the tea. It might be Margaret and Tufty.

Caroline   I hope they haven't brought that dog with them.

Barton *exits one way,* **Dulcie** *the other.*

Terry *goes to the biscuit tin and helps himself to a biscuit, putting it into his mouth whole.* **Caroline** *watches him.*

Barton *returns with* **Tufty**, **Margaret**, *and Bruno.* **Tufty** *has brought a bottle of sherry in a carrier bag.*

Barton   The travellers return.

Tufty   Come back, Bruno. You naughty boy. Sit.

Terry   Dog! Dog!

Caroline *steps back in alarm as Bruno jumps up at her.*

Margaret   Lie down.

Tufty   Hallo, Caroline.

Caroline   Oh!

Tufty   It's all right, he's just a bit boisterous.

Barton   You're not very brown.

Tufty   Too hot in India to sunbathe.

They all respond as Bruno apparently moves toward **Caroline**.

Margaret   Make him sit, Tufty. You know Caroline doesn't like dogs.

Caroline   It's all right.

Barton   You're looking healthy, though.

Caroline   Did you have a good time?

Margaret   Marvellous. We just picked up the slides from the chemist on the way over.

Bruno approaches **Caroline** *again. They all react.*

Margaret   Tufty, keep him away from Caroline.

Tufty   Here. Good boy.

Margaret (*to* **Caroline**) I wanted to leave him in the car but she wouldn't hear of it.

Caroline It's OK. Honestly.

Margaret He'll get hairs on Mrs Barker's furniture.

Tufty (*to* **Barton**) How was your holiday? Greece, wasn't it?

Barton That's right. Very restful.

Tufty Everyone told us we'd get ill in India. Proved them wrong.

Margaret Tufty, are his paws clean?

Tufty Yes, miss. Barton says you had a good time in Greece.

Caroline It was very restful.

Tufty (*to* **Terry**) And how are you, mister?

Barton Bruno must've missed you.

Margaret I don't think so.

Tufty Mrs Carter from the school looked after him.

Margaret He's terribly fickle.

Tufty They're very loyal actually, border collies.

Margaret Must be that bit of Alsatian then, mustn't it? (*To Bruno.*) You'll go with anyone, won't you?

Terry Dog.

Margaret (*to* **Barton** *and* **Caroline**) Where's Mrs Barker?

Barton (*to* **Margaret**) Getting some tea.

Tufty (*to* **Terry**) That's Bruno.

Barton (*to* **Caroline**) Perhaps she needs some help, darling.

Caroline Who?

Barton Aunty.

Caroline *looks at him.*

Tufty I'll go and see.

Caroline   No, no.

Caroline *exits.*

Barton   Has the procession started yet?

Tufty   They were still up at the car park when we went past.

Margaret   They hadn't finished the judging.

Tufty   Elaine was helping Gwen up onto the float. She waved and said she'd be along later.

Terry *starts to choke on his biscuit.*

Tufty   You all right, mister?

She hits him on the back. He coughs more.

Margaret   Mind your own business, Bruno. Sit.

Barton   I'll get some water.

Barton *exits.*

Margaret   You should have left him in the car.

Tufty   He doesn't like it in the car.

Margaret   She's too soft on you. Yes, she is.

Tufty   Couldn't leave you out there could we, old boy?

Margaret   She's very naughty.

Tufty   And she's bossy, isn't she?

Barton *and* **Dulcie** *return with a glass of water.*

Tufty   Something went down the wrong way. Here you are.

Terry *takes the glass and drinks.*

Dulcie   He's been at those biscuits again.

Tufty   Better?

Terry   Better.

Dulcie   You're greedy. Tea?

Margaret } (together) { Lovely.
Tufty   }   { Please.

Dulcie Barton, I can't open the bathroom door properly with the washing machine there. I think you'd better leave it on the landing.

Barton I did say that.

He exits.

Dulcie (*quietly and confidentially*)   I don't really want a washing machine. I prefer to wash by hand.

Dulcie *exits.*

Margaret *starts looking at the slides.*

Tufty Have you missed me?

Terry Yes.

Tufty I'm back now.

Terry We going Day Centre?

Tufty Yes, next week. I'll be picking you up in the minibus as usual, won't I?

Margaret Some of these look like they're really good.

Tufty *goes to look at the slides.*

Margaret This is Jaipur. These must be Delhi.

Tufty Here's a good one of you.

Margaret Let's see.

Tufty It's the one in the rickshaw. (*She laughs.*) That hat!

Margaret Tufty, give it to me.

Tufty Yes, miss.

Margaret It's awful. I look enormous. And you never get me when I'm smiling.

Tufty I wonder why.

Margaret These are all Agra and the Taj Mahal.

Terry *puts on his coat.*

Tufty   Where are you going, Terry?

Terry   Day Centre.

Tufty   Not today.

Margaret   He misses the Day Centre during the holidays. Must get bored.

Tufty   I haven't got the minibus today. Next week.

Margaret   They've come out well. (*She starts to put the slides down.*)

Caroline *enters with some teacups.*

Caroline   Did you take lots of pictures?

Tufty   A few rolls.

Caroline   Be interesting to see them.

Tufty   Once you've seen one temple, you've seen them all.

Margaret   Maybe we'll do a slide show.

Tufty   So make sure you haven't got any free evenings.

Dulcie *brings in the teapot and pours tea.*

Caroline   Well, I'd love to see them.

Tufty   There's one here you might like.

Margaret   Tufty, don't you dare.

They wrestle over the slides.

Dulcie (*worried that they're going to knock over the tea things*)   Mind . . .

Caroline   I suppose you saw an awful lot of poverty.

Margaret   Yes. Tufty, don't.

Dulcie   Terrible.

Tufty   It is terrible. So many beggars.

Margaret (*to* **Caroline**) The shocking thing was that apparently some parents maim their own children to make them more effective as beggars.

Tufty (*to* **Dulcie**) There's not really a shortage of food in India either. The problems are caused by rich landowners driving people into the cities.

Margaret The worst thing about all the poverty was the way you became hardened to it.

Tufty I didn't get hardened.

Margaret No. She says she was brought up to help out people less fortunate than herself.

Tufty Very generous, us Brummies.

Margaret She'd have given away all our money if I hadn't stopped her.

Tufty She was so strict with me. Here it is, Caroline. (*She holds up the slide to the light.*)

Margaret Stop it. (*She grabs the slide and knocks the tea in* **Dulcie**'s *hand.*) Oh, I'm sorry.

Dulcie It's all right.

She exits to get a cloth.

Margaret Now look what you've done.

She follows **Dulcie** *out.*

Tufty *laughs.*

Dulcie *returns with the cloth and starts mopping up the tea.*

Tufty *is trying to stop giggling.*

Margaret *returns and glares at* **Tufty**. **Barton** *enters, followed by* **Elaine**.

Barton Look who's here. The Queen Mother.

Everyone greets **Elaine**.

Caroline How does she look?

Elaine   All right. I was going to walk some of the way beside the float but she said I was making her nervous.

Dulcie   Well, you'll get a good view from there. Where's Harold?

Elaine   He's driving the float. Didn't trust anyone else to.

Barton   He's come round to the idea, then?

Elaine   Yes.

Caroline   He wasn't going to let her do it at first.

Dulcie   Such a lovely girl.

General agreement.

Elaine   Nice holiday?

Tufty   Yes, thanks.

Elaine   You're not very brown.

Margaret   Goodness me, we didn't go all the way to India to sunbathe.

Elaine   No. I suppose not. Barton came back from Greece looking very tanned.

Tufty   That's because Barton wants to look bronzed and handsome.

Barton (*mimicking her accent*)   That's right, Tufty. I do.

Elaine   You don't go brown either, do you, Caroline?

Caroline   I thought I did quite well this time.

Barton   But you weren't brown.

Caroline   I was.

Barton   She wasn't.

Elaine   I just get burnt. I've got very sensitive skin.

Dulcie   They say you have to be careful though now, don't they, with the sun's rays?

Tufty   They do, Mrs Barker.

Dulcie Nice for you to have a rest though, Margaret.

Margaret Yes.

Dulcie You deserve it.

Margaret Do I?

Dulcie All those years looking after your father. Never having a break.

Tufty Did you get away, Elaine?

Elaine No.

Dulcie It's nice you've got a good friend like Tufty to go away with.

Elaine Harold was working.

Tufty That's a shame.

Margaret Well, I hope you're feeling fit. Ready for the new intake of infants.

Tufty Here we go.

Elaine Oh, yes.

Margaret There shouldn't be so many this year. I thought you and Mrs Carter could change rooms because her class will be bigger than yours.

Tufty The holiday's not over yet, headmistress.

Dulcie I've never even been in an aeroplane.

Elaine Me neither.

Dulcie And I've got cousins in Australia.

Margaret Really?

Dulcie Yes. My uncle Billy emigrated in nineteen twenty-eight. Went sheepshearing.

Elaine Don't know where I'd rather go, India or Greece.

Margaret I went to Greece in the sixties. I hear it's changed a lot since then.

Caroline Well, it's still very beautiful.

Margaret   Oh, I'm sure.

Dulcie   How many sheep do you think he sheared in one day?

Margaret   I don't know.

Elaine   I think I'd've liked to live in ancient Greece.

Tufty   Why's that?

Elaine   Oh, I don't know. All those ideals. It must have been so pure.

Dulcie   Course it was handclippers then, mind. Not electric.

Elaine   Beauty and truth. People living up to ideals.

Dulcie   Go on, guess.

Margaret   Guess what?

Dulcie   How many sheep my uncle Billy could shear in one day.

Margaret   Five hundred.

Dulcie   Five hundred, she said, Bart. You'd be hard-pressed to shear five hundred with electric clippers.

Margaret   I don't know then.

Dulcie   A hundred. A hundred sheep in one day.

Elaine   Must be funny coming back here after being in those inspiring places.

Tufty   It's certainly quieter here.

Margaret   Never changes this town.

Dulcie   A hundred sheep in one day.

Pause.

Tufty   I think I can hear the band.

Tufty *goes out onto the balcony to look.* **Terry** *follows her.*

They all listen again.

Dulcie Let's hope it doesn't rain.

Margaret It usually pours.

Tufty *returns.*

Tufty Seems to be some sort of holdup.

Dulcie Alaric's been all over the world. Went to Greece years ago. Just after he left school, didn't he, Bart.

Barton He did.

Dulcie Nineteen sixty . . . something.

Pause.

He's supposed to be down this weekend.

Margaret That will be nice.

Dulcie You'll have to come round and see him this time. He always asks after you.

Caroline Of course you were all in the same year at grammar school, weren't you?

Tufty Not me. I went to secondary modern. Hated school work.

Dulcie Alaric, Barton and Margaret were all in the same form.

Elaine You were head boy, weren't you, Barton?

Dulcie No, Barton was deputy. Alaric was head boy.

Tufty And guess who was head girl.

Margaret Be quiet.

Caroline (*to* **Barton**) I thought you said you were head boy.

Dulcie (*to* **Margaret**) Of course he went to Greece with you, didn't he?

Margaret Yes.

Dulcie My memory.

Barton   You wouldn't have had a very good time in ancient Greece, Elaine.

Elaine   Mmmm?

Caroline   Why not?

Barton   Women didn't get a look-in, did they?

Elaine   I don't understand.

Caroline   Neither do I.

Tufty   He means men were more interested in each other than in women.

Elaine   Oh.

Barton   It's true.

Caroline   How do you know?

Barton   It's well known – Socrates, all that lot – queer as coots.

Margaret   I can definitely hear something.

Margaret *goes out on to the balcony.*

Elaine   Most men aren't very interested in women.

They all look at her.

I mean they like other men's company more than women's.

Caroline   Honestly. The things she says sometimes.

Elaine   Don't you agree?

Caroline   No.

Elaine   But then, I think I prefer men's company to women's.

Caroline   Oh, thank you very much.

Tufty   I brought some sherry, Mrs Barker.

Dulcie   There are glasses there, my dear.

Elaine   I just mean there's more trust . . . less competitiveness.

Tufty Barton, sherry?

Barton Yes, please.

Caroline So men make better friends?

Elaine In some ways.

Dulcie My husband was a wonderful friend to me.

Elaine They see the world differently, so they seem more exciting.

Dulcie He never spoke a cross word to me.

Barton What do you think Tufty?

Tufty We make too much of our differences. (*She pours the drinks.*)

Elaine Most people in this town wouldn't even talk about things like this.

Caroline No.

Barton Caroline thinks we've got narrow minds and lead narrow lives. But that's because she was brought up in Bristol and then went to college in London. She yearns for the cosmopolitan life.

Dulcie No sherry for me, my dear. Gives me gastric.

Margaret *enters.*

Margaret There's a cattle lorry in the way. The parade can't get through.

Dulcie That's Kingdom. He's not supposed to park in the street. It's against the law. But his uncle is mayor, isn't he? So he gets away with it.

Barton Do you want some of Tufty's sherry?

Margaret When did you get that?

Tufty Down the off-licence last night.

Margaret No, thank you, Barton.

Tufty Here we are then. Barton.

Barton   Ta.

Tufty   Elaine.

Elaine   Harold doesn't like people drinking.

Barton   Live dangerously, Elaine.

Tufty   You sure you won't have one, Mrs Barker?

Dulcie   All right, just a little one.

Margaret   Did you know the phone was off the hook, Mrs Barker?

Dulcie   No, I didn't.

Margaret   Shall I put it back on?

Dulcie   Yes. (*She goes to the balcony. To* **Terry**.) Did you take this phone off the hook?

No answer.

Alaric might have been trying to phone. (*To the others.*) He's always doing that.

Tufty (*quietly; to* **Dulcie**)   Shall I give Terry a sherry?

Dulcie *shakes her head.*

Terry *quickly appears.*

Terry   Yes, please.

Dulcie   Just a little one.

Tufty *pours some sherry into the glass for* **Terry**.

Barton   What shall we drink to?

Tufty   Love and friendship.

Dulcie   Very nice.

They drink.

Tufty   Funny name, Alaric.

Dulcie   The vicar we had during the war was called Alaric Harper. Lovely man. Then when my Alaric was born they put him in my arms and he looked so beautiful. I just thought, 'You're a very special baby. I'm going to call you Alaric.'

Tufty   He's younger than Terry, isn't he?

Dulcie   Oh yes. Terry was three when Alaric was born.

Pause. They all look at **Terry**.

Terry   More.

Dulcie   No.

Caroline   There was something of Alaric's on TV lately.

Dulcie   There was one about all the forests that they're chopping down.

Caroline   No, it wasn't that.

Dulcie   Did I tell you he'd moved to Blackheath, Margaret?

Margaret   No.

Dulcie   Beautiful house, apparently.

Caroline   What was it about, Bart?

Barton   Homelessness.

Elaine   You said it was ... what was the word?

Barton   Can't remember.

Elaine   Facile. (*She giggles.*)

Barton   No, I didn't.

Elaine   You did. I remember clearly.

Tufty   So does he work for the BBC?

Dulcie   No. What is it he is, Barton?

Barton   Freelance. A freelance producer and director.

The doorbell rings.

Dulcie   Wonder who that is?

She exits to the front door.

Tufty   Perhaps it's him!

Elaine *giggles*.

Barton   That drink can't have gone to your head already.

Tufty   Want another, Elaine?

Elaine *holds out her glass*. **Margaret** *watches*.

Elaine   It's a funny word, facile, isn't it?

Caroline   Did you really say that?

Barton   Probably. His programmes usually are.

Caroline   They're not.

Barton   No, well, I didn't think you'd agree.

Margaret   The one on homelessness was excellent.

Barton   I forgot this was the Alaric Barker appreciation society.

Margaret   It made me very angry.

Barton   Me too. Such hypocrisy.

Dulcie *returns with* **Matt**.

Everyone greets **Matt**.

Matt   Kingdom's cattle lorry's in the way. Parade can't get through.

Tufty   Have a sherry, Matt.

Matt   Ta.

Elaine   They say homelessness is caused by the break-up of the family.

Dulcie   That's very true.

Caroline   What do you want, darling?

Matt   Got any money?

Caroline   Of course.

Barton   What for?

Matt   I'm going to Jason's on the bus later.

Caroline *gets her handbag*.

Matt 'Lo, Bruno. (*He crouches down to pet Bruno.*)

Tufty He's always pleased to see Matt.

Matt 'Lo, boy.

Dulcie Matt always wanted a dog, didn't you?

Matt Wouldn'ta minded.

Caroline He had rabbits.

Barton Only because you wouldn't let him have a dog.

Matt *leaves Bruno.*

Caroline Here. (*She gives* **Matt** *some money.*) Are you sure you're going to be warm enough?

Barton Leave him alone. You're fussing around him like a mother hen.

Caroline It might rain.

Elaine That makes you cock of the roost.

Margaret Are you working, Matt?

Barton Good question.

Caroline You're not sure what you want to do, are you?

Matt No.

Barton I've got him an interview for a job at the stables.

Margaret Aren't you doing your A-levels?

Caroline He doesn't want to go to university so he's not sure there's a point.

Barton That's his favourite phrase – 'What's the point', eh, Matt?

Matt Yeah.

Dulcie Alaric's Miranda goes to university this year.

Margaret How time flies.

Dulcie Archaeology.

Margaret Fascinating.

Caroline   Matt and his friend Jason have formed a band.

Margaret   Really?

Caroline   Yes. They played down at the Carpenters' Inn last month. But we haven't been allowed to hear them.

Matt   You wouldn't like it.

Dulcie   You could give us a little song now, Matt.

Matt   I don't know anything.

Dulcie   Course you do. What about the solo you sang in church?

Matt   That was years ago.

Barton   He won't do anything if he thinks you want him to do it.

Caroline   Hasn't got his guitar, have you, love?

Matt   No.

Barton   Can't you sing without your guitar? Pathetic.

Elaine   Barton will give us a song, won't you?

Barton   Me?

Elaine   Yes.

Dulcie   Barton's got a lovely voice.

Barton   I'm not singing.

Dulcie   What was the one you sang at the concert?

Elaine *sings 'Bless Your Beautiful Hide', from* Seven Brides for Seven Brothers.

Barton   Very good, Elaine.

Dulcie   He sounded just like Howard Keel.

Caroline *laughs.*

Barton   Oh pardon me, we didn't all go to music college. Why don't you give us a song then?

General expression of enthusiasm.

Caroline   I'm not warmed up.

Dulcie   It's the breathing, isn't it?

Caroline   What is?

Dulcie   That's the secret. You can always tell Caroline's been trained to sing. She breathes properly.

General agreement. Pause.

Matt   Bye, then.

Caroline   Have a nice time.

Matt *exits.*

Margaret   Doesn't he want to go and do a course somewhere?

Caroline   He doesn't seem to, at the moment.

Barton   Caroline's worried that he'll get stuck here.

Dulcie   There's not much here for the young people.

Caroline (*to* **Barton** *and* **Margaret**)   You both went to university.

Barton   And she thinks we're such stick-in-the-muds because we came back.

Elaine   *The Return of the Native* – I read that at school. (*She laughs.*)

Pause.

Dulcie   We should get out there.

They all move towards the window.

Tufty   Better leave our glasses behind. Don't want people thinking all these members of the church choir are alcoholics.

Margaret   No.

She goes out on to the balcony. The others follow her out, with **Barton** *and* **Elaine** *last.*

Barton   Now you've done it.

Elaine   Done what?

Barton   She'll be jealous now.

Elaine   Why?

Barton   What you said about men and women. Sounded like you prefer my company to hers.

Elaine   You flatter yourself.

Barton   You're tiddled.

Elaine   Come on.

Barton   What are you doing tomorrow afternoon?

Elaine   Don't know.

Barton   We're going up to the moors. Will you come?

Elaine   Why?

Barton   Things are easier when you're there.

Elaine   Oh, thank you.

Barton   What?

Elaine   I thought you enjoyed my company, Barton.

Barton   We do.

Elaine   I'm not a referee. (*Pause.*) I don't know what Gwen and the boys will be doing.

Barton   Have to ask Harold's permission, eh?

Caroline *enters.*

Caroline   You're going to miss her. She's coming.

Barton *goes on to the balcony.*

Caroline   All right?

Elaine   Yes.

Caroline   What's he been saying?

Elaine   Teasing me, as usual.

Caroline   Do you fancy coming for a drive with us tomorrow?

Elaine   Ummm . . .

Caroline   We're going up on the moors.

Elaine   All right, then.

Caroline   Don't if you don't want to.

Elaine   No, I'd love to.

Tufty *enters.*

Tufty   Here she is. Quick.

Elaine *and* **Tufty** *exit.*

Caroline *starts to cry.*

Dulcie (*off*)   Here they come.

Tufty (*off*)   Wave, Terry.

Caroline *sobs. There is the sound of a brass band.*

Alaric *enters.*

Alaric   Hallo.

Caroline *looks up.*

Alaric   Had to fight my way through the crowds.

Caroline   Alaric.

Alaric   Tried to phone. I couldn't get through.

The brass band music gets louder.

Dulcie (*off*)   Doesn't she look a picture?

Margaret (*off*)   Oh no, it's starting to rain.

Curtain.

Act Two

The moors 1

Afternoon. By the river – a place to swim.

Elaine *and* **Caroline** *are sitting on a blanket.* **Matt** *is strumming idly on his guitar.*

Caroline The river looks freezing, doesn't it?

Elaine Mmm.

Caroline Are you going for a swim, Matt?

Matt Don't want to.

Caroline It's probably not that cold.

Matt Don't feel like it.

Caroline Please yourself.

Elaine Barton's still quite tanned.

Caroline He uses a sunlamp.

Pause.

What's Harold doing today?

Elaine Taking Gwen out for a driving lesson.

Caroline Hope he doesn't lose his temper with her.

Elaine Why should he?

Caroline I thought he was a bit fussy about his car.

Elaine It'll be all right.

Caroline Did he mind you coming out on the moors with us?

Elaine Of course not.

Caroline I just needed someone to talk to.

Matt Can I have an apple?

Caroline   Of course, darling.

Matt   Ta.

Caroline   What did you think of Alaric?

Elaine   I don't think I like him.

Caroline   Really? (*To* **Matt**.) Perhaps your dad would like one. (*Calling to* **Barton**.) Do you want an apple, darling?

Elaine   He seemed a bit superior.

Caroline   You'd like him if you got to know him.

Elaine   Maybe.

Caroline   Funny to think that he and Margaret were boyfriend and girlfriend.

Elaine   She never talks about it.

Caroline   No. I sometimes think she and Tufty are the only happy couple in this town.

Elaine   Maybe.

Caroline   Matt, love, go and give your dad an apple.

Matt   Make him come and get it.

Caroline *exits to take the apple to* **Barton**.

Pause.

Elaine   Don't you like swimming?

Matt   It's all right.

Elaine   Lovely day.

Matt   Yeah.

Pause.

Elaine   So you've decided against going to college?

Matt   Dunno.

Elaine   Plenty of time, I suppose.

Pause.

Matt   I wanna make a record with the band.

Elaine   Oh, is that difficult?

Matt   Have to get a manager or a deal with a record company.

Elaine   How do you do that?

Matt   Send them stuff on tape.

Elaine   So do you get someone to record you when you play at the Carpenter's Inn?

Matt   No. You have to do it at a recording studio.

Elaine   Oh, I see.

Caroline *returns*.

Caroline (*to* **Matt**)   You never want to do anything I ask you, do you?

Matt   What?

Caroline   So truculent.

Matt   I haven't done anything.

Caroline   Exactly. He says he's waiting for you to go in, Elaine.

Elaine   Really?

Caroline   Yes. He wants to duck you.

Elaine *laughs*.

Caroline   He obviously thinks you're more fun than I am. He didn't ask me to get in. Do you think he's in love with you?

Elaine   Caroline!

Caroline   He might be.

Elaine   Don't be ridiculous.

Caroline   I wouldn't mind.

Elaine   I would.

Caroline   Why? You like him.

Elaine   As a friend.

Caroline   All the better.

Elaine   I'm not having this conversation.

Caroline   Why not?

Elaine   Because it's ridiculous.

Caroline   Or is it too near the bone?

Matt   Where's the frisbee?

Caroline   Where do you think it is? In the car.

Matt *exits.*

Elaine   How can you say all that in front of Matt?

Caroline   I'm sorry. (*Pause. She collects herself and prevents herself from crying.*) I think I'm going mad sometimes. The way Barton looks at me. It's as if he despises me.

Elaine   I'm sure he doesn't.

Caroline   He accused me of undermining him last night. He says I'm not interested in his work. That I never have been. He should have married a local girl.

Elaine   I don't know about that.

Caroline   Of course you know what it was really about.

Elaine   What?

Caroline   Alaric turning up like that. He's got such an inferiority complex about him. It's ridiculous. So then he takes it out on me. (*She starts to cry.*)

Elaine   All marriages go through bad patches.

Matt *returns with Bruno.*

Matt   Come on, Bruno. Good dog.

Elaine   Oh, there's Bruno. What's he doing up here?

Matt   Dunno. Yeah, come on. (*He jumps around with Bruno.*)

Elaine   Margaret and Tufty must be around.

Matt   There they are. Hallo! Over here.

Bruno is licking **Caroline**'s *face.*

Caroline   Go away, Bruno. Matt, get him away.

Elaine   You've got him over-excited, Matt.

Matt   Come on, boy. (*He moves away with Bruno.*)

Elaine   You all right?

Caroline   Yes. Thanks. I don't know what I'd do without you to talk to.

Bruno has the frisbee in his mouth and **Matt** *is trying to get it back.*

Margaret *enters with a rucksack.*

Margaret   Hallo, there.

Caroline   Hallo.

Elaine   Been for a walk?

Margaret   Yes. From the top road right over the moor.

Elaine   Long way.

Margaret   Only took a couple of hours.

Tufty *enters and throws herself on the ground.*

Tufty   Three. I need a fag.

Margaret   Here, Bruno, lie down. We were hoping to see some deer.

Caroline   Any luck?

Margaret   No.

Tufty (*holding out a pack of cigarettes*)   Fag anyone?

Caroline   Not for me.

Elaine   No thanks.

Tufty   Matt?

Caroline   He doesn't smoke.

Matt (*taking a cigarette*)   Ta.

Margaret   All this fresh air and she has to smoke.

Tufty   I've had enough fresh air for one day.

Margaret   Mrs Barker not here yet?

Caroline   Is she supposed to be?

Margaret   Yes.

Tufty   And the celebrity.

Margaret   After church this morning, Alaric said he was going to take her for a drive so we arranged to meet up here.

Elaine   Don't you like him either?

Tufty   Who?

Elaine   Alaric.

Tufty   Don't know him.

Caroline   Elaine thinks he's a snob.

Margaret   That's the last thing Alaric Barker is, a snob.

Pause.

Caroline   Sometimes you see the deer in that copse over there.

Elaine   It's lovely up here at night.

Margaret   Yes, it is.

Elaine   Harold used to bring me up here when we were going out.

Caroline   Very romantic.

Elaine   The road was a ribbon of moonlight
  Over the purple moor,

Margaret   And the highwayman came riding,

Margaret *and* **Elaine**   Riding, riding,

Elaine   The highwayman came riding,

Margaret, **Caroline** *and* **Elaine**   Up to the old inn door.

They giggle.

Tufty (*to* **Margaret**)   How do you know what it was like up here at night?

They laugh more.

Barton *enters in swimming trunks.*

Barton   What's the joke?

Elaine   He looks like a highwayman, doesn't he?

Caroline   Does he?

Barton   Who me?

Tufty   Not dressed like that, he doesn't.

Barton (*to* **Matt**)   Put that out.

Matt *stubs out the cigarette. Pause.*

Caroline   Is it cold in?

Barton   It's always cold, you know that.

Caroline   Get your dad the big towel, Matt.

Matt   Where is it?

Caroline   Where you left it. In the car.

Matt   Ohhhh.

He exits reluctantly.

Tufty   Sorry Barton, didn't know smoking was against the rules.

Barton   Not your fault.

Elaine   Matt tells me he wants to make a record.

Barton   What?

Elaine   With his band. He was talking about getting a manager or something.

Barton   That's Caroline's doing.

Caroline   What is?

Barton   Encouraging that nonsense.

Pause.

Margaret Well, does anyone want a swim? (*She gets her costume from her rucksack.*)

Elaine I haven't got my costume.

Margaret Tufty?

Tufty Too cold for me. I'll watch.

Margaret Hold the towel then.

She starts to get changed.

Caroline He enjoys his band.

Matt *returns with the towels, etc.*

Barton (*as* Matt *enters*) He's going to get a job.

Margaret You coming in, Matt?

Matt OK.

Caroline I think I'll come with you. (*She starts to strip down to her bathing costume underneath.*)

Matt *attempts to change into his swimming trunks while holding a towel around his waist. He takes every precaution to be modest and gets himself into a tangle.*

Caroline You sure you don't want to come in, Elaine?

Barton She hasn't got her costume.

Caroline Couldn't she borrow yours, Tufty?

Tufty Sorry, didn't bring one.

Caroline I'd've brought an extra one if I'd known.

Barton I think yours would be too big for her, darling.

Tufty Ooops, I nearly saw your bum then, Matt.

Matt *is embarrassed. His underpants are stuck to his foot and he is trying to kick them off. The towel nearly slips off.*

Barton Look at him.

Caroline You want me to hold the towel, love?

Matt No.

Barton   Nobody's watching you. Don't make such a fuss.

Caroline   Barton thinks we're all too prudish. He was especially taken with the topless sunbathing in Greece.

Margaret   I'm ready.

Caroline   Me too.

Barton (*to* **Matt**)   Hurry up.

Margaret   See you in there.

Tufty *whistles to Bruno.*

Margaret *and* **Tufty** *exit.*

Elaine   I'll come and watch.

Barton   What, and leave me here on my own?

Caroline   Come on, Matt.

Caroline *and* **Matt** *exit.*

Elaine   I think we're the same size, actually.

Barton   Who?

Elaine   Caroline and me.

Barton   She's put on a lot of weight lately. (*Pause.*) What's she been saying?

Elaine   She's a bit run-down.

Barton   Been trying to get your sympathy?

Elaine   No.

Barton   She resents me, you know.

Elaine   I'm sure she doesn't.

Barton   She blames me for the fact that she gave up the Music Academy and a singing career.

Elaine   She's never said that to me.

Barton   I don't know why she married me. She should have married someone like Alaric if she wanted to lead an arty life. She's forever comparing me with him.

Elaine   That's not true.

Barton   The way she looks at me. So superior. Full of contempt. As if I'm some sort of ignorant brute. And she's turned Matt against me. Encouraging him in this ridiculous idea of being a pop star.

Elaine   It's what he wants.

Barton   Guess what he wanted to be when he was small.

Elaine   What?

Barton   A vet. Always had pets. He used to come out on my rounds with me, you know. He loved it. Got spoilt rotten. The farmers used to slip him fifty p and wives would give him sweets and cakes and God knows what. And we used to drive over these moors together in the car singing. Of course, she hated it. Jealous. I feel as if she's stolen him from me, you know. Cow. (*Pause.*) Thank God I've got you to listen to me ranting.

Pause.

Elaine   In marriage you have to take the rough with the smooth, Barton.

Barton   Good old Elaine.

Pause.

Elaine   Do you think the deer will come out today?

Barton   Too many people around.

Alaric *and* **Terry** *enter. They have a folding chair and a blanket.*

Alaric   Hallo, there.

Barton   Alaric.

Alaric   Thought it was you. And it's Elaine, isn't it?

Elaine   That's right.

Alaric   The mother of that very pretty carnival queen. (*Calling off.*) Over here, Mum. Are Margaret and Co. here?

Barton   They're having a swim.

Alaric   Bet it's bracing in there.

Barton   It's very invigorating.

Alaric   I may go in later.

Dulcie *enters carrying a bag.*

Alaric   Here we are, Mother.

Dulcie   Didn't know you were coming up here, Barton.

Alaric *puts the chair up for her.*

Dulcie   Thank you, my love. Looks after me, my boy, doesn't he?

Alaric   You want the blanket?

Dulcie   Not in this heat. I'm boiling.

Alaric *lays out the blanket.*

Barton   That's a very smart car you've got there, Alaric.

Alaric   Thank you.

Dulcie   He drives too fast.

Barton   Makes mine look like an old heap.

Alaric   I thought the choir sounded very good this morning.

Barton   Thank you.

Alaric   Caroline was in fine form.

Barton   Yes.

Alaric   She should have carried on with her singing.

Elaine   What about the sermon?

Alaric   What about it?

Barton   Our vicar probably seems a bit simple-minded to you sophisticated Hampstead types.

Alaric   Blackheath actually, Barton.

Dulcie   He just preaches the gospel. (*She takes drinks and food out of a bag during the following.*)

Barton   He believes that once you start questioning the Bible then people lose faith.

Alaric   Dangerous stuff.

Elaine   Dangerous, why?

Alaric   Unquestioning faith in anything is dangerous.

Barton   That's what we'd expect from a Bohemian.

Alaric   Bohemian? That's a word I haven't heard in a long time.

Elaine   Does it make our lives any better, though?

Alaric   Pardon?

Elaine   Questioning everything all the time.

Alaric   That's an ontological question in itself.

Dulcie   Juice, anyone.

Barton   No thanks.

Elaine   What does ontological mean?

Barton   Oh, Elaine, don't show us up.

Elaine   Do you know?

Barton   Course I do.

Elaine   What is it, then?

Barton   It's about religion.

Alaric   Let me see . . . it's the branch of metaphysics relating to the study of the nature of existence.

Dulcie   Want some juice, Al?

Alaric   Not at the moment.

Terry   Juice.

Dulcie *hands some orange juice to* **Barton**, *who hands it to* **Terry**.

Barton   Here you are.

Dulcie   Don't drink it all.

Margaret, **Matt**, **Tufty** *and* **Caroline** *enter with Bruno*.

Margaret   Ah, there you are. That water is freezing.

Tufty   Bruno! No!

Bruno stands among them and shakes his coat out.

All   Ugghhh!

Tufty   You naughty boy. Sorry about that, folks.

Terry *giggles and shakes himself like a dog.*

Margaret   Brrr. Where's my towel?

Tufty   Here.

Caroline   Refreshing, though.

Margaret, **Matt** *and* **Caroline** *dry themselves off.*

Alaric   Lovely spot. Can you still see deer up here?

Margaret   Sometimes.

Barton   Did you ever come up here at night?

Alaric   Ummmm? Yes.

Barton   They used to call it Lovers' Layby.

Alaric   So they did.

Matt   Still do.

Pause. **Terry** *drinks some orange juice.*

Elaine   Do you think there were ever highwaymen on these moors?

Dulcie   What she say?

Alaric   Did there use to be highwaymen on these moors, Mother?

Dulcie   Ooooh, I don't know. I expect so. Don't remember.

Tufty   Stagecoaches were a bit before your time, weren't they, Mrs Barker?

Dulcie   Just a bit, Tufty.

Elaine   Funny to think it was all here before us and will be here after we've gone.

Terry *belches.*

Caroline   That's a morbid thought.

Dulcie   He's going to drink all that, Barton.

Barton   Terry! Not too much.

Alaric   I was just saying how much I enjoyed your singing this morning, Caroline.

Caroline   Oh, thank you.

Dulcie   Beautiful voice.

Barton   I don't think it's morbid. It's good to be reminded how insignificant we all are.

Margaret   Let's hope it is still here after we've gone. That we don't destroy it all.

Barton   More likely to destroy ourselves.

Tufty   The planet would be better off if we did.

Margaret   That's a terrible thing to say.

Dulcie   It's in Revelation, isn't it? The end of the world.

Terry *belches again.*

Dulcie   Terry!

Tufty   Steady, old chap.

Margaret   I saw this really good programme on TV the other night about the end of the world. Did you see it, Alaric? What was it called?

Tufty   *Apocalypse Then.*

Alaric   Oh yes, a friend of mine made it.

Margaret   It showed how from time immemorial people have thought the end of the world was coming.

Elaine   I saw it too. It was really interesting.

Margaret   It was very well made.

Alaric   Well, he had a lot of money to make it. He's very good at fundraising and selling his ideas.

Tufty   I thought it was fantastic.

Barton   It was good.

Alaric   Really? It didn't work for me.

Tufty   Best thing I've seen on telly for ages.

Pause. **Terry** *burps and then farts.* **Elaine** *and* **Tufty** *try not to giggle.*

Margaret   We don't know how lucky we are.

Elaine   Mmmm?

Margaret   Having all this beauty around us.

Caroline   Have you been to the opera lately, Alaric?

Alaric   I heard Carreras in Barcelona when I was there.

Caroline   How wonderful!

Alaric   It was sheer magic.

Caroline   You lucky thing.

Margaret   Do you like Placido Domingo? He's my favourite.

Tufty   Look at Matt – he's gone all red.

Margaret   Tufty!

Tufty   What?

Alaric (*to* **Caroline**)   And I heard Montserrat Caballe at the Liceu as well.

Tufty (*covering her nose with her hand*)   Pooh, Terry.

Margaret   Stop it.

Tufty   Sorry, miss.

She catches **Matt**'s *eye and starts giggling.*

Margaret   Listening to beautiful singing can be like communing with nature.

Alaric   It can.

Barton   Opera leaves me cold.

Margaret   We've become too far removed from nature. Don't you agree, Alaric? That's where all our problems stem from.

Matt *is sitting with his head bowed trying to hide his laughter.* **Terry** *realises that something is funny and starts to join in the laughter. He farts again, which makes* **Tufty**, **Matt** *and* **Elaine** *laugh more.*

Dulcie (*trying to keep some decorum*)   Really!

Barton   Man's alienation. That's ontological too, isn't it?

Alaric   Yes.

Margaret   Yes. We're alienated from the natural world.

Tufty *is lying on the ground laughing helplessly.*

Margaret   Oh, honestly . . .

Tufty   That's why when you go to the toilet . . .

Barton   What'd she say?

Margaret   I've no idea.

Tufty   When you go to the toilet . . . (*She laughs.*)

Barton   What?

Tufty   That's why when you go to the toilet, you say, 'Nature calls'. (*She lies back on the grass again, helpless with laughter.*)

Elaine   I'd never thought of that.

Barton *and* **Dulcie** *also laugh.*

Margaret   Are you making a film at the moment, Alaric?

This attempt at conversation makes the others laugh more. Suddenly **Terry** *stands up and points.*

Terry   Animals.

Dulcie   What's he say?

Alaric   Shhhhh. (*He points.*)

Tufty   What?

Alaric (*whispering*)   Coming out of the wood. Six of them.

Tufty   Oh, yes.

They all sit or stand in silence, entranced by the deer.

The lights dim to indicate the passage of time.

The moors 2

Late afternoon.

Dulcie *is asleep.* **Elaine** *is sitting and sketching. In the background* **Tufty**, **Matt**, **Margaret**, **Caroline** *and* **Terry** *are playing frisbee.* (*NB. The game should not be intrusive; if this is a problem, it can move off stage so that it is still heard in the distance.*)

Eventually **Alaric** *returns from having a swim and picks up his towel. He moves to* **Elaine** *and looks over her shoulder.*

Suddenly she becomes aware of him and is startled.

Alaric   I'm sorry.

Elaine   It's just a sketch.

Alaric   Let's see.

Elaine   I'd rather you didn't.

Alaric   Why not?

Elaine   Because I'm not very good. (*Pause.*) Enjoy your swim?

Alaric   Very invigorating. (*Pause.*) They were fantastic, weren't they?

Elaine   Yes. Pity they didn't stay longer. The stag looks more like a horse with horns and twice as big as the tree. I was never very good at perspective.

Alaric   In the end it's important to communicate what it made you feel.

Elaine   Oh, you draw as well, do you?

Alaric   It's what my artist friends tell me.

Pause.

Elaine   So you make films.

Alaric   For my sins.

Elaine   Must be a very exciting life.

Alaric   Exciting? Maybe. I sometimes wish I did something really ordinary.

Elaine   Like teaching?

Alaric   Why not?

Elaine   I don't know that I want to be ordinary.

Alaric   I bet your work is much more useful, much more real than anything I do. People are so impressed when you say you work in television. They think you're special. But it's a terrible rat-race.

Elaine   But you go all over the world, see all those different countries.

Alaric   Most of the time you're worrying about your next proposal and whether anyone's going to fund it. Gets a bit obsessive. You're always on the look-out for ideas. I was watching those deer and I was thinking, 'I wish I had a camera crew here.' And then I was trying to decide what music I'd use behind it to create the mood of mystery and wonder. It puts you at one remove all the time.

Pause.

Elaine   Why can't you hold on to moments like that?

Alaric   How do you mean?

Elaine   Well, it was like magic the way they just stood there. But then as soon as you think that, that it's magical, then ... oh, I don't know what I'm trying to say really. I'm just rambling.

Alaric   No, you're not. You mean as soon as you become aware of yourself experiencing something you remove yourself from the experience.

Elaine   That's it. That's exactly what I mean.

Alaric   It's because we try to fix things for all eternity rather than living in the moment.

Elaine   Yes.

Alaric   It's like me with my filmmaking. I'm always –

Elaine   I must write it down. How did it go?

Alaric   Oh, ummm, I've forgotten.

Elaine   When you become aware that . . . I can't remember it.

Alaric   As soon as you become aware of yourself experiencing a moment . . . um . . .

Elaine (*writing*)   '. . . of yourself experiencing a moment . . .'

Alaric   As soon as you become aware of yourself experiencing a moment then you remove yourself from the experience.

Elaine   '. . . yourself from the experience.' That's so wise.

Alaric   Sometimes I even imagine that my whole life is a film. The camera's there over your shoulder shooting me in close-up. Always at one remove.

Elaine   I wish I could say things so clearly.

Alaric   Don't put yourself down. You do that a lot, you know.

Elaine   Do I?

Alaric   Yes, you do.

Elaine   Really?

Alaric   Yes. I've noticed.

Pause.

Elaine   Still, it must be wonderful to make films.

Alaric   Why?

Elaine   It means you can express yourself.

Alaric   Believe me Elaine, it's a very unhealthy world. Maybe I should move back here and be a teacher.

Barton *approaches and taps* **Elaine** *on the head with the frisbee.*

Elaine   Owww!

Barton   I'm sorry.

Elaine *rubs her head.*

Barton   Sorry, did I hurt you?

Elaine (*annoyed*)   No.

Barton   Aren't you going to come and play?

Elaine   No, thank you.

Matt   Come on, Dad.

Barton (*noticing* **Elaine**'s *sketch*)   Let's have a look. Oh, very good.

Elaine   It's not.

Barton (*showing the drawing to* **Alaric**)   What does the connoisseur think?

Alaric   Who me? I'm no expert. But I like it.

Barton   You see, Elaine? Blackheath has spoken.

Elaine (*ignoring* **Barton**; *to* **Alaric**)   Can I draw you?

Alaric   Me?

Elaine   Yes, I'm better at portraits.

Alaric   I'd be flattered.

Matt   Dad!

Barton   All right. Just wait.

Matt   Throw us the frisbee back then.

Barton   Don't talk to me like that.

Matt   You just walked off with it.

Barton   That's no reason for you to behave like that.

Matt   Like what?

Barton   Like a spoilt child.

Matt   Selfish git.

Barton   What did you say? (*He moves towards* **Matt** *threateningly.*)

Caroline   Barton, don't.

Barton   Don't know why we brought him with us.

Matt   I didn't want to come. She made me.

Barton   Well, you're welcome to walk home. Go on.

Matt   Piss off.

Barton   Don't use language like that. (*He hits* **Matt** *over the head with the frisbee.*)

Caroline   Stop it, you two. Matt!

Matt   What? It's not me, it's him. Bastard.

Matt *walks off.*

Caroline   Matt! Matt!

Barton   He'll soon cool off.

Caroline   I'll just go and see if he's all right.

Barton   Leave him.

Caroline   Where's he going?

Barton   For a walk. Here, catch, Tufty. (*He throws the frisbee to* **Tufty**.)

Caroline   Matt!

Barton   Stop fussing.

Tufty *picks up the frisbee and stands looking after* **Matt** *with* **Caroline**.

Barton   We stopped playing?

Margaret *approaches* **Dulcie**. **Elaine** *is still sketching* **Alaric** *on the other side of the stage.*

Margaret   Look at Mrs Barker. She's still asleep.

Barton   Getting a bit chilly now. (*He puts on a sweater.*)

Dulcie (*opening her eyes*)   I could do with that blanket, Barton.

Alaric   I'll get it.

Barton   The artist's model isn't supposed to move. (*He tucks the blanket around* **Dulcie**.)

Caroline   He's going up over the moor.

Dulcie (*to* **Alaric**)   Ought to be getting home soon.

Alaric *doesn't respond.*

Tufty   Fancy a stroll?

Caroline   Oh, yes.

Elaine   Shall I come?

Caroline (*looking at* **Elaine**; *after a pause*)   It's all right.

Caroline *and* **Tufty** *exit in the same direction as* **Matt**.

Barton   Don't be long.

Caroline (*as she goes*)   We won't.

Barton   Kids, eh?

Pause. **Terry** *lies down in the grass.*

Dulcie   How's Gwen today?

Elaine   Tired. Her boyfriend brought her back from the dance at half past two. Harold's taking her out for a driving lesson today.

Alaric   I still can't believe you've got a daughter that age.

Dulcie   She's got three lovely children.

Elaine   You've just got the one, have you?

Alaric   Yes. Just Miranda. She lives with my ex-wife.

Dulcie   She worships her dad.

Elaine   Do you see a lot of her?

Alaric   Not as much as I'd like to.

Dulcie   There's nothing more important to you than your family as you get older. Be lonely without your children.

Barton   Parenthood's a trial. You're well out of it, Margaret.

Dulcie   Oh, but Margaret's a teacher. That's different. I mean, they're all your children, aren't they, at that school. I could never be a teacher. Don't know where you get the patience. You must be a saint.

Margaret   You should see me with them some days.

Dulcie   Anyway, Margaret's not lonely. She's got Tufty.

Pause.

Alaric   Can I scratch my nose?

Elaine   Of course.

Pause.

Margaret   I'm just going to go and get changed.

She exits.

Alaric   Mother!

Dulcie   What?

Alaric   Did you have to do that?

Dulcie   What have I done?

Alaric   Nothing.

Dulcie   She is a marvellous teacher. Don't know what that school would do without her.

Alaric   We ought to be making a move.

Dulcie   All right, all right.

Elaine   I should get home as well. They expected me back at four.

Alaric   We'll give you a lift.

Dulcie   What am I supposed to have said, anyway?

Alaric   Nothing.

Dulcie   People shouldn't be so sensitive.

Alaric   Come on, Mother.

Dulcie   All right, I'm coming. Don't rush me. Looks like I've said something so I've got to be rushed off before I do any more damage. Oh, well, that's how it is when you're old. You're dispensable.

Alaric   Don't be daft, Mother.

Dulcie   Come on, then, let's get going. I'd hate to cause any more embarrassment.

Dulcie *exits.*

Elaine *starts to pack up her sketching things.*

Alaric   Can I see it?

Elaine   No. I want to finish it first.

Barton   I'm sure Caroline won't be long, Elaine.

Alaric   We've got plenty of room.

They continue gathering things together. **Alaric** *folds up the chair and the blanket.* **Barton** *also starts picking up towels, clothes, etc.*

Tufty *runs on.*

Tufty   Has he come back?

Barton   Who?

Tufty   Matt.

Barton   No. Why?

Tufty   We can't see where he's gone.

Barton   Where's Caroline?

Tufty   She thought he might have gone into the wood.

Alaric   Maybe he's walking home.

Barton   Too far. I'll go up and look.

Alaric   You want any help?

Barton   No, you go on. We'll find him.

Barton *exits.*

Alaric   He's very hard on Matt.

Elaine   Yes. Pity they didn't have more children, really.

Alaric   I don't think Caroline could. She was very ill having Matt, I remember.

Elaine   Must be difficult being an only child.

Alaric   Mmmm. We'd better not keep Mother waiting.

They start to leave.

Tufty   Bye.

Alaric   Oh, goodbye, Tufty.

Elaine *and* **Alaric** *exit.*

Tufty *opens a can of beer. She drinks some and burps, then laughs to herself, remembering* **Terry**'s *performance earlier.*

Margaret *enters.*

Margaret   They're all leaving.

Tufty   I know. Matt's disappeared.

Margaret   Is Elaine going home with the Barkers?

Tufty   Think so. Her and Alaric seem to be hitting it off after all.

Margaret *starts picking up her things.*

Tufty   Lovely day.

Margaret   Yes.

Tufty *sighs with satisfaction.*

Margaret   Well, are you coming?

Tufty   We could get a lift back to the car with Barton.

Margaret   It's not far to walk.

Tufty   It's even less far to ride. It's nice just sitting here, looking.

Barton *can be heard calling* **Matt**, *off.*

Margaret You sound so middle-aged sometimes.

Tufty I am middle-aged.

Margaret You don't have to talk like it.

Tufty Sorry, miss.

Margaret I wish you wouldn't keep saying that. Drives me mad.

Tufty What's got into you?

Margaret Nothing's got into me.

Tufty Upset you, has it?

Margaret What?

Tufty Seeing your ex-boyfriend.

Margaret Don't be ridiculous.

Tufty I suppose it's a bit of a comedown really, isn't it?

Margaret What is?

Tufty Ending up with someone who's just a driver for social services when you could have been married to a telly producer.

Pause.

Margaret Can I have the car keys?

Tufty Don't blame me if you feel like a failure.

Margaret *waits.* **Tufty** *gives her the keys.*

Tufty I'm sorry.

Margaret I'll see you back at the car.

Margaret *exits.*

Tufty *is left on her own and expresses her frustration.*

Tufty (*to Bruno*) Here, boy. (*She strokes the dog and finishes her drink.*)

She gets up and exits after **Margaret**.

Barton *and* **Caroline** *can be heard calling* **Matt**. **Terry***, who has been lying in the grass, sits up and looks around, enjoying the feeling of being outside. He sings his own version of 'You Are My Sunshine'.*

Terry   Sunshine . . .
   Sunshine . . .
   Yappy . . .
   Skies are blue.
   Sunshine . . .
   Sunshine . . .
   'Appy, skies are blue.

The lights fade. Curtain.

Act Three

The garden 1

*Early evening. The garden of **Margaret**'s and **Tufty**'s house.*

Tufty *is adjusting a slide projector (practical) on a step ladder. Bruno is about the garden somewhere. On the garden table there is a punch bowl and glasses, slides and the cassette for the projector. The projector is switched on and is directed at an imaginary screen in the audience.*

Margaret *enters with a book.*

Margaret   Is this one thick enough?

Tufty   We'll try it.

Margaret   I still think this is a ridiculous idea.

Tufty   What?

Margaret   Showing slides in the garden.

Tufty   Put it under this end.

Margaret   It will be too bright out here.

Tufty   Not when it gets dark. We'll put off the outside light. Be cooler anyway.

Margaret   It's still not right. It needs to go up.

Tufty   I know.

Margaret   Adjust the legs.

Tufty   They're broken. You know that. That's why I'm using the book.

Margaret   I don't know why we're using your old projector.

Tufty   What are Caroline and Elaine doing?

Margaret   Elaine's brought a trifle round. They're putting whipped cream on the top.

Tufty   Why's Elaine wearing those ridiculous sunglasses?

Margaret   I don't know. (*She goes to the table and looks at the slides.*)

Margaret   You're not showing this one.

Tufty   Which one?

Margaret   The one of me getting out of the rickshaw in Agra.

Tufty   Why not?

Margaret   Because it makes me look enormous.

Tufty   Alaric musn't see that one then.

Silence.

(*In exasperation with the projector.*) Aowhhh.

Margaret   We should have borrowed the one from school.

Tufty   This one's fine.

Margaret   Except you can't adjust the legs.

Tufty   It's a stronger bulb.

Margaret   It wouldn't need to be so strong if we showed them indoors.

Tufty   Pour me a drink.

Margaret   Bit early, isn't it?

Tufty *goes and gets herself a drink of the punch and then returns to fiddle with the projector.*

Margaret   It's coming off the edge of the screen.

Tufty   I know. (*She plays with the focus and sips her drink.*)

Margaret   Shall I bring the screen nearer?

Tufty   No! Out of the way, Bruno. Go and lie down.

Margaret   You can't adjust the lens properly with that projector either.

Tufty This is a really good projector. I paid a lot of money for it.

Margaret Twenty years ago.

Tufty Oh, shut up.

Margaret Shut up yourself.

Elaine *enters wearing quite ostentatious sunglasses.*

Elaine Have you got any hundreds and thousands?

Tufty Pardon?

Elaine You know, to sprinkle on top of the trifle.

Margaret Vermicelli? You could grate some chocolate.

Tufty We haven't got any chocolate.

Margaret Yes, we have.

Tufty No, we haven't.

Margaret We have.

Tufty You scoffed it all the other night.

Margaret Oh yes.

Elaine It's all right.

Elaine *exits.*

Tufty (*putting the slides in the cassette*)   Do you want a drink?

Margaret *doesn't answer.*

Tufty Maggie?

Margaret Might as well.

Tufty That dress suits you.

Margaret Thank you.

Tufty She looks very tasty, doesn't she, Bruno? Cheers.

Margaret Cheers.

Tufty *reaches out and touches* **Margaret**'s *cheek.*

Margaret   Don't. (*She looks towards the house. Pause.*) How much gin did you put in this?

Tufty *doesn't reply.*

Margaret   It's very strong.

Elaine *and* **Caroline** *enter.*

Elaine   That's that done.

Caroline   The food looks lovely.

Tufty   Come and have some punch, you two.

Caroline   I thought Barton was out here.

Tufty   He's gone to have a look at the fish in our pond.

Caroline   You've got a fish pond?

Margaret   Don't get her started, Caroline. The hours we spend in garden centres buying plants and fish for that pond. She's even got a waterfall with lights.

Caroline   How sweet. I must have a look later. Matt used to have fish.

Elaine   Is Matt back yet?

Caroline   No.

Tufty   Where's he been?

Caroline   He went up to Bristol this morning with Alaric.

Margaret   Bristol?

Caroline   Yes.

Elaine   Alaric had to go for a meeting. He took Matt because he knows a record producer up there who's got a recording studio.

Caroline   You're well-informed.

Tufty (*handing out the drinks*)   There you are. (*She picks up her own drink.*)

Margaret   The salad's still got to be made.

Tufty *exits.*

Caroline   I thought you might have gone with them, Elaine.

Elaine   Gone with who?

Caroline   Alaric and Matt.

Elaine   Had some preparation to do for school.

Caroline   He asked you then, did he?

Elaine   Who?

Caroline   Alaric.

Elaine   He mentioned they were going.

Caroline   Thought he might have.

Margaret   There's a book on special needs teaching you must read for next term.

Elaine   Right.

Caroline   Have you seen much of Alaric since last Sunday on the moors, Margaret?

Margaret   I've been at the school getting things ready.

Caroline   I thought you were old friends.

Margaret   We haven't been in touch for years.

Caroline   Sad how people drift apart, isn't it?

Tufty *returns.*

Tufty   The Barkers are here. They've brought Matt. Can you come and help, Maggie?

Margaret *and* **Tufty** *exit.*

Caroline   This punch is rather wonderful, isn't it?

Elaine   Are you angry with me?

Caroline   Why should I be angry with you?

Caroline *exits.*

Elaine, *left alone on stage, behaves in an agitated manner. She moves toward the house to see if she can see* **Alaric**. *She takes a mirror out of* *her handbag and looks at herself, adjusting her sunglasses. She puts on some lipstick and smiles at herself brightly.*

Barton *enters.*

Elaine   How are the fish?

Barton   They look healthy enough to me. Not that I'm an expert. (*He looks towards the house.*) I need to talk to you.

Elaine   I should see if Margaret and Tufty need any help.

Barton   It won't take a minute.

Tufty *enters with* **Terry, Alaric** *and* **Matt.**

Tufty   Here we are.

Alaric   Hallo there.

Barton   Hallo.

Tufty   Help yourself to punch.

Alaric *pours himself some punch.*

Tufty   Look who's there under the bush, Terry.

Terry   Dog.

Tufty   That's your friend Bruno.

Terry *sticks his tongue out and pants like a dog.*

Tufty   Yes, he's hot.

Terry (*seeing* **Alaric**'s *drink*)   Drink.

Alaric   All right, not too much. (*He gives* **Terry** *some punch.*)

Elaine   How was Bristol?

Matt   Brilliant. Twenty-four track digital recording studio, everything computerised. We'll be able to do a really good demo tape.

Barton   And when are you planning to do that?

Matt   Monday and Tuesday.

Barton   I arranged for you to go to that job interview at the stables on Tuesday.

Matt   I forgot.

Elaine   Won't they change it?

Barton   We'll have to see.

Pause.

Tufty   Come on, Terry, let's go and have a look at the fish.

Terry   Fish.

Tufty   Shall we take Bruno with us?

Terry   Yes.

Tufty   Here, boy.

Terry *edges around as if he is slightly scared of Bruno.*

Tufty   Coming, Matt?

Matt   Yeah.

Tufty, **Terry** *and* **Matt** *exit.*

Alaric   Sorry about that, Barton. Don't want to tread on anyone's toes.

Barton   I'm sure you don't.

Alaric   He seems pretty keen on his music.

Barton   You think so?

Alaric   Yes. Don't you?

Barton   He hasn't got any real staying power. Bit lazy, our Matt. Needs to get some work experience.

Alaric   Work isn't everything.

Barton   Is that what you say to Miranda?

Alaric   Yes. (*Pause.*) How are you, Elaine?

Elaine   I'm all right.

Barton   Why didn't you bring her with you?

Alaric   Miranda?

Barton   Yes.

Alaric   She's with her mother.

Barton   Things must have been difficult in that quarter since the divorce.

Alaric   Not at all. It's all quite amicable.

Barton   Very civilised.

Alaric   Actually, Barton, don't you think it would be good if Terry had some sort of work?

Barton   Why? He's happy.

Alaric   He's very dependent on Mother.

Barton   He's company for her.

Alaric   Mmmm. Did you get your work for school done, Elaine?

Elaine   Some of it. I got a bit sidetracked.

Barton   Has Miranda got over it do you think?

Alaric   Got over what?

Barton   The divorce. Losing her dad.

Alaric   She didn't lose me. Sidetracked?

Elaine   I finished your portrait.

Alaric   I must see it.

Barton   Because she was seeing a psychiatrist, wasn't she?

Alaric   Yes.

Elaine   I'll bring it to church on Sunday and show you.

Pause.

Caroline *enters.*

Caroline   Did you bring that bottle of wine from the car?

Barton   No.

Caroline   Can you get it?

Barton   In a minute.

Caroline   Now. It should go in the fridge.

Barton *follows* **Caroline** *into the house.*

Alaric   I enjoyed the beach yesterday.

Elaine   Yes, so did I. Do you think divorce harms the children?

Alaric   It needn't.

Elaine   Mmmm.

Alaric   Yes. It was good to escape. Relax. I was feeling a bit tense.

Elaine   Harold says I'm tense.

Alaric   Been getting a bit irritable with Mother. Then I feel so guilty. I'm not a very good son, I'm afraid. I always feel a bit of a misfit when I come down here.

Elaine   That's what Harold calls me – a misfit.

Alaric   And then, of course, there's Barton being the dutiful nephew – just to make me feel worse.

Elaine   Last night Harold and I had a bit of a row.

Alaric   Oh dear.

Elaine   Well, he gets a bit jealous.

Alaric   Jealous?

Elaine   Of my friends.

Alaric   I see.

Elaine   I suppose I make things difficult, really.

Alaric   How come?

Elaine   He says I'm abnormal.

Alaric   Why?

Elaine   I could do without the bed side of things altogether.

Alaric   Maybe that's to do with him.

Elaine   I don't know why I'm telling you all this.

Alaric   I'm flattered you feel able to.

Margaret *enters from the house.*

Margaret   The food's nearly ready. Where's Tufty?

Elaine   Down by the pond.

Margaret   I might have known.

Elaine   I'll go and get her.

Margaret   Thank you.

Elaine *exits.*

Margaret   She's a funny thing, isn't she?

Alaric   Mmmm. What's her husband like?

Margaret   Bit hot-tempered.

Alaric   Tufty seems nice.

Margaret   Oh, yes she is.

Alaric   Known her long?

Margaret   She used to help look after my father. Meals on wheels. Home help. He thought the world of her.

Alaric   Do you have friends in this area?

Margaret   Who?

Alaric   You and Tufty.

Margaret   Most people we know are either from the choir or from work.

Alaric   So no other gay friends?

Margaret   I beg your pardon?

Alaric   You don't have any lesbian friends.

Margaret   No.

Alaric   I just thought there might be some sort of group.

Margaret   I've never been a person for groups.

Alaric   No.

Pause.

Margaret Actually, Michael Kingdom proposed to me.

Alaric Did he?

Margaret Yes.

Alaric His father used to drive the cattle lorry?

Margaret It's quite a thriving business now.

Alaric Really?

Margaret Of course, I refused.

Alaric Yes?

Margaret Too wide a gap.

Alaric Of course.

Margaret So there were others, Alaric.

Alaric I'm sure there were. (*Pause.*) You always used to terrify me, you know? When we went out together.

Margaret Terrify you?

Alaric Yes, you made me feel that I had to be extremely sensible. No nonsense. You just weren't like other girls. You hated being flattered, I remember. You always seemed to see through me. It made me very edgy. Then when I saw you with Tufty, I understood.

Margaret Understood what, exactly?

Alaric Well, that you weren't really interested in men, sexually, I mean. That's why you didn't want to play all those courtship games. I think I sensed that even in those days.

Margaret How very observant of you.

Alaric I'm sorry, Margaret, have I offended you?

Margaret Not at all.

Alaric Oh, good.

Margaret I think you're rather jumping to conclusions.

Alaric Ah.

Margaret   People are always so ready to do that, aren't they? They see two people living together and they make assumptions. When it's really none of their business.

Alaric   I have offended you.

Margaret   I just can't bear labels.

Alaric   That's your right.

Margaret   What is?

Alaric   To define yourself in whatever way you choose.

Margaret   I don't need to define myself, thank you.

Alaric   That's what I meant.

Margaret   I suppose you think we're rather grotesque.

Alaric   No.

Margaret   I know what goes on in people's heads. I mean, how dare people assume . . . Who I live with is my business.

Alaric   Of course it is.

Margaret   Don't patronise me.

Alaric   I'm sorry, I wasn't.

Margaret   Oh, but I think you were. It's certainly not what you think. Some cosy quaint little ménage. The spinster schoolteacher living with her best friend and their dog.

Alaric   No.

Margaret   How dare you come down here and judge me and my life.

Alaric   But I –

Margaret   You think I'm a failure, don't you? Just because I'm not married and I haven't got a job that impresses people. I chose to come back here and look after my father. No one forced me. I like this town. I like being a primary school headmistress. Strange as it may seem to you. I'm happy in my work, in my life. I've no complaints, thank you. I certainly wouldn't want to be running around seeking prestige all the time. I don't need people's approval for the choices I've made in my life. I'm perfectly happy.

Tufty *enters with* **Matt**, **Terry** *and* **Elaine**.

Tufty   One of our little babies is dead.

Margaret   What?

Tufty   One of the ghost carp.

Margaret   Oh, for goodness sake, stop harping on about your silly fish. The dinner's ready.

She exits.

The others look after her. Blackout.

The garden 2

Night.

The slide show is in progress. Everyone is looking at the imaginary screen in the audience.

Margaret   That's Tufty on an elephant in Jaipur.

General response.

Tufty   You were so far off the ground. You could see why they used elephants for tiger hunting. It felt very safe.

Margaret   After that we went to Varanassi. Benares as it used to be called by the British.

Tufty *changes the slide to a landscape. There is general response to the new slide.*

Margaret   This one's out of order, Tufty. It's Agra again. Taj Mahal.

Tufty   That's the view across the river from the back of the Taj.

Elaine   I recognize that.

Dulcie   Beautiful, isn't it?

Margaret   Tufty, it's slipped again. You can't see the people wading through the water at the bottom.

Tufty   Help me move the book, then.

Margaret (*going to help her*)   Sorry about this. Everyone OK? I hope we're not getting bitten by the midges. Tufty insisted on us sitting in the garden to look at the slides. I think she wanted you to get the genuine experience of India. Including getting eaten alive by insects.

Tufty   It's cooler out here.

Barton   I suppose you need to have a lot of jabs going somewhere like that.

Tufty   Quite a few.

Margaret   Hepatitis. Typhoid. Meningitis. Tetanus booster.

Tufty   We decided not to have the cholera jab because it's only fifty per cent effective.

Margaret   Malaria.

Tufty   You had to take tablets all the time for that.

Dulcie   The vicar before last, his daughter married a missionary and he got malaria out in Africa. Remember, Margaret?

Margaret   I don't.

Dulcie   It's a terrible disease.

Margaret   Tufty?

Tufty   What?

Margaret   It still needs to go up.

Tufty   I know.

Margaret   This is Tufty's old projector that she's had for years and you can't adjust the legs properly.

Tufty   Are you helping me or not?

Margaret   There, can you see the people?

Barton   Those little dots? I thought they were birds.

Margaret   No, they're people.

Dulcie It keeps coming back, you see, malaria.

Margaret Next. Ah, now this is Varanassi. That's by the Ganges where they burn people when they die.

Dulcie Very public, isn't it?

Tufty There was a smell of hamburgers in the air. Bit unnerving.

General response.

They just brush all the ashes and bits into the water afterwards.

Margaret They have a completely different attitude to death. It's not hidden away and sanitised. It's there, part of life.

Tufty And then people bathe in the water and wash their pots in it. It's a bit all-purpose, the Ganges.

Dulcie That must spread disease.

Tufty *changes the slide.*

Margaret Hang on, Tufty, go back. I want to show them the little man who talked to us about reincarnation.

Tufty Sorry, memsahib. (*She changes the slide back.*)

Margaret It's out of focus.

Tufty Blast.

Margaret I told you we should have borrowed the one from school. Anyone want another drink?

Dulcie Not for me, my dear.

Caroline *gives* **Margaret** *her glass to be filled.*

Barton No thanks, not yet.

Terry Yes.

Dulcie He mustn't have any more.

Tufty I'll have one. (*She holds out her glass.*)

Margaret *looks at her and then takes it and goes and gets her a drink.*

Dulcie   That wine we had with dinner's gone to my head.

Tufty (*fiddling with the projector*)   Is that any good?

Margaret   Not really. Shall I move the screen?

Tufty   No.

Margaret   That's better. More, more. No, it's gone out again. No, that's worse.

Barton   You ought to get a video camera, Margaret.

Margaret   Tufty, it's just getting more blurred.

Tufty   I know. I'm trying to turn it the other way.

Margaret   For goodness sake. That's better. That'll do.

Tufty   Hang on.

Margaret   That'll do. Leave it. It'll only go out again.

Tufty   There we are.

Margaret   Yes, there he is. He was a priest, I think. Reincarnation is fundamental to Hinduism. It's everyone's aim to be born at a higher level in their next life. And that depends how you lead this life. If you're not careful you can be born lower down the scale.

Tufty   Finished?

Margaret   Yes.

Matt (*putting his hand up*)   Uh, Margaret?

Margaret   Yes?

Matt   Can I use your phone?

Caroline   Matt! Don't be so rude.

Matt   I want to phone Jason.

Barton   Can't it wait?

Tufty   Go ahead, Matt.

Matt   No, it's all right.

Tufty   You sure?

Matt Yeah.

Tufty (*changing the slide*) There's only a few left now. That's Varanassi again. (*She changes the slide.*) Ganges. (*She changes the slide.*) Ganges. (*She changes the slide.*) Temple near Ganges.

Margaret Not so fast.

Tufty *changes the slide.*

Dulcie Oh my, look at Margaret.

Barton That's what I call a candid shot.

Dulcie They're funny things those rickshaws, aren't they?

Margaret Yes.

Tufty Margaret didn't want me to show you this one. I must say I rather like it.

Barton It's like a motorbike with a cab on it.

Margaret That's what it is. Shall we carry on?

Caroline What's that hat you're wearing?

Tufty It was the only one we could find in the market.

Margaret Are there any more?

Tufty I think it suited her.

Barton Very fetching.

Margaret Can we carry on?

Tufty That was the last. (*She changes the slide.*)

General response to the blank screen.

Barton What were the roads like in India?

Caroline Why on earth do you want to know that?

Dulcie That was interesting. A real education.

Elaine Wonderful.

Caroline I'm surprised you could see anything with those sunglasses on. Did Alaric enjoy it?

*Everyone looks at **Alaric**, who has fallen asleep. He suddenly starts.*

Alaric   Pardon?

Barton   You nodded off.

Alaric   No I didn't.

Barton   What was the last slide?

Alaric   Ummm . . .

Barton   He doesn't know.

Alaric   It was the elephant, wasn't it?

Laughter.

Tufty   That was no elephant, that was my wife.

Elaine   The elephant was ages ago.

Tufty   How many elephants can you get in a rickshaw?

Alaric   I was watching.

Matt   Can I phone Jason now?

Barton   What's the hurry?

Matt   I want to tell him about the studio.

Barton   You've got to sort out that interview. You should phone up about that.

Caroline   He can't do that at this time of night, can he?

Tufty   Go on. You know where the phone is.

Matt *exits.*

Elaine   It's nice to see him smiling for a change.

Caroline   You see, Alaric, you've brightened up all our lives.

Terry *puts his arms around* **Alaric**.

Alaric   Get off me, Terry, it's too hot.

Dulcie   Leave him alone, Terry.

Alaric   His mouth needs wiping.

Dulcie   He's had too much to drink. Come here.

Terry *goes to* **Dulcie** *to have his mouth wiped.* **Alaric** *helps himself to more punch.*

Dulcie   Alaric keeps on saying Terry should be working.

Alaric   I didn't say that.

Dulcie   You did.

Alaric   I just think it might be good for him to be more independent.

Dulcie   He couldn't do a job. Look at him.

Pause.

Tufty   Still so warm.

Dulcie   Lovely for the holidaymakers.

Alaric   It was beautiful on the beach yesterday.

Caroline   I bet.

Alaric   Look at those stars. You don't see them like that in London.

Everyone looks up. A long silence.

Elaine   I'm not sure I believe in reincarnation.

Alaric   No?

Elaine   I prefer to believe that we become part of all that again when we die.

Alaric   So you don't think the soul lives on?

Elaine   I don't think the person who is me carries on.

Alaric   Sounds like you're questioning the existence of the immortal soul. I don't know what your fundamentalist vicar would make of that.

Dulcie   I know that your father is waiting for me.

Alaric   What a morbid thought!

Dulcie   It's true. Sometimes I know he's there. I can feel him.

Alaric   He's had a long wait.

Dulcie   You can laugh.

Tufty   Oh dear.

Margaret   What?

Tufty   I hope I don't have to come back again.

Caroline   Guess who Barton wants to come back as.

Barton   Matt's running up Margaret's bill.

Caroline   Go on, guess.

Elaine   The vet on TV, what's his name?

Tufty   I know the one you mean.

Caroline   No, not him.

Dulcie   The man that does the nature programme?

Caroline   No.

Dulcie   Attenborough.

Caroline   No.

Margaret   Saint Francis of Assisi.

Laughter.

Caroline   No.

Alaric   Robert Redford.

Caroline   Alaric's closest. He knows you, darling. Harrison Ford.

Everyone finds this hilarious.

Tufty   I can just see Barton doing all those stunts in *Raiders of the Lost Ark*.

Barton   You're just jealous because you want to come back as Harrison Ford, too.

Tufty   Do I? I've got this horrible feeling we wouldn't be able to choose. You might come back as a beggar in Calcutta.

Elaine   No one wants to be who they are, do they?

They all look at her.

I mean, we're all looking for something else.

Alaric Our generation has got that particularly badly.

Elaine Yes?

Alaric Yes. I mean, we were actually very lucky with the time and place of our birth. We haven't had to suffer real hardship – not like those beggars. We've got healthcare, education, a good standard of living. Maybe our lives are too easy.

Tufty Speak for yourself.

Elaine It doesn't always feel easy.

Dulcie They didn't have penicillin when I was a child.

Alaric And we've never been through a war, either. We've lived through a period of comparative peace. And yet all the time we feel that something's missing.

Elaine Yes.

Dulcie My little brother died of scarlet fever.

Tufty What are you saying, Alaric? That you want a war to shake you out of yourself?

Alaric No. But I sometimes feel that nothing touches us, nothing can touch us.

Tufty Perhaps an earthquake, then.

Barton Or the collapse of the BBC.

Dulcie Wouldn't want to go back to those days. People don't know how lucky they are now. Washing machines and dishwashers. Want, want, want. More, more, more.

Alaric Mother, for God's sake! You talk too much.

Silence.

Matt *enters.*

Caroline Did you get through, darling?

Matt Yeah. Can I go over to see him?

Caroline Who?

Matt   Jason.

Caroline   At this time of night?

Barton   It's ten miles.

Caroline   It might be misty on the moors as well.

Alaric   I'll take him.

Barton   You mustn't.

Alaric   I'd enjoy the drive.

Matt   Thanks.

Barton   You're not dragging Alaric all that way at this time of night.

Caroline   You take him.

Barton   No one's taking him.

Alaric   It's no problem. I'll be back in no time. Come on. Won't be long, Mother.

Dulcie   Don't worry about me. I'm all right. I'll go and look at the fish pond. Anyway, Barton will give me a lift home.

Matt *and* **Alaric** *start to leave.* **Caroline** *presents her face to be kissed.* **Matt** *kisses her.*

Matt (*to* **Barton**)   Bye.

Barton *doesn't respond.* **Terry** *goes and kisses* **Matt**.

Dulcie   Come here, Terry.

Matt *and* **Alaric** *exit.*

Elaine   He's very excited, isn't he?

Tufty   So much hope. He's just starting out.

Dulcie   Yes.

They all look at her. Pause.

Caroline   Did you go to the beach with Alaric yesterday, Aunty?

Dulcie   Oh no, my dear.

Caroline That's a shame. Didn't you want to go?

Dulcie I stayed at home and looked after Terry.

Caroline I thought he'd have taken you both.

Dulcie It was far too hot.

Caroline Did he go on his own, then?

Elaine I went with him.

Caroline Really? That was nice. I hope you didn't get burnt – what with your sensitive skin. (*To* **Barton**.) You see, darling, I knew there'd be a good reason for her not coming round yesterday. Elaine comes to tea on Thursdays. It's our little routine.

Margaret Yes, I know.

Caroline I'm surprised you didn't go, Margaret. Oh, but you're busy getting ready for your little children, aren't you? Our lives must seem so uneventful to people like Alaric. We're bound up in our little world. Can hardly blame Elaine for running off to the beach with him.

Dulcie It was the hottest September day for twenty years, yesterday.

Caroline Barton really missed you, Elaine. He was quite grumpy when you didn't turn up, weren't you, darling?

Barton Not that I remember.

Caroline Oh, you were. You got quite short with me when I said that she didn't want to spend a nice hot day having tea with two old fogeys like us. He nearly bit my head off, Elaine.

Barton That's enough, darling.

Caroline I told him, familiarity breeds contempt. Who wants old friendships when there are new ones on the horizon?

Barton Caroline.

Caroline Oh, it looks as if I'm misbehaving. Naughty girl.

Dulcie The hottest place in England was Heathrow Airport. Course, it would be, with all that tarmac.

Margaret   Doesn't Harold mind you spending all this time with Alaric?

Dulcie   They'll be putting us on standpipes soon.

Caroline   You're talking too much again, Aunty. Good job Alaric isn't here.

Barton   Caroline.

Pause.

Tufty   Would you like to see the fish now, Mrs Barker?

Dulcie   That would be lovely.

Tufty *and* **Dulcie** *exit.* **Terry** *helps himself to some punch and then follows them.*

Caroline   Charity obviously doesn't begin at home where Alaric's concerned.

Elaine   Pardon?

Caroline   Well, he doesn't seem to be putting himself out much for his mother and his brother.

Elaine   He's being very kind to Matt.

Caroline   Yes. I wonder what he's getting out of it. I suppose he's doing it to impress.

Elaine   You ungrateful bitch.

Silence.

Caroline *bursts into tears and exits.*

Barton   There go the waterworks again.

Margaret *exits after* **Caroline**.

Elaine   Maybe I should go and see if she's all right.

Barton   Leave her. Margaret's gone.

Elaine   I feel awful.

Barton   She deserved it.

Elaine   All the same –

Barton Don't go. You've become a stranger this last week.

Elaine Don't you start.

Barton I've got to talk to you. Please.

Elaine What about?

Barton I want you to come away with me.

Elaine Where?

Barton Around the world.

Elaine You're mad.

Barton Yes, let's do something mad, before it's too late.
There's nothing to keep us here. I've got some savings. I'm
going to buy a motorbike and then we can just take off.

Elaine Barton!

He grabs her and kisses her. She struggles and pushes him away.

What are you doing?

Barton I love you, Elaine.

Elaine Stop it. Stop it.

Pause.

Barton It's because of him, isn't it?

Elaine Who?

Barton Alaric. You're so impressed by him, like everyone
else. Did you hear him just now? He practically admitted that
he's a phoney.

Elaine You're jealous.

Barton Yes, I'm jealous. I can hardly breathe when I think
of you with him. I've been lying awake all night just thinking
of you. I've been so stupid, I can't believe it. I've known you
so long and I just didn't realise what you meant to me. I've
wasted so much time. I can't think straight, I can't work. I
was giving some inoculations this morning and I started to
think of you and him, together, and my hand shook so much
that I couldn't carry on. I had to tell the farmer that I was

sick. And I am, in a way. Sick with love. I can't bear the thought of you being taken in by him. He's just bored. He'll pick you up and then drop you again when it suits him.

Elaine   No one's picking anyone up or dropping anyone. You seem to forget that I'm already married, Barton. Alaric and I enjoy each other's company. That's all. He's not the phoney. He's not the one who's deceiving his wife.

Barton   At least I'm not deceiving myself as well.

He removes her sunglasses. She has a black eye.

You trying to tell me you're happily married?

Elaine   I'm going to find Caroline.

She puts the sunglasses back on again and exits.

Barton *is left on his own. He shakes his fist at the sky or hits himself. Eventually he pours himself a drink.*

Margaret *enters.*

Margaret   Has she come back?

Barton   No.

Margaret   I couldn't see her down there. I think she might have gone into the field.

Barton   She'll be all right.

Margaret   I hope so.

Barton   Everyone's a bit jumpy tonight.

Margaret   Yes.

Barton   Do you remember those parties we used to have?

Margaret   In the sixth form?

Barton   Yes. There was always someone in the garden bawling their eyes out.

Margaret   Or locked in the toilet.

Barton   Mmmm.

Tufty *enters.*

Tufty Mrs Barker's cross with Terry because he's drunk and Caroline's sitting all by herself in Webber's field. What's wrong with her?

Margaret Perhaps she wants to be on her own.

Tufty She seems upset. Someone should go and see if she's all right.

They both look at **Barton**.

Barton Oh, OK.

Barton *exits*.

Margaret Bit of inter-marital strife going on.

Tufty Not half.

Margaret *starts to go*.

Tufty Sit with me.

Margaret What are the others doing?

Tufty Looking at the waterfall.

Margaret *sits*.

Tufty I miss you. (*Pause.*) Margaret.

Margaret What?

Tufty Talk to me.

Margaret What about?

Tufty I know you don't like talking about it.

Margaret About what?

Tufty Us.

Margaret Ughhh.

Tufty Maybe you're right. Maybe talking does no good. (*Pause.*) But we do have some good times.

Margaret Of course we do.

Tufty So why aren't you happy?

Margaret *does not respond*.

Tufty   What do you want?

Margaret   I don't know.

Pause. **Tufty** *looks at her.*

Margaret (*emphatically*)   I don't know. (*Pause.*) It wasn't meant to be like this. My life.

Pause.

Dulcie *and* **Terry** *enter.*

Dulcie   Look at him. He's been sick in the pond.

Margaret   Oh no.

Dulcie   He doesn't know when to stop.

Tufty   Come on, I'll take you indoors and clean you up.

Dulcie   He's so sly. He must have been drinking when we weren't looking.

Tufty *and* **Terry** *exit to the house.*

Margaret   Put some music on while you're in there.

Dulcie   I'm sorry, Margaret.

Margaret (*thinking she's referring to* **Terry**)   You don't have to be.

Dulcie   I know I talk too much.

Margaret (*realising what she means*)   Oh.

Dulcie   I can't help it. It's because I get embarrassed. And now I've spoilt your dinner party.

Margaret   No you haven't.

Dulcie *cries. Music comes from inside the house: Placido Domingo singing 'Our Love Is Here to Stay'.* **Margaret** *attempts to comfort* **Dulcie***, who continues crying.*

Barton *enters and helps himself to another drink. After a moment* **Elaine** *wanders back. She and* **Barton** *avoid each other. After a moment* **Tufty** *and* **Terry** *return from the house.*

Tufty   There's someone at the door.

Margaret   Must be Alaric.

Tufty *exits to the house.*

Dulcie   I was beginning to wonder where he'd got to. Come on, Terry, we're going home now.

Margaret   I must give you your trifle dish, Elaine.

Elaine   Don't worry about that tonight.

The music is switched off abruptly. General response of regret.

Tufty *returns.*

Tufty   Barton. Can you come, please?

Barton   What is it?

Tufty   It's someone for you.

Barton   For me?

He exits with **Tufty**.

Dulcie   Isn't it Alaric?

Margaret   Apparently not. (*She moves to look into the house.*) It looks like a policeman.

Dulcie *gasps.*

Margaret   I'm sure it's nothing.

Dulcie   Why's a policeman coming at this time of night?

Silence.

Tufty *returns.*

Tufty   Can you get Caroline?

Margaret   What's wrong?

Tufty   Just get her.

Margaret *exits.*

Tufty   There's been an accident. They came off the road in the mist.

Dulcie   I knew.

Tufty Alaric's fine, Mrs Barker. He's with the police. He's all right.

Dulcie Thank God.

Tufty It's Matt.

Elaine Oh no.

Tufty I'm afraid he's dead.

Margaret *returns with* **Caroline**. *Pause.*

Caroline What's going on?

Barton *enters from the house.*

Barton Caroline.

He returns into the house. Silence. **Caroline** *looks at everyone and then follows him.*

The lights fade. Curtain.

Act Four

Early evening, two and a half years later. The Saturday before Christmas. Behind the church looking at the graveyard.

A bench.

Elaine and **Alaric** *enter.* **Elaine** *is pushing a pram.*

Alaric   She's sound asleep.

Elaine   She always goes to sleep when you take her for a walk.

Alaric   I still can't believe you're a grandmother.

Elaine   You could have a grandchild. Miranda's older than Gwen.

Alaric   True.

Elaine   I don't feel like a grandmother.

Alaric   It was a beautiful walk. Thank you.

They sit.

What time does choir practice start?

Elaine   Half past five. We're rehearsing the carol service.

Alaric   Mmmm.

Elaine   Are you going to come?

Alaric   I told Mother I might.

Elaine   That's wonderful. We need more basses.

Alaric   All right. I'll come then.

Elaine   What's your mother been doing this afternoon?

Alaric   Christmas shopping with Tufty and Margaret. (*Pause.*) So quiet up here.

Elaine   Peaceful. (*Pause.*) They've switched on the Christmas tree lights in the square.

Alaric   I used to come up here sometimes after school.

Elaine   On your own?

Alaric   Yes. I was going through that moody adolescent phase. I used to sit up here and look down on it all. Watching the street lights come on.

Elaine   Were you lonely?

Alaric   I felt as if I didn't belong here. It all seemed so narrow and joyless. Drab. There's something so depressing about English towns.

Elaine   Don't you think small towns are the same all over the world?

Alaric   Maybe. I used to think I'd never escape.

Elaine   So why do you want to come back and live here?

Alaric   Hmmm?

Elaine   If you find it so depressing.

Alaric   I don't want to come and live here, actually in the town. We're looking at places near the sea.

Elaine   Do you think your mother wants to move out of town?

Alaric   She says she does. Why?

Elaine   I just wondered.

Pause.

Alaric   Did you think of moving when you left Harold?

Elaine   No. My job's here. And my children.

Alaric   You ought to get away.

Elaine   Why?

Alaric   Pastures new.

Pause.

Elaine   I've got a Christmas present for you.

Alaric   Oh, really?

Elaine (*taking a roll of paper from the pram*)   Here.

Alaric   This is a surprise. (*He unrolls the paper. It is the sketch of him on the moors.*)

Elaine   I always meant to send it to you and never got round to it.

Alaric (*looking at the sketch*)   You put the deer in the background.

Elaine   Yes.

Alaric   Thank you. It's very flattering.

Elaine *looks at it.*

Alaric   Or perhaps I looked like that then. (*Pause.*) It's like seeing someone from another age. I've changed so much since then.

Elaine   Yes?

Alaric   Oh yes.

Elaine   I suppose I have, too. Now I'm on my own.

Alaric   You've still got the youngest two living with you?

Elaine   Yes. And Gwen and little Eleanor live nearby.

Alaric   Hmmm.

Elaine   How's your daughter?

Alaric   Miranda? She dropped out of university and is back living with her mother.

Elaine   Oh no.

Alaric   She came and visited me a few times in prison and I realised I didn't know how to talk to her any more. She stopped coming in the end. I don't think she trusts me.

Elaine   You mustn't give up.

Alaric   No. That's one thing I decided in prison . . . to face up to my responsibilities: Mother . . . Miranda . . .

Elaine   Terry?

Alaric   Of course. (*Pause.*) Afterwards, all I could think was, 'Why wasn't it Terry?' In the car with me. Do you think that's awful?

Elaine   No.

Alaric   It's what I felt. (*Pause.*) I wrote to Barton and Caroline, you know.

Elaine   But you still haven't seem them since?

Alaric   No. Mother said they've stopped coming to choir.

Elaine   Yes.

Alaric   What's the point of all this suffering, I wonder?

Terry *enters.*

Alaric   Hallo there. Where did you come from?

Terry   Christmas.

Alaric   Yes, it's Christmas.

Terry   Christmas tree.

Alaric   Down in the square. Can you see it?

Dulcie *enters.*

Dulcie (*calling off*)   They're round here. (*To* **Alaric** *and* **Elaine.**) Wondered where you'd got to.

Elaine   We're looking at the view.

Tufty *and* **Margaret** *enter. Bruno is with them.*

Tufty   That's our bench. Maggie and I used to sit there.

Dulcie   Oh, this is Gwen's baby then. Isn't she lovely?

Tufty (*looking in the pram*)   Hallo. What's your name, then?

Elaine   Eleanor.

Tufty   Hallo, little Eleanor. Aren't you good? Look, Maggie.

Margaret   She's beautiful.

Dulcie Sit down, Terry. He's over-excited. He was driving me mad in the supermarket. Kept losing him. Here, let me wipe your nose. He's had this terrible cold for days. He caught it going down that garden centre – working in the cold. (*She wipes* **Terry**'*s nose with a handkerchief.*)

Alaric It's been quite mild.

Dulcie Alaric found out they wanted a bit of extra help so he persuaded them to take Terry on two days a week.

Alaric Did you get everything?

Dulcie Apart from the veg.

Tufty You'll be eating well over Christmas, I can tell you that.

Dulcie Ridiculous, isn't it, the amount of money we spend?

Margaret Yes. We'll never eat all we've bought.

Tufty We'll manage.

Dulcie People go mad. Spend, spend, spend.

Margaret What do you mean, 'We'll manage'? You won't be here after Boxing Day.

Dulcie And the presents they buy. Little boy Webber next door to me is getting a computer. He's only six. And he's getting a bike from his grandparents.

Tufty Are you down for long, Alaric?

Alaric Just until we find somewhere we both like.

Tufty Oh, that's right. Mrs Barker was telling us.

Dulcie And she's just as bad, the mother. Her husband's got her a new cooker. The one they had was perfectly all right but it didn't go with the new fitted kitchen. So out it goes.

Alaric Mother, shhhh.

Dulcie Oh, sorry.

Tufty So your mother and Terry may be going to live with you.

Alaric They *are* going to. That's the whole idea.

Dulcie Do you think Mr Potter's arrived with the key yet?

Elaine I'll go and see.

Elaine *exits*.

Dulcie They never used to lock the church.

Margaret It's since the font was vandalised.

Dulcie What's the world coming to?

Tufty At least it's not quite as cold as it was.

Dulcie There's snow forecast. Perhaps we'll have a white Christmas.

Margaret I hope not.

Dulcie You'll have to think of us shivering in the snow while you're lying in the sun, Tufty.

Alaric (*to* **Margaret**) You going away?

Margaret Not me.

Dulcie Tufty's going to Spain for New Year.

Alaric Where in Spain?

Tufty A villa near Almeria.

Alaric Did some filming there once. It's beautiful. Going on your own?

Tufty No. With a friend. It's her villa.

Alaric It will be nice at this time of year.

Margaret I heard it can rain a lot.

Tufty Sit, Bruno.

Alaric Bruno's getting old.

Tufty Yes, we're a bit worried about him.

Margaret Let's hope he doesn't get worse while you're away.

Tufty Have you found a house you like yet?

During the following **Terry** *moves to look in the pram.*

Alaric   We looked at somewhere this morning but you weren't too keen, were you, Mum?

Dulcie   It was too big. And the price they wanted for it!

Alaric   Look, I told you not to worry about the price. Once I've sold the house in Blackheath it will more than cover it.

Dulcie   It would be so much work to keep clean.

Alaric   We'd be able to get someone in.

Dulcie   Oh no. I want to do my own housework thank you very much. I'm not that old. Anyway, you said you wanted somewhere near the sea.

Alaric   Well, the house we saw yesterday was right on the cliff.

Dulcie   Oh, but it was so poky. You should have seen it, Margaret.

Alaric   It wouldn't be too big to clean though, would it?

Dulcie   Hmmm. Terry, come away from that baby! You'll give her your cold.

Elaine *returns.*

Elaine   There are a few more people there now. But Potter still hasn't turned up with the key.

Tufty   We'll have to practise out here. How are you doing on your descant, Elaine?

Elaine   'Once in Royal David's City' is still a bit shaky.

Margaret   It's quite easy. (*She starts to sing the descant.*)

Tufty (*over* **Margaret**'s *singing; to* **Dulcie** *and* **Alaric**)   I only have to sing the tune on that. They only ever give me the tune.

Elaine *joins in singing.*

Margaret   No.

They start again. **Tufty** *joins in with the tune.* **Elaine** *goes wrong.*

Margaret (*to* **Tufty**)　You're putting her off.

Tufty　I was singing the tune. Sometimes it's easier if you sing the other part as well.

Margaret　Not when you sing it off-key.

They start again. **Dulcie** *joins in singing the tune.*

Elaine　Darn.

Dulcie *carries on singing.*

Margaret　From the beginning again.

Dulcie *continues singing.*

Alaric　Mother.

Dulcie　What?

Margaret　I think it would be easier if we just sing the descant on its own, Mrs Barker.

Dulcie　Sorry, my dear.

Margaret *and* **Elaine** *sing the descant again. They manage to get through the first verse and start on the second verse.* **Dulcie** *and* **Tufty** *join in. They all laugh.* **Alaric** *claps.*

Barton *and* **Caroline** *enter.* **Caroline** *holds a bunch of flowers. Pause.*

Caroline　That sounded very good.

Elaine　We thought we'd practise out here seeing that we couldn't get into the church.

Barton　Good idea.

Dulcie　Lovely flowers.

Caroline　Yes, aren't they? (*Pause.*) This must be little Eleanor.

Elaine　Yes.

Caroline　Isn't she beautiful?

Barton　Very bonny.

Pause.

Tufty You coming to carol practice then, Barton?

Barton Yes, we thought we might.

Margaret We've missed your bass.

Tufty Potter hasn't arrived with the key yet.

Dulcie So we're locked out in the cold.

Barton Oh dear.

Dulcie And there's snow forecast.

Barton Yes, I heard.

Pause.

Elaine New coat?

Caroline Yes.

Dulcie Very smart.

Tufty Christmas present?

Caroline Yes. From Barton.

Margaret Suits you.

Dulcie She's got lovely skin, hasn't she? Wish I had skin like that.

Caroline Thank you.

Pause.

Tufty Perhaps someone ought to go and ask the vicar if we can borrow his key.

Elaine He doesn't like you disturbing him at teatime.

Tufty Well, it's not our fault Potter's so unreliable.

Pause.

Barton How are you settling into your new house, Elaine?

Elaine It's all right. It's a bit cold.

Barton You ought to get on to the landlord. You should have central heating at the price you're paying.

Elaine The rent's about average for around here.

Dulcie　I think it's daylight robbery.

Dulcie (*to* **Margaret**)　Do you know how much she's paying?

Margaret　Yes, it's scandalous.

Dulcie　She ought to try and get somewhere cheaper.

Margaret　That's what I said.

Dulcie　The prices they charge. Lucky she's got a well-paid job.

Tufty　You know there's a flat going down West Street overlooking the park, don't you?

Elaine　No.

Barton　That's a much better location.

Elaine　I wouldn't want to move again.

Barton　Bet it's cheaper.

Elaine　Why does everyone want to tell me how to live my life now I'm on my own?

Barton　Sorry.

Pause.

Tufty　Come on, Elaine. Let's go and face the vicar. I'll go if you go. He likes you.

Elaine　All right. Keep an eye on the baby.

Dulcie　We will.

Tufty　No, Bruno. Stay.

Tufty *and* **Elaine** *exit.*

Margaret　It can't be easy.

Barton　What?

Margaret　Setting up home on your own after you've been married for all those years.

Caroline　No.

Margaret　Can I ask you a favour, Barton?

Barton　What's that?

Margaret   Will you have a look at Bruno again sometime?

Barton   I'll do it now.

Margaret   Oh, thank you. Quick, while Tufty's not here.

Barton   OK.

Margaret   She hates me mentioning it, but I'm sure he's getting worse.

Barton   Poor old boy. Let's have a look at you. (*He crouches down beside Bruno.*)

Terry *comes and watches.*

Caroline   Have you been down long, Alaric?

Alaric   About ten days.

Caroline   Nice for you to have him here for Christmas, Aunty.

Dulcie   Yes, it is.

Alaric   It's good to be here.

Pause.

Margaret   That growth's getting bigger, isn't it?

Barton   Yes. He's probably in pain.

Margaret   He's off his food as well.

Barton   You'd better think about bringing him in.

Margaret   She's so fond of him. (*She cries.*)

Pause.

Dulcie   Come away, Terry.

Alaric   How old is he?

Margaret   Eleven.

Dulcie   That makes him seventy-seven, doesn't it?

Barton   It doesn't really work like that.

Dulcie   That's what they always say. Multiply the age by seven.

Barton   He's old for a dog.

Dulcie *shivers.*

Margaret   Would you like to go and wait in the car, Mrs Barker? You'll be warmer there.

Alaric   That's a good idea, Mother.

Dulcie   What about the baby?

Alaric   Oh, ummm . . .

Dulcie   At least she's wrapped up warm.

Caroline   We'll watch her.

Alaric   Thanks.

Dulcie   Come on then, Terry.

Margaret   And you, Bruno.

Margaret, **Alaric**, **Dulcie** and **Terry** *exit.*

Caroline *looks in the pram.* **Barton** *sits in silence.*

Caroline   Elaine warned me he was coming down.

Barton   Yes.

Caroline   You knew?

Barton   Aunty phoned me at work.

Caroline   You didn't tell me. (*Pause.*) He can't have been back for ages.

Barton   No.

Caroline   Not since the court case. Two years.

Barton *picks up the sketch and looks at it.*

Caroline   What's that?

Barton   Nothing. (*He rolls it up and puts it to one side.*) Did you get a turkey?

Caroline   No, I didn't bother.

Barton   Don't you want one?

Caroline   I suppose we should have one.

Barton   Farmer over at Verraby gave me one today.

Caroline   That was kind. (*Pause.*) Elaine says he's going to buy a house down here.

Barton   Alaric?

Caroline   Yes. Didn't Aunty tell you? She and Terry are going to live with him.

Barton   Here in town?

Caroline   No. Somewhere by the sea.

Pause.

Barton   I could get a tree as well.

Caroline   What?

Barton   A Christmas tree. I could get one tomorrow.

Caroline   Do we have to have a tree?

Barton   Not if you don't want to.

Caroline   They make so much mess. (*Pause.*) I hate Christmas.

Barton   Don't –

Caroline   I don't know why we came.

Barton   You miss the choir.

Caroline   Do you think he'll be coming carol singing with us?

Barton   Who, Alaric? I shouldn't think so. (*Pause.*) Maybe we should have him over.

Caroline   Why?

Barton   I don't know. Aunty would be pleased.

Caroline   No. (*Pause.*) Are you going to take the flowers down to the grave or shall I?

Barton   I will. Won't be long.

Barton *picks up the flowers and exits.*

Caroline *sits looking at the baby. She sings, under her breath, the first two lines of 'Eleanor Rigby' by the Beatles. Then she stops, lost in thought.*

Elaine *enters.*

Elaine   Is she all right?

Caroline   Yes.

Elaine   Where is everyone?

Caroline   They've taken Aunty to the car to keep warm. Did you get the key?

Elaine   The vicar wasn't there. Tufty's gone to look for Mr Potter.

Caroline   Bit of a disaster. (*Pause.*) He doesn't look any different, does he?

Elaine   Alaric?

Caroline   Yes.

Elaine   No, he doesn't.

Caroline   Be nice to have a house by the sea.

Elaine   Wonder if he'll do it.

Caroline   What?

Elaine   Move back here.

Caroline   I was surprised.

Elaine   We'll see.

Caroline   You shouldn't let Barton annoy you like that, you know.

Elaine   I know.

Caroline   He means well.

Elaine   I know. Where is he anyway?

Caroline   He's taken the flowers to the grave. (*Pause.*) Christmas is the worst time.

Elaine   I'm sure.

Caroline   I was thinking of the year we bought him his first guitar. And a Beatles songbook. The three of us sat by the fire singing all afternoon.

Elaine   He had a lovely voice.

Pause. **Elaine** *takes her hand.*

Caroline   At least I don't want to lie down and die any more. You've got to carry on living, haven't you? Might have to come back and do it again otherwise.

Margaret *and* **Alaric** *return.*

Alaric   I'm sorry. I forgot something. (*He looks for the sketch.*)

Caroline   There was nothing on the bench.

Alaric   Perhaps it's fallen down behind.

Caroline   Oh, there was this. (*She holds up the rolled-up sketch.*)

Alaric   That's it.

Caroline   What is it?

Elaine   It's a sketch I did.

Caroline   Can I see? (*She unrolls it.*)

Margaret *joins her.*

Margaret   Oh, very good.

Caroline   It's a good likeness. (*She rolls it up and hands it to* **Alaric**.)

Margaret   Still no key?

Elaine   No. Tufty's gone off to find Potter.

Margaret   She'll be lucky.

Caroline   Excuse me.

Caroline *exits.*

Elaine   Oh dear.

Alaric   What?

Elaine   I wish she hadn't seen it.

Alaric   I shouldn't have left it there. I'm sorry.

Elaine   It's not your fault.

Alaric   I think I should go home.

Margaret   You should stay.

Alaric   I wouldn't have come if I'd known they were going to be here.

Margaret   You can't go through life feeling guilty.

Alaric   No?

Margaret   It was an accident.

Alaric   That's not what the judge thought.

Margaret   The judge was biased against you.

Alaric   I had been drinking.

Margaret   It's always tragic when someone so young dies. But it happens.

Alaric   I feel as if I've opened the wound.

Margaret   The rest of us just get older and greyer and sadder. Perhaps that's our tragedy.

Elaine   They thought of moving.

Margaret   Who?

Elaine   Barton and Caroline.

Alaric   Really?

Elaine   But they didn't.

Margaret   No.

Elaine   Wherever you go, you take yourself with you.

Tufty *enters.*

Tufty   Well, I can't find the vicar or Potter. So we need to have a little conflab with the others out the front. They're getting restless. They want to know how much longer we're going to wait.

Margaret   All right.

Elaine *goes to get the baby.*

Alaric   Leave her with me while you do that.

Margaret   Aren't you coming?

Alaric   I'll wait to see what you decide.

Tufty, **Margaret** *and* **Elaine** *exit.*

Alaric *sits. He looks at the sketch.*

Barton *enters and sits beside* **Alaric**. *Pause.*

Barton   It's getting dark.

Alaric   Yes.

Barton   I'm sure I saw a snowflake just now.

Alaric   I did too. (*Pause.*) They're having a little meeting because they still can't get in.

Barton   Sign of the times, isn't it?

Alaric   What?

Barton   A locked church.

Alaric *smiles.*

Barton   Not that I've wanted to go into churches much lately.

Alaric   No?

Barton   No.

Alaric   Funny, that.

Barton   Why?

Alaric   I went and stayed in a monastery this summer. On a retreat.

They laugh.

Barton   So you're returning to your roots?

Alaric   Maybe.

Barton   Big change for you, coming back here.

Alaric   Yes.

Barton   Won't you find it a bit quiet?

Alaric   I don't know. I thought that was what I wanted.

Barton   A bit of quiet?

Alaric   Yes.

Barton   A bit of peace.

Alaric   Yes.

Pause.

Barton   Well, I can't say I've forgiven you.

Alaric   No.

Barton   But I don't feel the same rancour. Not any more.
Towards you. (*Pause.*) As long as I blamed you, I didn't have
to face up to my own remorse. Awful thing, isn't it? Remorse.

Alaric   Yes.

Barton   Yes.

Alaric   And how's Caroline?

Pause.

Barton   We'll look after your mum and Terry, you know. I
know we haven't seen much of them the last couple of years
but they're family.

Alaric   Oh, but I'm –

Barton   So if you're worried about them down here on their
own, you don't have to be.

Alaric   Right.

Barton   We won't abandon them. (*Pause.*) That was
definitely a snowflake.

Alaric   It was.

It begins to snow lightly.

Dulcie *enters with* **Terry**. *She is embarrassed to see* **Barton** *and* **Alaric** *together.*

Dulcie   Oh, I was looking for the others.

Alaric   They're round the front.

Dulcie   It's snowing.

Alaric   We know.

Dulcie   There's no point hanging around any more.

Barton   I'll go and see what they've decided.

Barton *exits.*

Dulcie   I'm worried about Terry's chest. Look at his hands, he's blue.

Alaric (*to* **Terry**)   Oh yes, you're freezing, aren't you? Let me warm you up.

Dulcie   He can't carry on with this job if he's going to get ill.

Alaric *rubs* **Terry**'s *hands together.*

Alaric   Brrrrr.

Dulcie   Don't be too rough with him.

Alaric   Stamp your feet.

Dulcie   You and Barton have a chat?

Alaric   Yes. Come on, get that circulation going. Now let's go for a little run.

Terry *and* **Alaric** *run around the bench.* **Alaric** *sings to* **Terry** *to the tune of 'Singing in the Rain'.*

Dulcie   Careful . . .

Alaric (*singing*)   We're running in the snow,
    Just running in the snow . . .

Dulcie   Was that all right?

Alaric   What?

Dulcie   Your chat with Barton.

Alaric   (*stopping*)   Yes. I think so. (*He sits on the bench and hugs* **Terry**.)

Dulcie   I'm glad you talked. Especially if you're going to come and live down here. (*She goes and checks the pram.*) She's still warm as toast in there. (*Seeing the baby is startled.*) Oh, I'm sorry. Did I frighten you? (*She tries to console the baby.*)

Alaric   I had a letter from an old friend at the BBC. He wants me to do some work on a new series of documentaries.

Dulcie   Oh yes?

Alaric   It would mean being in London a lot.

Dulcie   I see.

Alaric   I wasn't going to reply.

Dulcie   You must.

Alaric   It might mean postponing any move.

Dulcie   Oh dear. Well, your work's got to come first.

Alaric   Yes.

Dulcie   You can always come and visit.

Alaric   Mmmm.

Dulcie   Need my umbrella. (*She puts up an umbrella.*) Here, Terry, put your hat on.

Alaric *puts* **Terry**'s *hat on for him.*

Alaric   Do you mind?

Dulcie   You must do what's best for you.

Alaric   But what about you?

Dulcie   I'm all right. You mustn't worry about me.

Alaric   I do.

Dulcie   Tell you the truth, Al, I think we'd be happier staying here in the town.

Alaric   I see.

Dulcie   We're all right, aren't we, Terry?

Terry   Snow.

Dulcie   Yes. Isn't it pretty?

Alaric   Can I have his hanky?

Dulcie *hands him the handkerchief.*

Alaric (*holding it to* **Terry***'s nose*)   Blow. (*He wipes* **Terry***'s nose.*)

Elaine *enters and goes to the pram.*

Elaine   Still no sign of Potter.

Dulcie   Don't worry. She's all right.

Tufty, **Margaret** *and* **Barton** *return.*

Margaret   Do you want a lift home, Mrs Barker?

Barton (*calling*)   Caroline!

Tufty   That's snow, little Eleanor.

Barton (*calling*)   Caroline.

Caroline (*off*)   Coming.

Elaine *picks up the baby.*

Tufty (*to the baby*)   You haven't seen that before, have you?

Elaine   She doesn't know what to make of it.

They all stand in the snow waiting for **Caroline**.

Caroline *enters.*

Caroline   The hills are completely white already.

Margaret   So they are.

They stand watching.

It's like a Victorian Christmas card.

Elaine (*singing quietly*)   Snow had fallen,
   Snow on snow,

Dulcie *joins in.*

Snow on snow.

Tufty *joins in.*

In the bleak midwinter
Long ago.

They laugh. An organ starts to play. They look at each other.

Barton   Someone's got into the church.

Tufty   Just as we were beginning to give up.

Pause.

Margaret   Let's go and sing then.

Elaine   Are you joining us, Alaric?

Alaric   No. I thought I'd take a little walk.

Dulcie   You wrap up.

Alaric   I'll come back for you, Mother.

Dulcie   That'll be nice.

Everyone but **Alaric** *heads off to the church. They start singing.*

In the bleak midwinter,
Frosty winds made moan.
Earth stood hard as iron,
Water like a stone.
Snow had fallen,
Snow on snow,
Snow on snow,
In the bleak midwinter,
Long, long ago.

Alaric *stands listening.*

Matt *enters and joins him.*

The snow continues to fall on the stage, thickly covering it in white. The lights fade. Curtain.

What I Did in the Holidays

Characters

Morley, *eleven*
Eileen, *Morley's sister, twenty-five*
Frank, *Morley's half brother, nineteen*
Robert, *Morley's brother, twenty-one*
George, *their father, sixties*
Catherine, *a visitor from Glasgow, twenty*
Andy, *a visitor from Glasgow, seventeen*
Peggy, *George's wife, mid/late forties*

Scene One	Late July
Scene Two	Early August
Scene Three	Late August
Scene Four	Late August
Scene Five	Early September
Scene Six	Early September

Setting: a farm in Devon

Time: the school holidays, summer 1963

What I Did in the Holidays was first presented by the
Cambridge Theatre Company in association with the
Wolsey Theatre, Ipswich, on 2 March 1995 at the Wolsey
Theatre, with the following cast:

Morley	Anthony Taylor
Eileen	Kate Byers
Frank	James Kerr
Robert	Steve Nicolson
George	Chris Crooks
Catherine	Penny Layden
Andy	Fergus O'Donnell
Peggy	Jacqueline Tong

Directed by Mike Alfreds
Designed by Paul Dart

Scene One

The farmhouse. A living room with a kitchen off it.

It is raining.

Kathleen Ferrier is singing 'Blow the Wind Southerly' on the radio.

Eileen *and* **Morley** *are looking out the window.*

Morley They've been out there for ages.

Eileen They must be getting soaked.

Morley No one will give them a lift.

Pause. They watch.

Eileen Awful weather for hitchhiking

Morley They must be on their holidays.

Eileen Mmmm.

Pause.

Morley Where do you think they're from?

Eileen I don't know. (*She switches the radio off and moves to fill the Aladdin lamp with oil.*)

Morley They might be from London.

Eileen Mmm.

Morley Or Bristol.

Eileen Hold this.

Morley *holds the funnel.*

Morley Or Birmingham.

Eileen Mmmm.

Morley Or Blackpool.

Eileen Hold it still.

Morley Or Bath.

Eileen Morley!

Morley   MMMMorley. Or Morecambe. Or Morchard Bishop.

Eileen   Stop it.

Morley   Or Moretonhampstead.

Eileen   Is that it?

Morley   Bit more. Mum always fills it right up. Or Minehead. Or Manchester.

Eileen   Shut up, Morley.

Morley   That's it.

Eileen   Where's the top?

Morley   Here. Or the Isle of Man. Or Moscow.

Eileen   Give me the matches.

Morley   Or Mexico. Or Outer Mongolia.

Eileen   If you don't stop, I'll smack you. Give them to me.

Morley   I'll do it.

Eileen   You know what Mum says about you playing with matches.

Morley   She's not here, though, is she?

Eileen *lights the wick and they watch the flame creep round the wick.*

Morley   Or the moon. Or Mars.

Eileen   You're driving me mad, Morley. Be quiet.

Morley   You're driving me mad, Morley. Be quiet.

Eileen   Stop it.

Morley   Stop it.

Eileen   If you don't stop –

Morley   If you don't stop –

Eileen   What did you do today?

Morley   What did you do today?

Eileen   Morley!

Morley   Morley!

They look at the lamp. **Eileen** *hums 'Blow the Wind Southerly'.*
Morley *imitates her.*

Eileen   That's Mum's favourite song.

Morley *stops humming and looks out of the window.*

Morley   We never go anywhere.

Eileen   Tell me what you did today.

Morley   Didn't do anything.

Eileen   First day of your holiday.

Morley   Read my book.

Eileen   You could have gone upover and helped Dad and
Rob look for the spring for the new well.

Morley   That's boring. Perhaps they're on an adventure.

Eileen   Who?

Morley   The hitchers.

Eileen   Come here. (*She turns up the light.*)

He goes to her and she starts pinning up the hem of his trousers.

Morley   Why are you doing this now?

Eileen   I want to see if they're going to fit.

Morley   It's ages before I start.

Eileen   Surprising how quickly September will come.

Morley   When you used to read *Famous Five*, did it make
you sad?

Eileen   No. Why should it?

Morley   'Cause they're friends.

Eileen   Why does that make you sad?

Morley   'Cause they're all together.

Eileen   Yes.

Morley   And even if they quarrel they like each other really.

Eileen   Mmmm.

Morley   Do you think I'll make friends at grammar school?

Eileen   Of course you will.

Morley   David Buckingham's mum is buying him long trousers.

Eileen   You don't need long trousers.

Morley   These were Rob's.

Eileen   They're all we can afford.

Morley   Mum would let me have long ones.

Eileen   We haven't got the money, Morley.

Morley   We haven't got the money, Morley.

She jabs him with the pin.

Aowwhhh.

Eileen   Sorry.

Morley   You're not.

She laughs.

You did it on purpose.

Eileen   I hardly touched you. (*She turns up the light.*) Can't see properly.

Morley   The electric never works.

Eileen   Perhaps Frank will let us have some of his diesel.

Morley   'Nother leak!

Eileen   Where?

Morley   There.

Eileen   My clean floor.

She runs out.

Morley *holds his hand out to the drip.*

Eileen *enters with a saucepan.*

Morley   There's a drip in my bedroom too. I had to put Dad's pot under it.

Eileen   That'll mean another damp patch on your ceiling.

Morley   Dad should have done the roof properly.

They look at the ceiling.

Mum wouldn't have gone away if he did things properly.

She looks at him.

Eileen   You want a treat?

Morley   What?

She gets a box of chocolates.

Wow!

Eileen   Just one, mind.

Morley   Where did they come from?

She takes the wrapping off the chocolates.

Elly!

Eileen   What?

Morley   Where did you get them?

Eileen   They were a present.

Morley   Did Derek Rudd give them to you?

They look in the box.

Eileen   Strawberry cream. That's your favourite.

He takes the chocolate.

Morley   You've gone red.

Eileen   I haven't.

Morley   You have.

They eat their chocolate.

Are you going to marry Derek Rudd?

She does not respond.

Are you?

Eileen Course not.

Morley What's sex appeal?

Eileen Where did you hear that?

Morley Rob said to Dad that Derek Rudd hasn't got any.

Eileen You shouldn't eavesdrop.

Morley What's eavesdrop?

Eileen Listening to things you shouldn't.

Morley Have you got sex appeal?

Pause.

Eileen Morley?

Morley What?

Eileen Don't say anything about these.

Morley Why not?

Eileen I don't want everyone going on about it.

Morley Can I have another?

Eileen Promise?

Morley Yes.

She lets him choose another chocolate and then hides the box.

I don't want you to marry Derek Rudd.

Eileen Mum will come back, Morley. She always comes back in the end.

Morley I know. Don't go on about it.

Eileen *returns to pinning up the trousers.*

Frank *enters singing. He is carrying a bucket of milk.*

Frank   We're going where the sun shines brightly,
We're going where the sea is blue.
You've seen it in the movies
Now let's see if it's true oooo.

Eileen   You're late, Frank.

Frank (*singing*)   Everybody has a summer holiday
Doing things they always wanted to . . . (*He takes off his boots and wet clothes.*)

Eileen   Where are Dad and Rob?

Frank   Still upover looking for this spring.

Eileen   They shouldn't be out in this.

Frank   I've been out in it. No 'lectric?

Eileen   There's no diesel for the generator.

Frank   Told him we were getting low. (*Singing:*)
Fun and laughter on our summer holiday
For me and you ooo ooo.
Had to get the cows across the road on my own. And feed Rob's pigs. Not doing that every night. (*Singing:*)
For a week or two.

Frank *goes into the kitchen.*

Eileen   Supper's nearly ready.

Frank (*off*)   I'm having supper at Rosemary's.

Frank *enters with a jug and some muslin.*

Had to get them two hitchhikers to stop the cars while I got the cows across. (*Singing:*)
We're going where the sun shines brightly. (*He sets up the jug with the muslin over it.*)

Morley   Where they from?

Frank   Dunno. Sounded Irish.

Morley   Irish?

Eileen   Give Dad and Rob a shout.

Frank *goes to the window.*

Frank   Daaad! Daaaaaaad!

Eileen   No need to make it sound like there's been a murder!

Morley *giggles.*

Frank   Rohhhhb!

They listen.

Eileen   They hear you?

Frank   Dunno. Rohhhhhhb! (*To the hitchhikers.*) Just calling my dad into supper. No luck yet, then?

Morley   Where are they trying to get to?

Frank   Ilfracombe. Daaaaaaaaaaaaaaad.

Eileen   They must have heard you.

Frank *starts pouring the milk through the muslin into the jug.*

Frank (*singing*)   We're all going on a summer holiday
   Doing things we always wanted to
   Everybody has a summer holiday . . .

Eileen   Frank?

Frank   What?

Eileen   Can't we use some of your diesel?

Frank   I need it for the milking machine.

Eileen   I just thought –

Frank   You know what thought thought. He thought if you stuck a feather in the ground a hen would grow.

Pause.

He's always doing this.

Eileen   All right.

Frank   And he never gives me the money for it. Why didn't he send Rob up for some.

Eileen   Mandy works on the pumps.

Frank   So just because Rob's fallen out with his girlfriend I have to suffer.

Pause.

I don't see why I should have to supply the diesel for the generator. I'm trying to save. Let Rob pay for it.

Eileen   Rob hasn't got any money.

Frank   He's always got enough money to buy petrol for that car of his. It's all right for you. You've got your job at the library. You get a wage packet every week. I'm fed up with it. I'm just a bloody dogsbody round here.

Morley   Don't get aereated.

Frank   I was in a good mood till I come in here. S'pose there's no water for me to wash either.

Morley   You going out?

Eileen   You'll have to go down and get some.

Morley   Going pictures?

Frank   Mind your own business.

Morley   Can I come?

Frank   No, you bloody can't.

Morley   He's going to sit in the back row snogging with Rosemary.

Eileen   What's on?

Morley   New Elvis film. Will you take me?

Eileen   Maybe.

Morley   Tonight?

Eileen   I'm going out tonight.

Morley   Who with? Derek Rudd?

Eileen   Shut up, Morley.

Morley   Nobody takes me anywhere.

Robert *enters.*

Eileen   Rob, you're soaking.

She goes to get him a towel. He takes off his boots and wet clothes.

Frank   Get Rob to take you to the pictures. He hasn't got anybody to go with.

Frank *goes into the kitchen. He sings 'Take These Chains From My Heart' off stage.*

Morley   Will you?

Eileen   You find a spring?

Robert   In the end.

Eileen   What's wrong?

Robert   Nothing.

Morley   Rob!

Robert   What?

Morley   Will you take me to the pictures?

Frank *enters with a pail.*

Frank   The ceiling's leaking in the kitchen.

Eileen   I've just washed the floor.

Frank   I put the milk bucket underneath.

Frank *exits. He sings 'Take These Chains From My Heart' off stage.*

Eileen   Honestly.

Robert   What?

Eileen   I get home from work. There's no electricity. No water. The roof's leaking and Morley's getting on my nerves.

Morley   I haven't done anything.

Robert   You sound like Mum.

Eileen *holds out* **Morley**'*s farm trousers.*

Eileen   Here, Morley.

Morley *takes off the pinned-up trousers and puts on his farm t.*

Robert Those my old school trousers?

Eileen I'm altering them for Morley. (*She takes the school trousers and starts tacking them up.*)

Robert Hated going to that school.

Morley You didn't go to grammar school.

Eileen Where's Dad?

Morley You went secondary modern.

Robert Talking to Mr Buckingham. He was over the other side of the stream watching us dig the well. He said to Dad, 'You want go get a mechanical digger, George.' Dad patted me on the back and said, 'This is my mechanical digger.' (*He laughs.*) Henry Buckingham stood there laughing. He's back from Agricultural College.

Eileen I know.

Robert Oh yeah?

Eileen Someone said in the library.

Robert Thing about Henry Buckingham is he thinks he's the cat's whiskers because he's been away to college. Pathetic, isn't it? That's the height of achievement round here. People round here got no imagination. Stick-in-the-muds all of 'em. And they laugh at anybody who wants to be a bit different. They go round in their old bangers that they've had for ten years covered in hen's mess and cow shit and they think you're a bloody good-for-nothing just 'cause you've got a car with a bit of oomph about it. Makes me sick. He said to me, 'I see you got a new car, then, Robert. Bit fast for our roads.' I told him I might take a trip up to London in it. 'What ee want to go to London for?' Typical. No ambition, see. Asked me if I was going to help organise the Young Farmers Club fancy dress. Bloody Young Farmers Club! All they do is sit around talking about the butter content of their milk. Bloody plodders. Wouldn't want to be like them.

What I Did in the Holidays

Morley Henry Buckingham went to grammar school.

Eileen You going out tonight?

Robert Dunno.

Morley You could take me to the pictures, then.

Robert Fancy a ride into town later?

Morley She's going out with her boyfriend.

Robert He's another plodder. (*In a high squeaky voice.*) I spend six days shearing sheep and on the seventh day I go preaching in the chapel.

Morley He gave her some chocolates. Look.

Eileen Morley!

Robert Oooohhh. He'll want a kiss tonight, then. Bet he's got a slobbery kiss.

Morley Ugghhhh.

Eileen Least he hasn't got engaged to somebody else.

Morley *makes kissing noises.*

Eileen (*she slaps him hard*) Stop that.

Morley Aowwwhhh.

Eileen You're a little tell-tale.

Morley And you're a ratty ratface. I hate you.

Robert Don't be a baby.

Morley I'm telling Mum.

Robert Fat lot she cares.

Morley Shut up!

Pause.

Robert Who told you?

Eileen 'Bout Mandy and Henry Buckingham?

Robert Yeah.

Eileen Everyone knows.

George *enters.*

Eileen Take your boots off, Dad. I washed the floor tonight.

George Why haven't you got the lights on?

Robert No diesel.

George Use some of Frank's.

Morley He won't let us have any.

Eileen Says he hasn't got enough.

George Frank!

Frank *enters. He has been washing.*

George We want some of your diesel.

Frank Haven't got any.

George Only want a little bit for tonight.

Frank That's what you always say. I need it for tomorrow morning.

George You can go up the garage first thing.

Frank They don't open early enough.

George Hour or so either way won't hurt.

Frank I'll miss the milk lorry.

Robert You know he doesn't like his little routine upset, Dad.

Eileen The lamp's lit now.

Robert Creature of habit, our Frank. Just like his cows.

Frank *ignores* **Robert** *and exits.*

George Go and get some, Rob.

Frank *enters.*

Frank You can't have it.

Robert Don't be such a miser. Little bit of diesel either way isn't going to make any difference to you.

Frank (*to* **George**)   Give me the money for it, then.

George   Now look, who do those cows belong to?

Frank   I have to milk them.

George   And whose grass do they eat?

Frank   And who buys the cake for them?

Robert   You're so petty, Frank.

Frank (*looking at* **Robert** *for the first time with surprising intensity*)   Shut up! Just shut up!

George   There's that temper again. We know where that comes from.

Eileen   Dad!

Frank *exits.*

George   That's Jerry temper. (*He fetches a petrol can and a piece of hose.*)

Eileen   You shouldn't say things like that.

George   Here, Rob.

Eileen   We can manage with the lamp.

Robert   He'll only fly off the handle, Dad.

George   Go and siphon off a bit of diesel.

Eileen   Don't, Rob.

Robert *puts on his boots and exits.*

George   That little runt, Manfred, had a temper like that. He was a vicious little bugger.

Eileen   Shhhh.

Frank *enters and puts on his boots.*

Frank   Where's he going with that can?

Morley   He's gone to get some of your diesel.

Frank *exits after* **Robert**.

Eileen   Morley!

Morley *exits after* **Frank**.

Eileen   You shouldn't go on about Frank's father in front of Morley.

George   You heard from your mother?

Eileen   Not since last week.

George   Saw Buckingham upover.

Eileen   Rob said.

George   He's got a pump he doesn't need.

Eileen   He's given Henry a partnership.

George   Who told you that?

Eileen   Mandy's mother came in the library. That's how Mandy and Henry can get engaged.

George   Did your mother say when she was coming back?

Eileen   No.

George   She'll be back.

Eileen   Mmmmm.

George   Once we get this water connected.

Eileen   She'll say she wants mains water. You know what she's like.

George   Shouldn't have to pay for your water. Falls from heaven. Should be free.

Eileen   Mmmm.

George   Soon have water on tap. Get the health inspector to pass it. Then you can write and tell her.

Eileen   Lot of work.

George   We'll find a way.

Eileen   Rob's upset.

George   What about?

Eileen   Mandy.

George   He'll get over it.

Eileen   Mmmm.

George   He wants thirty bob for it.

Eileen   What?

George   Buckingham. For the pump. Thought I'd go up and get it tonight.

Eileen   You shouldn't have kept Rob away from school so much.

George   I could teach him all he needs to know.

Eileen   He's got an inferiority complex about it.

George   You got any money?

Eileen   Bit.

George   Selling a calf tomorrow.

Eileen *gets some money from her purse and gives it to him.*

Eileen   He hasn't got anybody to go out with tonight.

Morley *runs in.*

Morley   Rob's hit Frank. Frank took the can off Rob and so Rob hit him with the pipe.

Frank *enters. He is nearly in tears.*

Frank   I'm fed up with it. It's not bloody fair.

Morley   Frank's lost his temper.

Robert *enters.*

Frank   You keep away from me.

Robert   I'm not going to touch you. Making such a fuss.

Frank   You bloody hit me.

Robert   I just tapped you.

Frank   Bloody bully.

Morley   You shouldn't bloody swear you bloody bugger.

Eileen   Shut up, Morley.

George   Give me back the can.

Robert *tries to get the can from* **Frank**. *They struggle*.

Eileen   Stop it! Stop it! Look at the mess you're making.

They stop.

You're driving me mad. All of you. I've had enough of it.

Frank *exits*.

Robert   I hardly touched him.

Eileen   You don't know your own strength.

Eileen *exits*.

Morley   You're a bully. Bobby's a bully.

Robert   It's your bedtime.

Morley   It's holiday. Ha ha ha.

George   She'll get over it.

Frank *enters and looks for his keys*.

Frank   Who's had the keys for my scooter? (*To* **Morley**.)
Have you been playing with them?

Morley   No.

Frank   You sure?

Morley   Yes.

Frank *looks at* **Robert**.

Robert   I haven't had them. Wouldn't be seen dead on
your scooter.

Frank   Someone's moved them. I'm going to be late.

George   She'll have to wait.

Morley *whispers in* **George**'s *ear*.

George   Go on, then.

Frank   Give 'em back, Morley.

Morley *goes to get the keys*.

George   You give us some diesel first.

Morley *gives the keys to* **George**.

Frank   You're a troublemaker. You know that?

Morley   And you're a liar.

Frank   What you mean?

Morley   You've got a whole can of diesel hidden in the loft.

Frank   You want to keep your nose out of things. Might get it chopped off.

Frank *grabs hold of* **Morley**'s *nose*.

Morley   Aowwwhhh.

Eileen *enters with plates and cutlery*.

George   Leave him.

Frank   You little bugger.

Frank *hits* **Morley**.

Morley   You're not my real brother.

Eileen   Morley.

Morley   You're a Jerry.

Pause.

George (*giving* **Frank** *the keys*)   Now, son, go and put that diesel in the generator.

Frank   I'm glad I'm only your half-brother. Maybe I won't turn out like the rest of you. Look at him, he's a laughing-stock driving around in his Riley. Can't even keep a girlfriend.

George   Go on. Let's get these lights on.

Frank *exits*.

Eileen   You're never to say things like that.

Morley   What?

Robert   I hardly touched him, Elly.

Pause.

Want some help?

Eileen   It's OK.

Robert   When's Derek picking you up?

Eileen   I said I'd ring him from the phone box.

Morley   Dad?

George   What?

Morley   Will you take me to the pictures?

George   Dunno, boy.

Robert   I'll do the washing-up tonight.

Morley   Please, Dad.

George   Maybe next week.

Morley   The Elvis film won't be on next week.

Eileen   (*to* **Robert**)   Aren't you going town?

Robert   No.

Eileen   I'll go with you.

Robert   Thought you had a date.

Eileen   Oh that . . . (*She laughs.*)

Robert   All right, then.

Morley   I want to go.

Robert   You can't.

Morley   I want to see the film. Dad!

George   Quiet, boy.

Morley   I want to see it. It's Elvis. (*He cries.*)

Frank *enters.*

Frank   Those hitchers want to know if they can camp.

George   Tell 'em to come in.

Frank *exits.*

Eileen *follows him out.*

Robert   You going to let 'em?

George   Why not?

Robert   Don't put them in the field with the bull.

George   He could go upover.

Robert   He'll get out on the road if you do that.

Eileen *enters with* **Andy** *and* **Catherine**. **Andy** *is wearing a cowboy hat.*

Catherine   Hope we're no bothering you.

George   You look a bit wet.

Catherine   Ay we're soakin'.

Andy *takes off his haversack.*

Catherine   OK?

Andy   Yeah.

Robert   Come far, have you?

Catherine   From Bristol the day. Cosy here, i'n't it? Look at that lamp. I've never seen a lamp like that.

George   Hitched all the way?

Catherine   Ay.

Eileen   On holiday?

Catherine } *(together)* { No exactly.
Andy   Yeah.

Catherine   My aunty used tae work in a hotel down here every summer. She always used tae say how nice it was here. So we thought we might get a job down here.

George   Ahhh. You hungry?

Catherine   A bit.

George   Spec' we've got enough to go round, haven't we, Elly?

Eileen   Think so.

Catherine   Thank you.

Eileen   You're from Scotland.

Catherine   Ay, Glasgow.

George   What sort of work you looking for?

Catherine   Anything, really. (*She starts to take her coat off.*)

Eileen   Robert!

Robert *helps* **Catherine** *take her coat off.*

Eileen   This is my brother Robert.

Catherine   I'm Catherine.

Robert   Hallo.

Catherine   Hi.

Eileen   I'm Eileen, and this is our Dad.

Catherine   How d'ye do.

Catherine *shakes their hands. She sees* **Morley**, *who is still tearful.*

Catherine   And who are you?

Eileen   That's Morley.

George   My youngest.

Catherine   How d'ye do.

Morley (*mimicking her*)   How d'ye do?

Laughter.

Catherine   This is Andy.

Morley   Andy Stewart!

More laughter.

Is he your boyfriend?

Catherine   No.

Eileen   Your brother?

Andy   No.

Catherine   My friend's brother. Wilma. She was going to come with us but she couldnae in the end. So we came anyway.

Eileen   All the way from Scotland.

Morley   I can sing 'The Scottish Soldier'. Do you know it?

Andy   Ay.

Morley   Ay.

Eileen   Morley!

Andy   What are those birds?

Eileen   Pardon?

Andy   The birds under your roof.

Robert   The what?

Eileen   Buds? On the roses?

Catherine   The birds. They've wee nests along under the slates on your byre.

Robert   They're house-martins.

Eileen   They come every summer.

Catherine   It's lovely here. I cannae get over that lamp.

There is the sound of an engine starting up.

George   Turn the switch, Morley.

Morley *does so. Slowly, a flickering light comes on, which gradually gets brighter and steadier. All the family respond with pleasure;* **Catherine** *with disappointment.*

George   That's better.

Scene Two

A field.

Morley *enters with* **Catherine**.

She stands looking.

Morley   That's the moor over there.

Catherine   Ay. Eileen took me up there last week. It's beautiful.

Morley   See that farm over there?

Catherine   Yes.

Morley   That belonged to Mr Kingdom.

Catherine   It's right up on the moor. Must be great to live up there.

Morley   He hanged himself in his barn.

Catherine   Oh dear.

Morley   Yeah. He shot his wife with a shotgun first.

Catherine   Why did he do that?

Morley   He was depressed. His face was blue when they found him. And that's Mr Buckingham's farm.

Catherine   Ah-ha.

Morley   His fields are greener than ours. That's because he's a proper farmer.

Catherine   Yes?

Morley   Mum says Dad isn't a proper farmer.

Catherine   I see. There's Andy in the well. Hallo! I've brought your dinner.

Morley   Hallo! Frank! Rob! Cathy's brought your dinner.

Catherine   Andy! Come and have your piece.

Morley   Your what?

Catherine   Piece. Do you not know what that is?

Morley   No.

Catherine   It's what my dad always took to work with him. A cheese piece.

Morley   A sandwich!

Catherine   OK. A sandwich. (*Shouting.*) Will I bring it down to you?

Morley   What did he say?

Catherine   Don't bother.

Morley   Don't bother wi' me piece!

She laughs.

They're going to get the pump working today.

Catherine   Why do they no just put the pump on the well in the orchard?

Morley   'Cause the man from the council said that water might have germs in it. It's too near the buildings and all the pigs' mess and cows' mess can just run into it.

Catherine   Ughhh.

Morley   That's why we have to boil all the water. Mum was doing cream teas but they closed us down. They said it wasn't hygienic. See that shed over there? That's my museum.

Catherine   Your museum?

Morley   It's where I keep my collection. Do you want to see it?

Catherine   Ay. When I've had a wee rest.

Morley   Shall we lie in the grass?

They lie in the grass.

Sometimes I lie in the grass and pretend that I'm on the run and I've got to hide. And if Dad or Rob or anyone sees me, then I'll get caught.

Catherine   All on your own?

Morley   Yes.

Catherine   Are there no other wee boys around here?

Morley   Only David Buckingham. I don't like him. Shall we play that?

Catherine   OK. Why don't you like him?

Morley   He made me put my hand in a cow-pat. There's Rob.

Catherine   That looks heavy.

Morley   It's a rock. They must have dug it up.

Catherine   It's huge.

Morley   Rob's really strong. He's stronger than anyone.

Catherine   Is he?

Morley   Yes. He can lift four bales at the same time.

Catherine   Really?

Morley   He stopped a fight at a dance once by knocking the blokes' heads together.

Catherine   Did he?

Morley   Yeah. Do you like his car?

Catherine   Ay.

Morley   Dad got it him for his twenty-first birthday from the car auction. Eileen paid for some of it though. He went a hundred and seven in it on the dual carriageway.

Catherine   Really?

Morley   Have you ever been that fast?

Catherine   Not in my boss's wee car. He had a fit if I went over thirty.

Morley   Can you drive?

Catherine   Ay.

Morley   Why were you driving your boss's car?

Catherine   He taught me.

Pause.

Morley   Rob goes courting in the Riley.

Catherine   Does he?

Morley   Yes.

Catherine   Has he got a lot of girlfriends?

Morley   Quite a few. His last one was called Mandy. He's doing a wee wee. Look.

Catherine *looks away.*

Morley   Rob!

Catherine   Don't.

Morley   You can't see anything. He's got his back to us.

She hides.

He's gone.

Catherine   What happened to Mandy?

Morley   Her father didn't like her going out with Rob because Dad sold him a sow that always eats her piglets.

Catherine (*jumping*)   Ughhhh.

Morley   What?

Catherine   A wee beastie.

Morley *laughs.*

Catherine   I don't like creepy-crawly things.

They lie in the grass.

Morley   What was your job?

Catherine   Eh?

Morley   In Scotland.

Catherine   I was a waitress. In an Italian restaurant.

Morley   Didn't you like it?

Catherine   It was OK.

Morley   So why did you come down here?

Catherine   I fancied a change.

Andy *creeps up behind them and jumps on* **Catherine**. *He is covered in mud.*

Andy   Aaaaarghhhh.

Catherine   Och. Don't. You gave me such a fright. Stop it.

Andy   (*putting mud on her and singing*)   Three wee craws,
Sittin' on a wa', sittin' on a wa', sittin' on a wa',
Sittin' on a wa' aw aw aw.

Catherine   Stop it, Andy.

Andy *lies on top of her.*

Andy   Three wee craws sittin' on a wa'
On a cold and frosty morning.

They stop and look at each other.

Can you feel it? Feel it.

Catherine   Don't.

They look at **Morley**. **Andy** *goes to put mud on him.*

Morley *runs away.*

Catherine   You've scared him.

Andy   He's a wee jessie, that one.

Catherine   Leave him. It's OK, Morley. He willnae touch you.

Andy   I'm famished.

Catherine   Are yees nearly finished?

Andy   There's a root of a tree in the way.

Catherine   Here.

She gives him a sandwich. He eats.

Andy That root's really thick. I tried tae pull it out with my hands. But it goes right down intae the earth. Frank says it probably comes from that tree way over there. You'd never believe the roots would go that far. It's amazing, i'n't it?

Catherine I went to the phone box this morning. Phoned Wilma at her work.

Andy And?

Catherine The naval whatchamecallems had been to the house.

Andy The reggies.

Catherine Them.

Andy I'm no going back.

Catherine OK.

Andy Ye didnae tell Wilma where we are?

Catherine She willnae tell.

Andy Did ye?

Catherine No.

Andy She's a big gob.

Pause.

Did you phone the restaurant and speak to Mr Capaldi as well?

Catherine Course not.

Andy Thought mebbe you'd be missing your sugar daddy.

Catherine Don't be stup't.

Andy Does he know where you are?

Catherine I didnae even tell him I was leaving.

Morley *enters.*

Andy (*splattering him with mud and singing*)   The first wee craw
  was greetin' for his maw
  Greetin' for his maw.
  Greetin' for his maw aw aw aw.

Catherine   Don't. It's OK, Morley. I'll wipe it off.

*She wipes **Morley** with her hanky. **Andy** picks his nose.*

Andy   Oh, look, a great big snotter. Look, Morley.

Catherine   Will ye stop that, Andy!

Andy *chases him.* **Morley** *runs away.* **Andy** *pretends to rub it in on* **Morley**.

Catherine   Stop it.

Andy *leaves* **Morley**.

Catherine   What's wrong wi' you?

Andy   Nothing.

Catherine   You're forever bullying that wee boy.

Andy   Do ye no like it, Morley?

Morley *does not answer.*

Andy   Your Aunty Catherine will kiss it better.

Catherine   Ye want tae grow up. You get so jealous, you.
He's just a wee boy.

Andy   Well, we all know about you and wee boys.

Pause.

I waited for ye last night.

Catherine   I couldnae, Andy. They'd hear us.

Andy   I thought maybe you and Morley.

Catherine   Shut it.

Catherine *hits* **Andy**. **Morley** *watches.*

Eileen *enters.*

Eileen   Thought you'd all be up here.

Catherine   You no at work the day, Eileen?

Eileen   Library closes midday on a Wednesday.

Catherine   Forgot.

Eileen   They finished?

Catherine   There's a wee problem with the root of a tree. I didnae bring you any dinner.

Eileen   I've had some. (*She sits with* **Catherine**.)

Andy *wanders off.*

Catherine   I put clean sheets on the bed the day.

Eileen   Thanks. You all right in Mum's room?

Catherine   It's great. You sure it's OK?

Eileen   I wished you'd said something sooner.

Catherine   Och, it was fine.

Eileen   It wasn't until you asked about sleeping in the barn that it even occurred to me. I feel awful. You been out there two weeks now.

Catherine   I feel awful that Andy's taken Morley's room.

Eileen   Morley's often had to share with Frank and Rob. Better than you having to share that tent with Andy.

Catherine   Ay.

Eileen (*quietly*)   He seems a bit young.

Catherine   Andy?

Eileen   Yes.

Catherine   I'm used tae sharing. I was forever having tae share at home.

Eileen   Big family?

Catherine   Yes.

Eileen   I always wanted to be Roman Catholic. It looks more . . . well . . . religious. Everyone's Methodist around here. (*In a very broad accent.*) Us all goes to chapel!

Catherine   A funny bloke called in the day.

Eileen   Who?

Catherine   I couldnae understand him. Speaks in dialect.
Got a really high squeaky voice.

Eileen   Blue car?

Catherine   Ay. He left a letter for you.

Eileen   I got it. It was my invitation to the Young Farmers
Club Fancy Dress Ball at the end of August.

Catherine   That's Derek?

Eileen   Yes.

Pause.

Catherine   A lot of the farmers round here I cannae
understand.

Eileen   No.

Catherine   He seemed very nice.

Eileen   If a boy takes you out and tries to be too nice I don't
like it.

Catherine   It's no a problem I've had to deal wi'.

Eileen   It just makes me nasty. I end up saying something
really spiteful. I told him he was too plodding the other day.

Catherine   What did he say?

Eileen   Nothing. Just sat there.

Catherine (*laughing*)   Oh dear.

Eileen   He said, 'I try, Eileen. I try.' (*She laughs.*) I wanted
to slap him.

They start giggling.

He always comes round to open the car door for me. The
other night I deliberately opened it myself and banged his
shin.

They roll around laughing.

Catherine   You're crazy, Eileen. I've never met anyone like you.

Eileen   He makes me want to say rude words. Like 'piss' and 'shit'.

Catherine *laughs.*

Morley   Eileen!

Eileen   Go away, Morley.

They laugh more.

You have many friends in Glasgow?

Catherine   Some.

Eileen   Who's Wilma?

Catherine   She's my sister.

Eileen   I thought you said she was Andy's sister.

Catherine   Did I? No. She's my sister. She's no Andy's sister.

Eileen   Always wanted a sister.

Pause.

Catherine   So are you going to go to the dance with Derek?

Eileen   Don't know. Will you come?

Catherine   Havenae been asked.

Eileen   Mmmmm.

Robert, **Frank** *and* **George** *enter.*

Catherine   Here's your piece.

Morley   That means sandwich.

Robert   Thank you.

They all take their sandwiches.

Catherine   I hear you found a tree root.

Frank   Bloody great thing. Us needs a chain saw, Dad.

George   Rob'll chop it out.

Morley   Yesterday Rob chopped down a tree this big in eleven minutes.

Catherine   Quite a man.

Eileen *giggles.*

Morley   I timed him.

Robert   Frank didn't believe his eyes.

Frank   Get off! Get off! Bloody wasp.

Robert   He went down to get the saw. Time he came back I'd chopped the whole tree down. Hadn't I, Frank?

Frank   Yeah. Get off.

Robert   If you flap at it, it'll sting you. He said, 'Yer, you'll rupture yourself if you're not careful.' All right, Andy boy?

Andy   Ay.

Robert   Ay. He's a good little worker.

He squeezes **Andy**'*s arm.*

Robert   Got quite a muscle there.

Catherine   He's been learning to box in the –

Robert   What?

Andy   In the Boys' Brigade.

Robert   I'll give you a fight.

Morley   Rob's muscle is really big.

The insect buzzes around **Eileen**. *She screams.*

Robert   Don't be daft. It's only a wasp. Come on, Andy.

Andy   What?

Robert   Let's see your muscle.

Eileen *raises her eyebrows to* **Catherine**. **Catherine** *giggles.*

Morley   Let's see yours, Rob.

Robert   Mmmmm?

Morley   Go on. Please.

Robert *flexes his arm.*

Eileen (*to the insect*)   Get off.

Robert   For God's sake! She's a farmer's daughter too.

Eileen   It looks bigger than a wasp.

Morley *feels* **Rob**'s *muscle.*

Morley   Look.

Robert *indicates his stomach.*

Robert   Go on.

Morley *punches him.*

Robert   Solid as a rock.

Eileen *screams and swats the insect.*

Robert   It won't hurt you.

Eileen   I don't like them.

Robert   Don't be daft.

Eileen   Shut up.

Robert   You get hysterical.

Eileen   Leave me alone.

Robert   Temper, temper!

Frank   There it is.

Catherine *and* **Eileen** *both scream.*

Catherine   I don't like them either, Eileen.

Andy   Don't send it tae me.

Robert   It won't sting you.

Frank   Looks more like a hornet. Get off!

Morley *hits* **Robert** *in the stomach when he is not expecting it.*

Robert   Aowwhhh.

Morley   What?

Robert   What did you do that for?

The others smirk. **Catherine** *giggles.*

George   I want you to drive me into town this afternoon, Cathy.

Eileen   Why you going town?

George   I want to see the planning people. They say the well's gotta be further from the stream.

Eileen   I told you.

George   They'll be all right once I've talked to 'em.

Catherine   I was going to wash the sheets.

George   Eileen'll do that. Won't you, Elly?

Catherine   It's her afternoon off.

George   She'll be all right.

Catherine   Can you no drive yourself?

Eileen   He's lost his licence.

George   Bloody policeman only stopped the car 'cause it was me.

Morley   There's the hornet.

Eileen   Where?

Eileen *gets up and runs away.*

Morley   It's on the back of your head, Cathy.

Catherine *screams.* **Morley** *laughs.*

Catherine   Where is it? Where is it? Get it off me. Andy!

Andy   I'm no touching it.

Everyone except **Catherine** *is laughing. She runs around with the insect chasing her.* **Morley** *laughs hysterically.* **Catherine** *is almost in tears with panic.*

Robert   Let me get it. (*He goes towards* **Catherine** *and tries to swat the insect.*)

Eileen   Careful. It'll sting you.

Catherine   Is it still there?

George   It's gone.

There is a brief moment of waiting to see if the insect has gone.
Catherine *listens and watches. Suddenly she hears it.*

Catherine   No, it isnae. (*She runs towards the others.*)

They all run away from her because the insect is following her. More
screams. **Catherine** *trips over.* **Robert** *trips over her.*

Robert   There it is. (*He swats it.*) All right?

Catherine   Where is it?

Robert   It's gone. You OK?

Catherine   Yes, thanks. I was stung by a bee once when I
was little.

Robert   Can be nasty. (*He smiles at* **Catherine**.)

Andy *watches* **Catherine**'s *face.* **Eileen** *is looking at* **Robert**
and **Catherine**. *They all sit again.*

Andy   Anything to drink?

Catherine   Here. (*She gets up to give him some lemonade.*)

George   Nice sandwich.

Robert   Yeah.

Morley   Eileen never puts enough butter on.

Robert   She always scrapes it on. (*He smiles at* **Catherine**.)

Eileen   The postman's been, Morley. Brought you this
card.

She gives him a postcard.

Robert   Who's it from?

Eileen   Who do you think?

Robert   Let's see.

Morley   No. It's mine.

George   From his mother?

Eileen   She says she might come down at the end of the month.

Morley   How do you know?

Eileen   I read it.

Morley   You shouldn't have. It's my card.

Catherine   Is she on holiday?

Robert   Something like that.

Eileen   She's working in Hastings.

Robert *takes the card.*

Morley   Give it back.

Robert   Nice picture of the pier.

Morley   Tell him to give it back.

Robert *teases* **Morley**, *keeping the postcard just out of his reach.*

Morley   Elly!

Robert   Don't be such a baby.

Eileen   Give it back, Rob.

Morley   You can't read it anyway. See if you can. He can't.

Robert (*reading*)   'Dear Morley, how's my – '

Morley   Told you he couldn't read it.

Eileen   Rob.

Robert   'How's my – '

Eileen   '. . . darling . . .'

Robert   '. . . darling boy?' Aaaahhhh. 'Bill's going to drive me down to see you on the last . . .'

Eileen   '. . . weekend in August.'

Robert   '. . . weekend in August. He wants to meet you.' More fool Bill.

Eileen *looks at* **George**.

Robert   'Hope you're being yourself.'

Morley   Being? It doesn't say that. Stupid.

Eileen   'Behaving'. You're not though, are you?

Robert   '. . . behaving yourself. I'm missing you. Lots of love and kisses, Mum.' Isn't that sweet? Are you missing your mummy too?

Morley   Shut up; it was my card.

Robert   Cry-baby.

Morley   Shut up. Shut up!

Robert   Here.

Morley   I hate you. I hate all of you.

Morley *runs off*.

Eileen   Now look what you've done.

Robert   She should be here looking after him.

Pause.

It was only a bloody postcard.

Catherine   Who's Bill.

Eileen   The man she's housekeeping for.

Pause. **Robert** *rests his arm on the ground and is stung*.

Robert   Aowwh.

Eileen   What?

Robert   That bloody hornet. It was there. Aowwwhhh.

Frank   Thought it was a wasp.

Catherine *nudges* **Eileen**, *who starts to giggle*.

Robert   It's not funny, Eileen.

This makes **Catherine** *and* **Eileen** *laugh more. The others join in.* **Robert** *shakes his head at them in disdain*.

Eileen (*laughing*)   Let's have a look.

Robert (*angrily*)   Get off.

Pause. **Robert** *sucks on his hand.* **Catherine** *tries not to giggle, hiding behind* **Eileen**. **Frank** *and* **Andy** *are also trying to hide the fact that they are laughing.* **Catherine** *snorts, which makes the others burst out laughing.*

Eileen   Do you want me to see if I can get it out?

Robert (*roughly*)   No.

Eileen   All right.

Robert   Leave me alone.

Eileen   Now you know what it feels like.

Robert   Don't be so bloody pathetic. You've never been stung, anyway.

Pause.

Catherine   I should have some cream here. (*She looks in her bag and takes out a tube.*) Let's see.

Robert *shows her his hand.*

Catherine   Does it hurt?

Robert   No.

Catherine   It's really swelling.

Frank *starts singing the chorus of 'It's Now or Never' to himself, unaware that what he is singing is apposite.*

Catherine   That better?

Robert   Bit.

Frank *is singing the first stanza of the song.*

Eileen   Do you dance, Andy?

Andy   Eh?

Eileen   You could take Catherine to the Young Farmers Club Fancy Dress. Derek could easily get two more tickets. He's secretary.

Catherine   He's two left feet when it comes tae ballroom dancing. He only knows the twist.

Robert   I'll take you.

Catherine   Oh.

Eileen   Thought you weren't going.

Robert   Never said that.

Eileen   Andy might want to go.

Andy   No.

Frank *is singing the chorus again.*

Catherine   You've a good voice, Frank.

Robert   He likes Elvis.

Catherine   I used to be a Cliff fan. I like John now, though. And Ringo.

Frank (*shocked*)   You don't!

Catherine   I went to see them.

Frank   Live?

Catherine   Ay.

Frank *finds this hilarious.*

Frank   Bloody hell! All that screaming!

Andy   She likes Susan Maugham an all.

Andy *sings two lines from 'Bobby's Girl'. They ignore him. During the following, he takes his shirt off and lies down, closing his eyes.*

George   Better get that pump going, Frank.

Frank   Idn any petrol in it.

George   Go up the garage on your scooter and get some.

George *and* **Frank** *look at each other.*

George   You got a half crown, Rob?

Robert   No.

George *looks at* **Eileen**.

Eileen I haven't got my purse.

Catherine Hang on. (*She looks in her bag.*)

George She's doing a grand job, this girl.

Eileen Mmmm.

Catherine Here you are.

She passes some money to **George**, *who gives it to* **Frank**.

Frank *exits, singing the next stanza of the song.*

George Helped me feed the calves this morning. We'll make a proper farmer of her.

Eileen *starts picking up the remains of the food.*

Catherine Leave all that, Eileen.

Robert I haven't had a drink yet.

Eileen Hurry up, then.

Catherine I'll bring it down.

Robert Leave it, for God's sake. Stop fussing.

Eileen You're so bossy, you. I'm fed up with it. Think you can tell everyone what to do. Maybe they don't want to do what you want them to do.

Robert What's up with you?

Eileen There's nothing wrong with me. It's you. You want to learn a bit of give and take. You're just a selfish pig.

Eileen *exits.*

Robert What's got into her?

George She'll soon cool off.

Catherine I'll go and help her with the washing. Eileen! Wait for me.

George Need to be in town before the town hall closes.

Catherine We'll manage. Eileen!

She picks up the food and exits.

George *and* **Robert** *stand watching her.*

George   Bloody good girl.

Robert   Mmmm.

George   Reminds me of Kate Ledger.

Robert   The one you used to take out in her pony and trap?

George   Lovely girl. Had hair just like that.

Robert   Why didn't you marry her?

George   Got TB.

Robert   You never told me that.

George (*singing*)   I'll take you home again, Kathleen.

Robert   So Mum's bringing this bloke.

George   Soon get rid of that bugger.

Robert   Yeah.

George   End of the month, she say?

Robert   Yeah.

George   Should have the water laid on by then.

Robert   Fancy bringing him with her.

George   He'll get my boot up his backside.

Morley *enters.*

Robert (*indicating* **Morley**)   Little pigs!

George   Better get into town.

George *exits.*

Robert (*to* **Morley**)   You're a selfish little bugger.

Morley *pokes his tongue out at him.* **Robert** *kicks* **Andy**.

Robert   Wakey, wakey.

Andy (*with surprising ferocity*)   You kick me again, pal, and you'll regret it.

Robert   All right, all right.

Robert *goes out, back to the well.*

Andy *lies on his back, looking straight up at the sky.*

Morley   I hate him. Do you?

Andy   You see that cloud way up there?

Morley   Which one?

Andy   That one. It looks like a man on a horse.

Morley   I can't see it. (*He lies down near* **Andy**.)

Andy   There. You see that wee bit sticking out?

Morley   Yes.

Andy   Well, just tae the top of that. That's the horse's head. He's got steam coming out of his nostrils. See it?

Morley   Yeah.

Andy   And there's the man on his back.

Morley   Oh yeah, I can see it now.

Andy   That's Matt Devine on his palomino stallion.

Morley   Who's Matt Devine?

Andy   Do ye no know Matt Devine? He's the fastest draw in the West.

Morley   And what's his horse called?

Andy   Ahh . . . that's . . . ahhh . . . that's Cloud, of course.

Morley   What, the horse is called Cloud?

Andy   Ay, what else? Kepaow. Kepaow. The bad guys are in the rocks above Devil's Canyon when Matt rides through. Kepaow. Kepaow. He takes cover behind a boulder. Kepaow. (*In Matt's voice.*) 'Steady, Cloud.' (*In Jake's voice.*) 'We're going to kill you, Matt Devine.' (*In Matt's voice.*) 'That's what you think, Jake.' Kepaow. Kepaow. (*In Jake's voice.*) 'Aaaaargghhhh. He got me.' The bad guy falls down. Dead. (*In Matt's voice.*) 'You wanna feel a bullet in your chest too, Trampas?' (*In Trampas's voice.*) 'You won't get me, Devine!' Kepaow.

Morley *giggles.*

Andy (*in Matt's voice*) 'You shot Cloud. That's it,
Trampas!' Kepaow. Kepaow. Kepaow. Kepaow. (*In Matt's
voice.*) 'Nobody hurts my horse, Trampas. You had to die.'

Morley *is entranced.*

Morley   Was Cloud dead?

Andy   No. Just hit in the leg. Matt Devine had to ride him
into town to see the horse doctor. (*He makes the sound of a horse
trotting lamely. He lies on the grass looking at the clouds again.*)

Morley *studies him.*

Morley   You've got a spider on you. (*He reaches out and takes
the spider on to his finger from* **Andy***'s arm. He looks at it on his finger.
He blows it off. He points at* **Andy***'s side.*) What's that?

Andy   What?

Morley   That scar.

Andy   That's where Jake's bullet got me. (*He closes his eyes.*)
Mmmm. It's great. That sun.

Morley *reaches out and touches the scar.*

Andy   What are you doing?

Morley   Nothing.

Pause.

Was it really a gunshot?

Andy   Ay.

Morley   Really?

Andy   No.

Morley   What was it?

Andy   A knife.

Morley *traces the scar.*

Scene Three

The living room.

Eileen *is scrubbing the floor.*

Robert *enters.*

Robert   Just wanted to use the looking-glass.

Eileen   Don't go where I've washed.

Robert   Aren't you going to get changed?

Eileen   Yes. After I've done this.

Robert   Trust her to arrive just when we're all trying to get ready. (*He looks at himself in the mirror.*) It's quite a good fit. Uncle Sonny's old tuxedo. You think I need a badge?

No response.

Elly!

Eileen   A badge?

Robert   O-o-seven.

Eileen   Thought you had a gun.

Robert   I can't wave that around all the time.

Eileen   Mmmmmm.

Robert   What's Cathy doing?

Eileen   Making some scones for tea.

Morley *runs in with a bunch of wild flowers.*

Morley   I've picked these. I'm going to do an arrangement.

Eileen   Careful.

Morley   Where's that pretty vase?

Eileen   Which one?

Morley   Mum's favourite.

Eileen   In the kitchen.

He runs towards the kitchen.

Don't make a mess. I've just cleaned up out there.

Morley   All right, Ratty.

Morley *exits.*

Robert   Don't know why you bother. She'll still complain however clean it is. Has Dad emptied his chamber pot?

Eileen   I don't know.

Robert   You know how she went on about that the last time she came home.

Eileen   They're only calling in, you know.

Robert   Isn't she staying the night?

Eileen   No. They're going down to Cornwall to see this Bill's mother.

Robert   Does Morley know that?

Eileen   I haven't said anything.

Robert   What a mother!

George *enters.*

George   Not here yet, then?

Eileen   Don't get mud on this floor.

George   Should be here by now.

Robert   Get the tank filled up?

George   Need more jubilee clips. You make much on the logs?

Robert   Four quid or so.

George   I want to get taps.

Robert   I gave Cathy and Andy ten bob each.

George   Just need a couple of quid.

Eileen   Frank's on the warpath. Wants his wages.

Robert   This arrived today from the solicitors.

George What is it?

Robert Tells you about how to draw up a partnership.

George Mmmm. Where's my black trousers, Elly?

Robert What you want them for?

George Wanted to put 'em on.

Robert I'm wearing them for my costume.

George Gave five bob for those.

Eileen Your suit trousers are clean.

George Need a clean shirt, too.

Eileen There's one in the chest of drawers on the landing.

George *starts to go.*

Eileen Don't forget to wash your neck first.

Robert You want to look at this?

George Better have me wash.

George *exits.*

Eileen Dad!

George (*off*) What?

Eileen Empty your pot.

She returns to her scrubbing.

Robert Pathetic, really, isn't it?

Eileen What?

Robert Him getting all spruced up for her.

Eileen Mmmm.

Robert God! Fancy being married to a woman like that. (*He looks at the forms.*) Looks fairly straightforward. What's that word?

Eileen Inheritance.

Robert Something about death duties. A partnership gets round that, you see.

Eileen   I hate talking about things like that.

Robert   Ought to get it sorted out. Sooner the better.

Eileen   He's not going to die for years.

Morley *enters with the flowers. He also has a very sharp knife.*

He puts the flowers in the middle of the table.

Robert   Very nice. Mummy will like them.

Morley *starts to go.*

Eileen   What you doing with that knife?

Morley   Andy needs it.

Eileen   What for?

Morley   He caught a rabbit in that trap. He's going to skin it and we're going to make a camp-fire.

Eileen   Don't get yourself dirty.

Morley *exits.*

Robert   First time I've known Morley interested in skinning a rabbit.

Eileen   That's Andy's influence.

Robert   'Bout time he started doing things normal boys do.

Eileen   They made a terrible mess in the bedroom. They've painted a cowboy on the wall. He's a funny boy, Andy.

Robert   S'pose.

Eileen   Don't really understand that relationship.

Robert   What relationship?

Eileen   Cathy and Andy.

Robert   He used to be her boyfriend, that's all. Nothing funny about it. What are you going as, anyway?

Eileen   Ruth.

Robert   Ruth who?

Eileen   Ruth from the Bible.

Robert   Oh.

Eileen   I've made one of those blue curtains into a long dress. And I'm going to wear that big white shawl over my head.

Robert   You'll look more like the Virgin Mary.

Eileen   I'm going to carry a basket with a sheaf of corn.

Robert   Why?

Eileen   Like I've been gleaning.

Robert   Gleaning?

Eileen   That's what she did.

Robert   Did she?

Eileen   Don't you remember Ruth and Naomi?

Robert   Vaguely.

Eileen   Naomi was her mother-in-law and when Ruth's husband died she stayed with her. (*She stops scrubbing.*) 'Whither thou goest, I will go; and where thou lodgest, I will lodge.'

Robert   Oh yeah.

Eileen   Then they fell on hard times and she had to go out picking up corn in the fields. Gleaning. Gran had that picture of *Ruth in the Alien Corn*.

Robert   Cathy's made herself a kilt.

Eileen   I know.

Robert   She was going to go as a geisha girl.

Eileen   Mmmmm.

Robert   Why don't you ask her if you can borrow her dressing-gown and go as that.

Eileen   I'm going as Ruth.

Robert   Please yourself.

Eileen   You haven't even seen my costume and you're already criticising it.

Robert   I'm not.

Pause.

What's Derek going as?

Eileen   Charlie Chaplin.

Robert *laughs.*

Robert   He's a good bloke.

Eileen   Mmm.

Robert   Reliable.

Eileen   I suppose.

Robert   Feel sorry for him, really?

Eileen   Why?

Robert   The way you treat him.

Eileen   What do you mean, the way I treat him?

Robert   He's obviously smitten.

Eileen   So?

Robert   You can't go through life looking for the perfect person, Elly.

Eileen *does not respond.*

Robert   Cathy thinks Derek Rudd would be very good for you.

Eileen   Does she?

Robert   She says you need someone who'll look after you. Treat you like a lady. She's a good judge of character. Shrewd, see? You should have seen her buttering up old Hetherington-Smythe this afternoon. We went up there to see if he wanted to buy some logs. He doesn't usually get any in the summer. She told him how nice his garden was and admired his lawn. Charmed him. Ended up buying half the load.

Eileen   Excuse me.

He moves. She scrubs.

Robert   Thing about Cathy is her independence. How many girls would be able to do what she did this summer? Just hitched to the other end of the country. Takes a lot of courage to do that, you know. Didn't have anything fixed up.

Eileen   I went to Bristol on my course.

Robert   You came home every weekend. Trouble with you, Elly, you're too self-sacrificing. You don't want to get stuck here. I mean, look at Aunty Pam. She lived for Dad and Uncle Sonny. Then when they got married, she never got over it. You don't want to end up like her.

Catherine *enters, wearing a kilt and carrying a plate of scones.*

Catherine   There we are.

Robert   A Scots girl in the Alien Corn, eh, Elly.

Catherine   What?

Robert   These look nice. (*He goes to take one.*)

They struggle.

Catherine   Don't. They're for tea.

He eats a scone.

Robert   Mmmmm. Lovely.

Catherine   You should wait.

They giggle.

Will I put some jam in your sponge, Eileen?

Eileen   I'll do that, thank you.

Eileen *exits with the bucket of water.*

Robert   I'll bloody kill her!

Catherine   Don't.

Robert   Going around with a face like a poker. It's not natural.

Catherine   What?

Robert   The way she behaves.

He kisses her.

Catherine   Careful.

Robert   Come on.

Catherine   I ought to get my make-up on.

Robert   You don't need make-up. (*He moves to kiss her again.*)

Catherine   Shhh.

Eileen *enters, crosses and exits.*

Robert *and* **Catherine** *giggle.*

Catherine   You havenae got your bow-tie on.

Robert   It's upstairs.

She kisses him.

Catherine   Go on. (*She looks at herself in the glass for a long time. Then she starts putting her make-up on.*)

Andy *enters with the knife. He has blood all over his hands and face.*

He stands looking at her. She suddenly sees him and jumps.

Catherine   What have you done?

Andy   Nothing. (*He finds a piece of string.*)

She returns to her make-up. He looks at her and starts whistling 'Bobby's Girl'. He has a rabbit's foot which he binds with the string.

Morley *runs in.*

Morley   Ugh. It was horrible. He took the rabbit's insides out. I'm going to put the rabbit's foot in my museum. I've got blood on my finger. Look.

Catherine   Get away, Morley.

Morley Yeeughhhh.

Catherine Stop it!

Andy Bring you good luck, a rabbit's foot. You should wear it round your neck.

Morley Ughhh.

Catherine You're revolting.

Andy Look at that, all the wee strings in its legs. Look.

Morley *draws away.*

Andy It willnae hurt you. Look. Touch it.

Morley *draws near.*

Andy Take it.

Morley No.

Andy Blood. Blood. Go on.

Morley No.

Andy *whispers to* **Morley**. **Morley** *takes the sinew and creeps up on* **Catherine**, *holding it out and singing 'Bobby's Girl'.*

Catherine (*angrily*) Get off, Morley.

Morley *is taken aback.* **Andy** *continues whistling.*

Catherine Which colour? (*She holds up two lipsticks.*)

Morley *does not respond.*

Catherine Morley.

He ignores her.

Andy We could chop its head off and mount it on a piece of wood like a trophy.

Catherine Do you like this colour, Morley?

Morley No.

Catherine This one?

Morley Yeah.

Catherine OK. (*She starts to put on the lipstick.*)

Morley *watches her.*

Morley   David Buckingham is going to the fancy dress.

Catherine   You wish you were coming?

Morley   Mum will be here.

Catherine   Of course.

Morley   Do you wish you were going, Andy?

Andy   No.

Morley   Anyway, Andy's taking me to the fair next week, so there.

Catherine   I think you were right about the colour.

Morley   You have to do that now on a piece of paper. (*He presses his lips together.*)

Catherine   You want to try it?

Morley *giggles.*

Andy   There you are, Morley. (*He holds up the rabbit's foot.*)

Catherine   Do you?

Morley *giggles again.*

Andy   Will we stretch the skin out to dry?

Catherine   Would suit you. Come here.

Morley *approaches.* **Catherine** *puts the lipstick on him.*

Andy   Will we, Morley?

Morley   Yeah.

Catherine   There. Look.

Morley *looks in the mirror.*

Catherine   Andy once put on all my make-up.

Morley *giggles.*

Catherine   Want some eye-shadow?

Morley   OK.

Catherine   Here. (*She applies the eye-shadow.*) Keep still.
(*She finishes.*)

He wants to look in the mirror.

Wait. (*She puts mascara on his eyelashes.*) There. What do you
think?

He shrugs.

Show Andy.

Andy   Very nice.

Frank *enters.*

Frank   You seen Dad?

Catherine   Is he no up at the well?

Frank   Been up there. He owes me my wages.

Catherine   Oh dear.

Frank   He's cashed the milk cheque and he hasn't given me
anything. (*To* **Morley**.) What are you doing?

Morley   Putting on Cathy's make-up.

Frank *shakes his head.*

Morley   Can I put on your ear-rings?

Catherine   Which ones?

Morley   The sparkly ones.

Catherine   OK.

Morley *exits.*

Catherine   I could lend you some money.

Frank   No. I'll get it off him.

Catherine   Mebbe he needs it.

Frank   But he always does it, you see, Cathy.

Catherine   Uh-huh.

Frank   You never know what you're going to get from one
day to the next. I'm trying to save up to buy a car, see. Saw a

little Morris in Westcott's garage in town. Needs a new throttle, new gasket, but I could do that meself. Mr Westcott only wants seventy-five quid for it. He said if I did a few jobs for him I could have it for less.

Catherine   Will your dad no buy it for you?

Frank   Don't know about that.

Pause.

Better go and get washed.

Catherine   Cannae wait to see your costume.

Frank *laughs.*

Catherine   I still think you should be going as Ringo.

Frank   I'm not that ugly.

Catherine   How dare you!

Frank   You seen the nose on him?

Catherine   Away wi' you.

Frank *exits singing the lines about a rabbit's foot from 'Good Luck Charm'.*

Catherine *returns to the mirror.*

Holding the knife, **Andy** *stands looking at her. They stare at each other.*

Catherine   You smell. You havenae washed for weeks.

Andy   Have you done it wi' him yet?

She does not reply.

Cannae be very comfortable doing it in that car of his. Not like that nice flat Mr Capaldi got you. With that great big double bed in it.

Catherine   I left some scones in the oven.

She exits.

Andy *looks at the knife. He pulls his shirt up. Slowly he draws the blade along his stomach.*

Catherine *enters.*

She looks at him. She takes the knife from him.

Catherine   I thought you were over that.

Andy   They used to shut me up in a dark room when I did it at the home. You could do that.

Catherine   Please, Andy.

Andy   You're just like everyone else. Mum and Dad didnae want me. My foster parents didnae want me. The Navy didnae want me. And now you don't want me.

Catherine   That's no true.

Andy   It is. (*He starts to cry.*)

She comforts him.

Catherine   Don't, Andy.

Andy   I don't know why you came down here this summer.

Catherine   I was worried about you.

Slowly, his tears subside.

Let me see that! (*She dabs at the cut with a handkerchief and applies the cream she used on* **Rob***'s sting.*)
    The second wee craw
    Fell and broke his jaw
    Fell and broke his jaw
    Fell and broke his jaw aw aw aw *etc.*

Andy   You used to say you'd run away wi' me to Australia.

Catherine   I'll always look after you. You know that.

Andy *does not respond.*

Catherine   Don't you?

Andy   Do you love me, though?

Catherine   Of course I do.

Morley *enters, wearing ear-rings and high heels.*

They look at him. **Catherine** *laughs.* **Andy** *starts laughing as well.*

Catherine   You look great, Morley.

Andy   You lookin' for me, Lily?

Morley   Who's Lily?

Andy   She's a bar girl at the Silver Dollar Saloon.

He dances with **Morley***, singing 'She'll Be Coming Round the Mountain'.*

Robert *enters.*

Andy   Oooh. There's a stranger just rode into town.

Morley   My name's Lily. Hallo.

They laugh.

What are you doing in our saloon?

Robert   The name is Bond. James Bond.

Catherine *straightens his bow tie.* **Andy** *whispers in* **Morley***'s ear.* **Morley** *walks up to* **Robert** *'seductively'.*

Morley   Hallo, James.

They laugh.

Would you like a drink of beer?

Robert   Scotch on the rocks.

Morley   Kiss me, James.

Robert   Get off.

Morley   I'm not a spy.

Robert   Stop it, Morley.

Morley   Kiss me.

Robert   Stop it.

He pushes **Morley** *away.*

Morley   Aowwhhh.

Andy *laughs.*

Catherine   You look great.

Robert   Thanks.

Eileen enters.

The others look at her for a moment. They all burst out laughing.

Eileen   What's so funny?

Andy   You look like the BVM.

Morley   What's the BVM?

Andy   The Blessed Virgin Mary. (*He crosses himself in front of her.*)

Morley   You look silly.

Eileen   Hark who's talking. You'd better get that off. Mum will be here soon.

Morley   I want her to see it. I look better than you.

Robert   You can't go like that.

Catherine   You look fine, Eileen.

Eileen   What's wrong with it?

Robert   Lend her your dressing-gown, Cathy. She could go as a geisha girl.

Morley *grabs* **Eileen**'s *shawl and puts it over his head.*

Morley   I'm a ratty ratface and I'm the BVM.

Eileen   Give it back.

Morley *refuses.*

Eileen   Morley. (*She smacks* **Morley**.)

Morley   What's wrong with you? Just because Cathy's costume is better than yours.

Eileen   Give it back.

She grabs the shawl. He pulls her hair.

Let go.

Morley   No.

She grabs his hair.

Eileen   Let go.

Morley   You let go.

Eileen   Not until you do.

Morley   Well, I'm not going to.

Robert   Stop it. Both of you. Morley!

Morley   I'm not letting go. Aowwwhhh.

Eileen   Let go, then.

Morley   No.

They crash around.

Eileen   Nasty little brat.

Morley   Ugly old maid.

Robert   Stop it.

Frank (*off*)   Give it to me.

George (*off*)   You just calm down.

Frank (*off*)   It's my money.

George (*off*)   You'll get it.

Morley *and* **Eileen** *stop fighting. Sound of doors slamming.*

Catherine   Frank wants his wages.

Robert   He's got money.

Catherine   It's not fair, Robert.

Robert   You should see. He's got a bank account with fifty quid in it.

Catherine   Ay, well, that's his savings.

Andy   Have tae get the union on to your dad.

Catherine   If Frank does the milking he should get the money.

Eileen   We don't need outsiders coming and telling us what to do.

George *enters with the pot in his hand.*

George   What?

Robert   Nothing.

George   I had to buy piping and get it laid.

Catherine   Could you no let Frank have some of the log money?

George   Need that to buy taps and jubilee clips.

Robert   Trouble with Frank is he's like an old miser. He's always got money when he needs a new shirt or a part for his scooter.

Catherine   Mebbe that's because he's good with money. Doesnae mean he shouldnae get his wages.

Frank *enters.*

Frank   Let me have it.

George (*holding out the pot*)   You keep away.

Frank   Bloody bastard.

Eileen   Frank!

Frank   What? You're all on his bloody side.

Catherine   Give him some log money.

George   He's not having that. Let me have it, Rob.

Robert *hesitates.*

George   Come on.

Robert   Tidn fair, Dad.

George   Give it to me.

Robert   No, Dad.

Robert *gives* **Frank** *a pound note.* **George** *snatches it from* **Frank**.

Robert   Dad!

George   He's not having it.

Robert   Give it to him.

George   This is my money. Those logs came off my land.

Robert *takes the money back and gives it to* **Frank**.

Frank *exits*.

George (*to* **Catherine**)   Now, look, I'm not having people coming here and interfering.

Robert   Don't talk to her like that.

George   You keep quiet, son.

Catherine   It was Frank's money.

George   You got a lot to learn, young lady.

Catherine   I already know what's fair.

George   You don't know anything.

Catherine   Here, take your bloody money.

She gets a pound note from her purse and holds it out to **George**.

Robert   Don't, Cathy. You earned that.

Catherine   I don't mind. Here.

George *takes* **Catherine**'s *money*.

Catherine *exits*.

Robert   You mean old bugger.

Robert *tries to snatch the money back. The pot spills. The note tears*.

Morley   Ughhhh.

Robert   Now look what you've done.

Eileen   Cathy should mind her own business.

Andy   What d'ye mean?

Eileen   Thinks she can tell us all what to do.

Andy   Don't worry, we willnae stick around. We don't need you.

Eileen   Go, then.

Morley   Elly!

Andy *exits.*

Morley *follows him.*

Eileen *gets her purse.*

Robert   You're pathetic, Eileen. (*To* **George**.) Give me the other half.

Eileen (*offering a pound note to* **George**)   Here, Dad.

Robert   Give it to me.

George *refuses.*

Eileen   Give her this one. Seeing as you're so worried about her. (*She gives* **Robert** *her note.*)

He takes it and throws the torn half into the chamber pot.

Robert   Hope you're satisfied.

Robert *exits.*

George *fishes the note from the pot.*

Eileen *takes the pot and exits.*

George *is left alone, drying the wet half of the note.*

Eileen *enters with the bucket and a floor-cloth.*

She starts cleaning up. **George** *is trying to put the note back together. A car drives up outside.* **George** *looks out the window.*

George   Your mother's here.

Scene Four

All, except **Frank**, *are seated around the tea table.*

Peggy   I'll never forget it. He was only three years old, weren't you, Morley? He stood up in front of the whole congregation and said it so loud and clear. What was it about? 'Bout a little boy in Africa who found Jesus, wasn't it? And the preacher pointed to all the other kids in the Sunday School and said 'You're all the cake, and this one,' and he pointed to Morley, 'this one's the cherry on the top.' It's true, Catherine.

Catherine   I believe you.

Peggy   Course, he's always been clever. Learnt to read way before he went to school. I always remember Robert bringing one of his books back from school and not being able to read one of the words and Morley told him what it said. Didn't he, Rob?

Robert   Mmmmm.

Peggy   Course, George says he takes after his family. No one else can have any brains. He forgets that my father was a very clever man. He was a butcher. Ran his own business. And my mum was a wonderful speller. She won a prize for spelling. Course she came from a very educated family. Her uncle was Lord Mayor, mind. What do you think of that?

Catherine   Amazing.

Peggy   Morley looks just like him. Same eyes.

Catherine   Right.

Peggy   Now he's going to grammar school.

Catherine   I know.

Peggy   Course, Eileen did quite well, went to grammar school. But Rob was hopeless.

Catherine   Mebbe he wasnae encouraged enough.

Peggy   He wasn't interested.

George   He learnt all he had to learn.

Morley   Mum.

Peggy   What?

Morley   Do I have to wear short trousers?

Peggy   What do you mean?

Morley   To grammar school.

Peggy   What does it say on the form?

Morley   It says you can wear long or short.

Eileen   All the boys wear short trousers until the second or third years.

Morley   David Buckingham isn't.

Eileen   Don't start, Morley.

Peggy   What is he going to wear?

Eileen   Rob's old ones.

Peggy   They had holes in them.

Eileen   I've cut them off and taken them in.

Peggy   He ought to have new trousers for a new school.

Morley   See.

Peggy   Mr Buckingham wouldn't have his son going to school in cast-offs.

George   When we've got this well built there'll be plenty of money. You'll be able to do cream teas without the health inspector coming snooping.

Peggy   I'm not doing cream teas. I've already got a job, thank you.

George   Cathy'll help out, won't you, Cathy?

Catherine   I don't know.

Morley   Andy, look. (*He blows down his straw.*)

Andy   Ay.

George   She's a good little worker, this one.

Peggy   See, Cathy, that's what he wants. Someone he can leave at home working while he goes off to market gallivanting.

George   You haven't got anything to complain about.

Peggy   Hear that? I haven't got anything to complain about. What do you think of this house, Catherine?

Catherine   It's great.

Peggy   What?

Catherine   Well . . . I mean . . . it's got a lot of potential.

Peggy   It might have potential. What do you think of it as it is?

Catherine   I suppose it's a wee bit basic.

Peggy   You've hit the nail on the head there, Catherine. Hear that? She can see what this house is like. It's basic. I'd say it was verging on the primitive, wouldn't you, Catherine?

Catherine   Well . . .

Peggy   No water. No proper electricity. No comfort. No nothing.

George   She's an ungrateful woman, Catherine.

Peggy   You leave Catherine out of this.

George   Cathy and I understand one another, don't we, Cathy?

Catherine   Do we?

George   You had one of her scones yet? Be able to sell these with a bit of clotted cream. Make a fortune.

Peggy   Who made the sponge?

Eileen   I did.

Peggy   Sunk in the middle, hasn't it?

Morley *blows down the straw again.*

Eileen   Stop it, Morley.

Morley   All right, ratty ratface.

George   So you gonna come up and see it?

Peggy   What?

George   The well.

Morley   Mum.

Peggy   I don't want to see a well.

Morley Will you come up and look at Andy's painting?

Peggy What do I want to see a well for?

Morley Will you, Mum?

Peggy What?

Morley Andy's done a painting on my bedroom wall. Will you come and look at it?

Peggy What do you mean, on the wall?

Andy It's a mural.

Peggy A what?

Andy A mural.

Morley It's a cowboy on a horse. He copied it from a book he's got. He's a really good drawer, Mum. The horse looks real.

Peggy I thought you didn't like cowboy stories.

Morley I do.

Peggy We only papered that room last year.

Pause.

Terrible smell of Dettol in here.

Morley That's 'cause Dad spilt his –

Eileen Shut up, Morley.

Pause. **Morley** *blows down his straw.*

Catherine Frank's no going to have time for his tea if he doesnae hurry up.

Peggy What time does this dance start.

Robert Eight.

Eileen We don't have to be there till nine.

Peggy You don't want to be late.

Eileen We'll have hardly seen you.

Peggy　You don't have to worry about me. You go off and enjoy yourselves.

Pause.

You going like that?

Eileen　Yes.

Peggy　You ought to go as Christine Keeler.

Eileen　Why?

Peggy　Topical, isn't it?

George　You know what they say about Christine Keeler, don't you?

Peggy　All right, all right. We don't want to hear any of your filth.

George　She was up to her neck in champagne . . .

Peggy　That's enough, George.

George　And he was up to his arse in cider.

Peggy　Really!

George　Get it, Cathy?

Catherine　Oh. Ay.

Morley　I don't. Do you, Andy?

Peggy　He's got a dirty mind, Cathy.

Morley　Why was it cider?

Eileen　Shut up, Morley.

Morley　Shut up, Morley.

Peggy　I don't know what the world's coming to. There's no standards any more. He was a government minister, mind. And she was sleeping with the Russians. Had a bloomin' KGB man as well as him. Never heard anything like it. That bloke who took the overdose, who was her whatchymecallit, pimp, what was his name? He was the son of a vicar. Just shows, though, doesn't it? They pretend to be so whiter than white all of 'em. And underneath they're as bad as anyone else. Worse.

Eileen   S'pose everyone's got skeletons in their cupboards.

Catherine *looks at her.*

Peggy   What's that supposed to mean?

Frank *enters in his Elvis costume.*

Catherine   Wow. Look at you.

Frank *sings three lines of 'Rock a Hula'.*

Catherine   It's great, Frank.

Frank   Thank you.

Robert   Your face doesn't look much like Elvis.

Catherine   That doesnae matter. It's the spirit of it he's got. Frank takes after you more than his dad.

Peggy   Mmmmm.

Catherine   The rest of the family's quite tall.

Peggy   Pass him some bread and butter, Morley.

Catherine   Not that Frank's short. It's just that his dad and Rob are quite tall. And Frank's sort of medium height.

Peggy   More trifle, Morley?

Eileen   He's already had two lots.

Morley   Yes, please.

Catherine   Was your father tall?

Peggy   He was fairly tall.

Catherine   It's funny that, i'n't it?

Peggy   Mmmmm.

Pause.

Catherine   My faether's quite tall.

Eileen   Is your father tall, Andy?

Andy   Ay.

George   I want you to get the pump going, Frank.

Frank   You'll be lucky. I'm not going upover in this. Haven't got time anyway.

George   Won't take a minute. Want to show your mother the water running into the tank in the barn.

Frank   Let me have me wages, then I might.

Peggy   Don't talk to him like that, Frank.

Robert   Before we go . . .

Peggy   What?

Robert   I got something to say.

Morley   Andy, look. (*He opens his mouth and shows* **Andy** *the contents.*)

Andy *laughs.*

Peggy   Morley!

Robert   I want a partnership in the farm.

Eileen (*impatiently*)   Ohhh.

Robert   What?

Eileen   Nothing. Do you want some more tea, Dad?

Peggy   Stop fussing over him. 'You all right, Daddy?'

Eileen *goes into the kitchen.*

Robert   I've got some stuff about it from the solicitor. We should get it sorted out.

George   There's plenty of time for that.

Robert   The sooner we do it the better.

Peggy   Why?

Robert   Death duties.

Morley *is showing* **Andy** *the contents of his mouth.*

Peggy   Morley!

Andy *opens his mouth at* **Morley.**

Peggy (*to* **Andy**)   Don't encourage him, please.

Andy *and* **Morley** *try to suppress their giggles.*

Peggy   There's more than just you to be considered, you know. There's Eileen and Morley. And I don't want to be left with nothing.

Eileen *enters with the teapot.*

Robert   He's always promised me this farm.

Peggy   I don't want to be dependent on you once he's dead.

Eileen   Do we have to talk about this now?

Robert   When else are we going to talk about it?

Peggy   I know you, Robert. You'll just spend it all once you've got it. Look at that car. The amount of petrol that must use. You don't need a car like that. Spend, spend, spend. That's you.

Morley   He bought Cathy a ring.

Peggy   Did he?

Morley   Yeah. She's wearing it on that chain around her neck.

Silence.

Robert   It's an engagement ring.

Peggy   Well, let's see it, then.

Catherine *takes it off the chain and hands it round.*

Peggy   Very nice. What are those little stones?

Robert   Diamonds.

Peggy   Mmmm.

Eileen   It's lovely.

Peggy   Well, congratulations.

Frank   Yeah, congratulations, Cathy. Good luck to you.

Catherine   Thanks, Frank.

Peggy   I never got an engagement ring. That's the sort of husband I had.

Morley   Are you going to come and live here?

Catherine   I don't know.

Peggy   If you've any sense you'll get as far away from here as possible. Take it from me, Catherine. I know. We lived with George's family when we got married. His sister, Pam, was always interfering. Never works out.

Robert   That's why I want to get it all settled legally.

Eileen   I'm sure Cathy doesn't want to listen to all this.

Robert   You don't understand. If we don't get it sorted out we could lose half this place when he dies.

Eileen   Why don't you just push him in his grave?

Robert   Don't be so bloody daft. We know why you don't want to talk about it. You're bloody jealous, that's your trouble.

Eileen   And you can't see what's going on in front of your eyes.

Peggy   Why anyone should want to marry into this family I don't know.

Eileen   Shut up! Just shut up!

Andy *exits.*

Morley *gets up.*

Peggy   What do you say?

Morley   Please can I leave the table?

Peggy   Mustn't forget your manners. Go on.

Morley *exits.*

Peggy   Don't you ever talk to me like that. Telling me I've got skeletons in my cupboard.

Eileen   I didn't say that.

Peggy   I know you and your little jibes. 'Everyone's got skeletons in their cupboards.' Sitting there with that little smile on your face. But underneath you're being catty. That's just like his sister, Pam. Your father's the one with skeletons in his cupboard. Not me. I haven't got any skeletons.

George   How many men would take a wife back after she's jumped into bed with another man and had a kid by him?

Peggy   That's right; throw that up again. You do anything wrong and it gets thrown up to you for the rest of your life. Course, you don't talk about what you've done.

Frank *starts to leave quietly.*

George   I haven't done anything.

Peggy   Oh, no? You know what he did, Catherine, while I was in hospital having Robert?

Eileen   Stop it!

Frank *has gone.*

Peggy   My sister, Lily, came and looked after him, and you know what he did?

George   Lily knows what happened. You ask her.

Peggy   He slept with my own sister. That's what your beloved Daddy did. That's the sort of man he is.

George   That sort of thing runs in your family.

Peggy   And what do you mean by that?

George   You know. All the women in your family have the same weakness. Your sister Lily's like it. Your precious mother was no better.

Peggy   You leave my mother out of this.

George   The Lord Mayor's niece had to get married from what I heard. She was pregnant when she married your father.

Peggy   How dare you.

George   Then there was Manfred. She went off with a bloody POW, Catherine. Had a little Jerry bastard.

Peggy   I'll kill you.

Catherine *starts to go.*

George   You stay here. You might learn something.

Catherine *stays.*

Peggy   Ohhh! (*She throws* **Morley**'s *flowers and then food at* **George**.)

Eileen   Mum!

Peggy   Don't you 'Mum' me. You think the same as him. You all take his side. He's a dirty old man and a liar. (*She goes to hit* **George**.)

George *holds her hands. They struggle.*

Eileen   Dad! Mum! Don't!

Morley *runs on.*

Morley   Leave her alone. Leave her alone! (*He kicks* **George**.)

Eileen   Morley, stop it.

George (*to* **Peggy**)   You behave yourself. This is what she gets like, Cathy. Hysterical.

Eileen   Dad.

Peggy *cries.*

Robert   Let's go.

Catherine *hesitates.*

Robert   Get your coat.

Catherine *exits.*

Robert *follows her out.*

George   You come and look at this well.

Eileen   Leave her, Dad.

George *and* **Eileen** *exit.*

Morley   It's all right, Mum.

Peggy   Your mother's a bad woman, Morley.

Morley   You're not. You're not.

Peggy   You say that now. But one day you'll think it like the rest of them.

Morley   I won't. I love you.

Peggy   I know. (*She hugs him.*) Would you like to meet Bill?

Morley   All right.

Peggy   He's been very good to me. He looks after me.

Morley   I'll look after you.

Peggy   Would you like to come and live with us?

Morley   Where?

Peggy   In St Leonards.

Morley   Where's that?

Peggy   In Sussex. Near Aunty Lily.

Pause.

Well?

Morley   Dunno. Where would I go to school?

Peggy   There's a nice school in Hastings . . .

Morley   I wouldn't know anybody.

Peggy   You'd soon make friends.

Pause.

You think about it.

Morley   OK.

Peggy   Bill's taking me down to Cornwall. We're going down there to stay with his mother for the week. You could come with us.

Morley   When?

Peggy   Tonight. Be a little holiday before you start school.

Morley   Tonight?

Peggy   Yes.

Morley   Andy's taking me to the fair this week.

Peggy   I expect there's a fair in Cornwall.

Morley   We were going to have a camp-fire and cook our rabbit.

Peggy   Oh.

Morley   And we haven't finished the mural.

Peggy   I see.

Morley   I promised.

Peggy   Oh, well . . .

Frank *enters*.

Frank   You want a lift into town?

Peggy   I'm not riding on that scooter. I'll get a lift with Rob.

Frank   He's gone.

Peggy   Oh.

Frank   So, you coming?

Peggy   In a minute.

Frank   I'm going now.

Peggy   Don't hurry me. (*She applies lipstick to her lips.*)

Frank   I thought Bill was waiting for you in the Rose and Crown.

Peggy   I don't know why you hang around here. There's nothing for you here. I don't know why you don't join the army or something. Do something useful with your life.

Frank   Morley going with you?

Peggy   You go and start up the scooter. I'm coming.

Frank *exits.*

Peggy *blots her lips with a piece of paper.*

Morley   I don't want you to go, Mum.

Peggy   It won't be for long. You can come to St Leonards and visit.

Morley   All right.

Peggy   So don't cry.

He shakes his head.

You have your camp-fire and go to the fair.

He hugs her. Sound of a scooter starting up.

I'd better go, love. Be a good boy.

She kisses him and exits.

Sound of a scooter revving and driving away. **Morley** *picks up the flowers and puts them in the vase.*

Scene Five

The yard. There is a pipe coming out of the ground.

Andy, **George** and **Morley** *are bending over it.* **Morley** *is wearing* **Andy**'s *cowboy hat.*

Morley   Is it coming?

George   No. (*He sucks on the pipe.*)

Morley   What you doing?

George   Seeing if I can suck it through.

Andy   Do ye no need a pump on the tank?

George   No, gravity does it, see. That's why we put the tank up in the loft.

Andy   You're a very clever man.

George   That's true, lad.

Andy   Mebbe there's a blockage somewhere.

Morley   Will it take much longer, Dad?

George   Is the tap on?

Andy   I think so. I'll get something to poke down there. (*He finds a stick which he pokes down the pipe.*)

Morley   Dad!

George   What, boy?

Morley   Andy and me are going to the fair tonight, you know.

George   Just get this done.

Morley   Eileen won't let me stay out very late. 'Cause of school tomorrow.

Andy   D'ye no want to see the water running, Morley?

Morley   Yeah.

Andy   I think there might be something down there.

Robert *enters. His hands are covered in oil.*

Morley   We're connecting up the water.

George   Can't get it to come through.

Robert *ignores them and exits.*

Morley   How long will it take them?

George   What?

Morley   To get to Scotland tomorrow?

George   Bloody hours.

Morley   He said they're going to see Loch Lomond.

Andy *and* **George** *do not respond.*

Morley   Do you wish you were going, Andy?

Andy   No.

George   You're going to stay and work for me, aren't you, son? Need a good strong bloke like you. Bloke with brains. Make a farmer of you, won't I?

Andy   Ye really think so?

George   Course I do.

Andy   I wouldnae mind trying.

George   I'll see you're all right.

Morley (*singing*)   You take the high road
  And I'll take the low road
  And I'll be in Scotland before you –

George   Quiet, boy.

Andy   Will I go and check the tap?

George   Good idea.

Andy *exits.*

Morley   Have you ever been to Scotland, Dad?

George   Nothing to see up there.

Robert *enters, carrying a tyre.*

George   Rob!

Robert   What?

George   Come and see if you can get this water to come through.

Robert   Thought you had all the help you needed.

George   Won't take you a minute.

Robert *comes and takes the pipe. He looks down it, then sucks.*

Morley   Ughhhh! Dad's been sucking that.

Robert *takes it out of his mouth, wipes it and sucks again.*

Robert   Nothing.

He hands the pipe back to **George**.

George   Go up to the loft and see if Andy's got it connected right.

Robert   I gotta get this car done tonight.

George   Where d'ee get that tyre?

Robert   Old Wolsey in the field.

George   I was going to put that one on my car.

Robert   Too bad.

George (*taking hold of the tyre*)   Hey boy, come on, no need to be like that.

Robert   Get off.

George   You go and give Andy a hand.

Robert   Cow's probably stepped on the pipe in the orchard. You haven't hardly buried it.

George   It'll be all right.

Robert   Come winter you won't have no water 'cause the pipes'll be frozen.

George   I know what I'm doing.

Robert   Oh, yeah, course you do.

George   Come on, son. You and me don't want to fall out. Don't want to let her come between us.

Robert   Tidn her. Can't you get that into your thick head? It's you. When I was his age you used to take me upover and point to it all and say, 'One day, all this will be yours, boy.' Soon as I want a share in it you won't let me have it.

George   We'll sort something out.

Robert (*almost pleading*)   Phone up the solicitor, then.

George   You don't want to let no solicitors start taking over. End up taking all your money off you.

Robert   Get your two new mechanical diggers to do it for you. You can give your bloody farm to Morley.

George   Rob! Rob!

Robert   Arsehole! (*He is not calling* **George** *an arsehole but saying the word as an oath.*)

George   Piss!

Robert (*answering him*)   Shit!

Robert *exits.*

George *returns to the pipe.*

Morley   Can I have my money, Dad?

George   What for?

Morley   The fair.

George   Haven't got any tonight.

Morley   You promised you'd let me have some if we helped you.

George   You'll get it, lad.

Sound of the scooter.

Morley   Elly! Frank! We're connecting up the water.

George   Frank! Frank!

Morley   He's putting his scooter away.

Eileen *enters. She has a crash helmet on.*

Morley   Andy and I are helping Dad.

Eileen   Tap working in the house yet?

George   Haven't got it running out the tank. Shouldn't be long. Need Frank to go up and help Andy get it running. He's s'posed to have fitted the pipe onto the stopcock.

Eileen   What's Rob doing?

Morley   He won't help us. He's getting the car ready for tomorrow. Elly, will you let me have some money?

Eileen   What for?

Morley   I'm going to the fair with Andy.

Eileen   You ought to be getting ready for school.

Morley   I'm going to the fair.

Eileen   Don't know what you're going to do next week. Frank's got this job. Rob'll be away.

Morley   And I'll be at school.

George   I've asked Andy to stay on.

Eileen   Oh. Don't know if that's a good idea.

Morley   Course it is. You don't know anything.

Pause.

Eileen   What if he doesn't come back?

George   He'll be back.

Eileen   They're talking about emigrating.

George   You ask Derek Rudd if he'll help out with the combining?

Eileen   His father won't let him.

George   Why not?

Eileen   You still haven't paid him for last year.

George   I'll pay him.

Pause.

Eileen   What did you think of Mum when you married her?

George   What do you mean?

Eileen   Had she had other boyfriends and things?

George   She wadn a virgin. Know that now.

Eileen   Would you have married her if you'd known?

George   I dunno. I'll go up and see old Rudd.

Eileen   No.

George   Why not?

Eileen   Don't start pestering Derek's father.

George   It's all in the family now, idn it?

Eileen   I don't want you to.

Pause.

We don't know anything about Cathy and Andy.

George   What's that s'posed to mean?

Eileen   Nothing.

Andy *enters.*

Andy   I cannae do it.

George   What's up?

Andy   That tap willnae move.

George   You put some oil on it?

Andy   Ay.

George   Frank! Frank!

Frank (*off*)   Coming.

George   Need your help.

Frank *sings two lines of 'As Long as He Needs Me' off stage.*

Andy   How'd it go?

Frank (*off*)   What?

Andy   Your first day.

Frank *enters, wearing his crash helmet and carrying a single.*

Frank   They had me changing the oil on the vet's car. Told Westcott I thought it was missing. Didn't believe me. Then we listened to the engine. He said, 'I think you'm right, boy.' Was too. Needed a new spark plug. Said to me after: 'You'll be an asset, boy, I can see that.'

George   I want you to get this tap turned on.

Frank   Only just got back. Gotta milk the cows yet.

Catherine *enters.*

Catherine   Frank, can we borrow your Stillson? We cannae get the wheel nuts off.

Frank   It's in my tool-box.

Catherine   We couldnae find your tool-box.

Morley   That's because he hides it in the loft.

Frank   Here. Look what I got today. (*He shows* **Catherine** *his single.*)

Catherine   It's out, then.

Frank   Released it yesterday.

Morley   What is it?

Frank *taps his nose.*

George   Come and have a look at the tank.

George *exits.*

Frank   Won't be a minute, Cathy. (*He sings four lines of 'As Long as He Needs Me'.*)

Frank *exits.*

Catherine (*to* **Andy**)   I'm making chips for dinner the night.

Andy *does not respond.*

Catherine   Andy's favourite meal. I'n't it?

Morley   He's not talking to you. Anyway, we're going to the fair.

Catherine (*to* **Andy**)   Hope you're going tae have a wash first.

Andy   Come on, Morley, let's go and help your dad.

Andy *and* **Morley** *leave.*

Catherine   Your dad and Andy seem to be getting on.

Eileen   Mmmm. (*She looks up at the birds.*)

Catherine   That's those birds again.

Eileen *does not respond.*

Catherine   There's a lot of them the night.

Pause.

My hands. They're covered in oil.

Eileen   What time you going in the morning?

Catherine   Early.

Pause.

Look, it's no me. It's Robert who wants tae go.

Eileen   Mmm.

Catherine   I like it here.

Eileen   Don't know how much longer I'll be here.

Catherine   No?

Eileen   Derek's asked me to marry him.

Catherine   Ay. Robert told me.

Eileen   Oh.

Catherine   Congratulations.

Eileen   Mmmmmm?

Catherine   If it's what you want.

Eileen   You can't spend your whole life looking for the perfect person.

Catherine   I think there's someone out there for everyone.

Eileen   Honesty's the most important thing in any marriage.

Robert *enters.*

Robert   Got that Stillson?

Catherine   He's gone tae get it.

Robert *kisses* **Catherine**.

Robert   Idn she lovely? Thank my lucky stars nobody gave her a lift that night. (*To* **Eileen**.) What you lookin' at?

Eileen   The house-martins. They're restless.

Robert *and* **Catherine** *look.*

Robert   They're just getting ready to fly off to Africa or wherever it is they go to.

They look up. Pause. **Robert** *kisses* **Catherine**. **Eileen** *cries softly. The other two stop kissing and look at her.* **Robert** *laughs.* **Catherine** *digs him in the ribs to make him stop. They look at the birds.*

Frank *enters.*

Frank   They were trying to turn that tap the wrong way. (*He stops to see what they're looking at.*) Ought to get those nests knocked out. (*He hands* **Robert** *the spanner.*) Make sure you give it back. Don't go driving off with it tomorrow.

Morley *runs on.*

Morley   Is it coming through? They've got the tap turned on.

Frank   Not yet.

Morley   What's wrong with you?

Eileen   Nothing.

Morley   You been crying?

Robert   Hold it in the bucket.

Frank *does so.*

Catherine   Is it blocked?

Frank *looks down the pipe.*

Catherine   Don't.

Frank *puts the pipe back in the bucket.*

Robert   Let's see.

Catherine   Careful.

Andy *runs on.*

Andy   Is it coming through?

Robert *takes the pipe and looks down it. The water shoots into his face. The others laugh. He puts his finger over the hole and squirts it at them.*

Frank   Get off.

Robert *pursues them.*

Eileen   Don't be silly, Rob. These are my clothes for work.

Robert   All right. (*He puts the pipe back in the bucket.*) It's all right. Honest.

The others approach.

Frank   How strong is it? (*He leans in to feel the water.*)

Robert *takes the pipe and squirts water at him again.*

Frank   Aowwhh. Get off!

Robert *squirts it at the others. They scream.* **Andy** *runs up to* **Robert** *and tries to get the pipe from him. They struggle.* **Catherine** *gets the bucket. Whilst the other two are fighting, she comes up behind them and pours the bucket over them.* **Robert** *squirts water. He misses* **Catherine** *and gets* **Eileen**.

Eileen   I told you not to do that. (*She pounds furiously on his back with her fists.*)

Robert   Sorry.

Andy *grabs him from behind.* **Robert** *slips.* **Andy** *kicks him ferociously.*

Catherine   Andy!

Frank   Hey, come on, Andy.

Catherine   Andy, stop it. Stop it.

Frank   Here, Andy, mate. That's enough now.

Catherine *and* **Frank** *pull* **Andy** *off* **Robert**. **Robert** *is curled up.*

George *enters.*

George   What's going on?

Eileen   You all right? Rob?

George   Go and turn the tap off, Morley. Use the wrench.

Morley *exits.*

Catherine *goes to* **Robert** *and helps him up.*

Robert   Bit winded. You won't get her back like that.

Robert *picks up the spanner and exits.*

Catherine *follows him.*

Frank   Better get those cows milked.

He exits.

George   (*quietly, to* **Eileen**, *so that* **Andy** *can't hear*)   What's going on?

Eileen   Leave it.

George   You know something I don't?

Eileen   It's probably all for the best, anyway.

She exits.

The water stops.

George   Can get this joined up now. Give me your screwdriver, boy.

Andy *gives him the screwdriver.* **George** *starts to join the two ends of the pipe.*

George   You don't want to lose your head like that, lad.

Andy *cries.*

George   'If you can keep your head when all about you,
   Are losing theirs and blaming it on you,
   You'll be a man, my son, you'll be a man.' (*He screws on the pipe.*)

All my life I've been surrounded by people who don't appreciate me. Many's the time I could have given up. Sat down and cried. But you gotta keep your head, you see.

Andy *nods.*

Morley *runs on.*

Morley   Can we go to the fair now?

George   Go and turn it on again.

Morley   I've just turned it off. Andy, can we go?

George (*to* **Andy**)   Just go and turn it on again, lad.

Morley   Aren't we going to the fair?

George   Won't take a minute.

Morley   Andy.

Andy   I don't really want to tonight, Morley.

Morley   But it finishes tonight.

Andy   Stop going on, Morley. Will you leave me alone!
You're a bloody pest!

Andy *exits.*

Pause.

George   How about you and me going to the fair, lad?

Morley *does not respond.*

George   'Member going to the fair with my old dad.

Morley   Andy was going to take me on the waltzer.

George   I'll take you on the waltzer.

Morley   Tonight?

George   Course.

Pause.

You spent a lot of time with Andy, haven't you?

Morley   Yes.

George   And Cathy.

Morley   Mmmm.

George   What do they get up to?

Morley   What do you mean?

George   Just wondered.

Morley   Does Andy love Cathy?

George   What do you think?

Morley   I saw them kissing in the loft once.

They laugh.

And . . .

George   What?

Morley   I don't think I should tell you.

George   Come on, lad. Course you can. (*He waits.*)

Morley   In Andy's cowboy book . . .

George   Yeah.

Morley   He's written his name.

George   And?

Morley   His surname isn't Mullen like he said.

George   Oh.

Morley   It's MacCusker. Like Cathy's . . .

George   I see.

Morley   It says this book belongs to Andrew James MacCusker.

George   Right.

Morley   Do you think they're married?

George   I don't know.

Pause. **George** *takes a coin from his pocket.*

Here's some spending money.

Morley   I don't want it.

George   Go on. You'll need it. All those rides.

Peggy *enters and watches them unseen.*

Morley   Did they have waltzers when you were a little boy?

George   Had the old carousel. And the rifle range. My dad won me a toy gun. Had it for years. And we went in to see the man with two heads.

Morley You won't tell, will you? About Andy.

George Course I won't.

Morley *takes the money.*

Morley Did he really have two heads?

George Saw it with my own eyes.

George *puts his arm around* **Morley**. *They laugh.*

Peggy What's going on?

Morley *starts, guilty that she has seen him sharing intimacy with* **George**.

Morley Mum!

George Where've you come from?

Peggy Just walked up from the station.

Morley You come home?

Peggy Here. I've brought you something. (*She gives him a bag.*)

Morley What is it?

Peggy Have a look.

Morley Is it trousers? It's long trousers.

Eileen *enters.*

Eileen Mum!

Peggy No need to look so shocked. Everyone's looking at me as if I've just got off the sputnik.

Morley Mum's bought me some long trousers.

Eileen The house is in a mess. Your bed hasn't got clean sheets.

George She can sleep in my bed.

Peggy Don't you start.

Andy *enters.*

Andy Oh, hi.

Peggy   Still here, then.

Andy   Ay.

Morley   Cathy and Rob are going to Scotland tomorrow.

Peggy   Are they?

Andy   The water's running out of the tank but there's nothing running in.

George   Ballcock's stuck I spec'.

Peggy   Haven't you got it all plumbed in yet?

George   You just go indoors and turn the tap on.

George exits with **Andy**.

Eileen   Bill drive you?

Peggy   No, I came on the coach.

Eileen   How long you staying?

Peggy   I don't know.

Eileen   When's Bill expecting you back?

Peggy   How many more questions? (*To* **Morley**.) So are you pleased?

Morley   Yeah.

Peggy   You still love your mum, then?

Pause.

Morley   He was just telling me about going to the fair.

Peggy   Give me a kiss, then.

Morley *kisses her.*

Peggy   Aren't you going to try them on?

Morley   OK.

Peggy   Put your blazer on as well.

Morley *exits.*

Eileen   Mum.

Peggy What?

Eileen Derek's asked me to marry him.

Peggy Oh.

Eileen You think I should?

Peggy How do I know? Only you can know that. He's dug up my lupins to put that pipe through the garden.

Catherine *enters.*

Catherine Hallo there.

Peggy I hear you're off to Scotland.

Catherine That's right.

Peggy Best thing you can do.

Andy *enters.*

Andy Cathy!

Catherine What?

George (*off*) Come back here.

Andy No.

George *enters.*

Catherine What is it?

George Want a word with you, Cathy.

Catherine Oh ay?

George I want you to tell Rob to unpack his bags.

Catherine We're leaving tomorrow. We're no changing our minds now.

George He belongs here, Cathy.

Catherine He's a grown man. He can make up his own mind.

Peggy Course he can.

Catherine You all make him feel that he's stupid.

George No, we don't.

Catherine Whose fault is it that he cannae read and write properly?

George I'm not going to stand by and see my son throw it all away. I've done all this for him. I'm not having you coming along and taking him off to God-knows-where.

Robert *comes in to see what is going on.*

Catherine He's the one that wants tae leave. No me. Let him have his share and then he'll stay.

George I've worked hard for this house and this land. I'm not giving it away till the time's right.

Robert How much older do I have to be, for God's sake?

George I didn't move into my own farm till I was forty-five. I stayed working for me dad.

Peggy Yeah, and the rows you used to have about it.

George You mustn't run before you've learnt how to walk.

Catherine Well, he's walking. Tomorrow. Out that door.

Frank *enters to see what is going on.*

George And what happens when he finds about what's been going on?

Catherine What d'ye mean?

George We got eyes, you know.

Catherine I don't know what you're talking about.

Eileen Dad! Don't!

George 'Bout you and your brother here.

Catherine What?

George You and Andy.

Robert Don't be bloody stupid.

George Mucking around in the loft.

Catherine What have you done?

Andy   I havenae done anything.

Catherine *looks at* **Eileen**.

George   Morley saw them.

Robert   Cathy?

Catherine *does not respond.*

Morley *enters.*

Morley   They're a bit long.

They all look at him.

Catherine   You nasty wee sneak.

Robert   Cathy. I don't understand . . .

Peggy   It's disgusting.

Catherine   Disgusting? You find me disgusting, do you? And what are you? Are you no disgusting? You're bloody hypocrites, the bloody lot of yees.

She exits.

Robert   Cathy!

George   You go and unpack your suitcase, Rob. You're better off without a woman like that.

Robert *advances on* **George** *with the spanner.*

Frank   Steady on, Rob.

Robert   You bloody bastard . . .

He picks **George** *up and shakes him.*

Robert   You bloody bastard.

Eileen   Rob.

Robert   You bloody bastard. You bloody bastard. (*He punches* **George**.)

Robert *exits.*

Eileen *goes to* **George**.

Eileen   Dad?

George   I'm all right.

Morley   You said you wouldn't tell.

George   Let's see if this tap's running.

He goes into the house.

Eileen *follows him.*

Morley   I didn't say anything.

Andy *hits* **Morley**.

Andy   You liar.

Morley   Andy.

Peggy   Here, that's enough of that.

Andy   Your wee daughter here is a sneak.

Peggy   You can stop that sort of talk.

Andy   You didnae think she was your son, did you?

Peggy   You want to watch what you're saying. After what you've been up to.

Andy   Is the wee girl going to cry.

Peggy   Here, I might just contact the naval police.

Pause.

Saw them at the railway station. Had a photo of the runaway they were looking for. You'd better get your bags packed. Wouldn't take me long to walk down to the phone box.

Morley   Mum! Andy!

Andy   Get off me.

Andy *exits.*

Morley *sobs.*

Peggy   Come on, Morley. Come in with me.

Morley   I don't want to.

He runs away upover.

Frank *looks at* **Peggy** *and exits.*

Scene Six

*Morley's bedroom that **Andy** has been using.*

*On the wall is the painting of the cowboy on the horse. **Andy** is lying on the bed.*

Catherine *enters with **Andy**'s jeans.*

Catherine   I brought these off the line. Will I put them in your rucksack?

Andy   I'll wear them.

Catherine   Here.

Andy   Have tae get a wash first.

Catherine   Frank's going to give us a lift up to the garage in the car. This long-distance lorry driver he knows will pick us up there.

Andy   You don't have tae come wi' me.

Catherine   I cannae stay here.

Andy   I'm going back to Portsmouth.

Catherine   Right.

Andy   The reggies will find me in the end. They always do.

Pause.

Catherine   What will happen to you?

Andy   They'll just lock me up for a while. It willnae be for long.

Catherine   I could come to Portsmouth wi' you.

Andy   No. Go back tae Mr Capaldi. He'll look after ye.

Catherine   I'm no going back there.

Andy   Where, then?

Catherine   I don't know. London.

Andy   There's lots of men like Capaldi in London.

Catherine   Mebbe.

She touches his hair.

Catherine *and* **Andy** (*sing*)   The third wee craw
Couldnae flee at aw
Couldnae flee at aw
Couldnae flee at aw aw aw aw
The third wee craw
Couldn't flee at aw
On a cold and frosty morning.

Eileen *enters.*

Eileen   Oh, sorry. I was just looking for Morley.

Andy   He's no here.

Andy *picks up his towel and goes.*

Eileen   Mum's worried because he ran away upover.

Pause.

Rob's out sitting in his car.

Catherine   I know.

Eileen   He locked the door when I went out to speak to him.

Catherine   What do you want me to do about it?

Eileen   What are you going to do?

Catherine   What do you think I'm going to do. Pack my bags. Get out. You must be feeling very pleased with yoursel. You never liked me, did ye? You were jealous of me right from the start.

Eileen   I didn't say anything. This isn't my fault.

Catherine   You didnae need Morley tae tell you though, did ye?

Eileen *doesn't respond.*

Catherine   Very convenient for you, wasn't it? That it was him who let the cat out the bag and no you.

George *enters.*

George   Ah, here you are.

Eileen   Get out, Dad.

George   I want a word with you, Cathy.

Eileen   Leave her.

George   You don't have to go, you know.

Catherine *laughs.*

George   Rob didn wanna leave here. He couldn live nowhere else.

Catherine   Aye, well, you're probably right about that.

George   Nobody wants you to go. You go out and tell Rob, you're staying.

She doesn't respond.

Rob doesn't want you to go.

Catherine   He hasnae said that tae me.

Peggy *enters.*

Peggy   Is he up here?

Eileen   No.

Peggy   Hope he hasn't fallen down that well.

She goes to the window.

Morley! Mooorley!

George   He'll be all right.

Peggy   I need some water for the kettle.

George   What'ee mean?

Peggy   There's no water coming out the tap.

Peggy *and* **George** *go.*

Eileen   Where will you go?

Catherine   I don't know.

Eileen   Back to Scotland?

Catherine   No. London. Mebbe.

Eileen   London?

Catherine   Aye.

Eileen   What will you do there?

Catherine   I'll be all right.

Eileen   And Andy?

Catherine   Back the navy.

Eileen   It's true then.

Catherine   Aye.

Pause.

Our mum put him in a home when he was ten. We didnae see him again till he was fifteen. Then he came back. My wee lost brother.

Robert *is standing at the door and has heard this.*

Eileen   And do you still . . .

Catherine   What?

Eileen   Love him.

She sees **Robert**.

Catherine *turns and sees* **Robert**.

Catherine   I love Robert.

Pause.

Eileen   Hello.

Robert *turns and goes.*

Eileen *runs after him.*

Catherine *takes the ring from the chain and looks at it.*

Eileen *returns.*

Eileen   He's gone to his bedroom.

Catherine   Uhhuh.

Eileen   He's so proud. And he's old-fashioned, really, when it comes to women. Wants us all to be whiter than white.

Catherine   Aye well give him this.

She holds out the ring.

Eileen   He'll never forgive us, you know.

Catherine   Mebbe.

Eileen   You could stay.

Catherine   Your dad would never let me forget.

Eileen   A girl on her own in London. Anything could happen.

Catherine   Aye.

She holds out the ring again.

Here. Take it. This is what you really want, isn't it?

Eileen   You lied to us. You lied to Rob.

Catherine   Well, now you've got him back.

Eileen   Yes. And you've got Andy.

Catherine   Aye, well, mebbe we've got more in common than we thought.

Pause.

I did start tae think of you like a sister, ye know.

Eileen *doesn't respond.*

Catherine   Mebbe you're doing the right thing.

Eileen   What?

Catherine   Getting out. Marrying Derek.

Eileen   Huh!

Catherine   You have tae get out, Eileen.

Eileen   Everyone's so quick to tell me what to do. I can make up my own mind, thank you. I hardly think you're qualified to advise anyone.

Catherine   No. Here.

She makes **Eileen** *take the ring.*

Morley *enters.*

Eileen   There you are. Mum's looking for you. Mum! Mum!

She exits.

Catherine   What do you want? Come tae get your room back? Don't worry, we'll be gone soon. You won't have many friends in this life, if you carry on being a sneak, you know. D'ye hear me?

Morley *nods.*

Catherine *exits.*

Morley *has the rabbit's foot. He curls up on the bed and strokes it.*

Peggy *and* **Eileen** *enter.*

Peggy   There you are. I've been worried sick about you.

Morley   I've been upover.

Peggy   Hope you haven't got those trousers dirty.

Morley   No.

Peggy   Where are his pyjamas?

Eileen *exits.*

Peggy *straightens the bedclothes. She hums a few bars of 'Blow the Wind Southerly'.* **Morley** *strokes the foot.*

Peggy   What's that you've got?

Morley   Nothing.

Eileen *enters with the pyjamas.*

Peggy (*looking out of the window*)   So quiet. Hate the quiet. Makes you feel like you're buried alive.

Eileen   Was it quiet in Cornwall?

Peggy   What you mean?

Eileen   Where Bill's mother lived.

Peggy   She's got this great big house in the town. She's a real snob.

Eileen   Oh.

Peggy   Got Bill under her thumb, as well.

Eileen   Yeah?

Peggy   Wouldn't do anything without asking her. What sort of man's that?

Frank *enters.*

Frank   Andy ready?

Peggy   How should I know?

Frank   Need to get a move on. Else my mate will have gone.

Eileen   I'll go and see what they're doing.

Eileen *exits.*

Peggy   So you've got a job.

Frank   Yeah.

Peggy   'Bout time you got away from here.

Frank   You never wanted me here, did you?

Peggy   Don't know what you're talking about.

*'Wooden Heart' starts playing in **Rob**'s bedroom.*

George (*off*)   Rob! Rob!

Peggy   Leave him alone.

Frank (*calling to **Robert***)   Be careful with my records!

George (*off*)   Rob! Open this door.

George *enters.*

He's put the chair up against the door.

Frank (*calling to **Robert***)   It's my room, too.

Peggy   Is there any water yet?

George   Andy's been having a wash and it's caused an air-block, Frank.

Frank   What you want me to do about it?

George   Need someone to help drain the system.

Frank   I'm taking these two up to the garage.

George   I was talking to the people from the petrol company the other day.

Peggy   What people?

George   They reckon I could get permission to build a petrol station in the lower field.

Peggy   Where are you going to get the money for that?

George   I'd need somebody mechanically-minded to run it. What'ee think?

Peggy   You don't know anything about petrol stations.

Frank   You wouldn't get me back here. Not if you paid me a million pounds.

Frank *exits.*

Peggy   Come on, Morley. Past your bedtime.

George   Soon be your bedtime, too.

Peggy   Are you going to get this water fixed or not?

George   What do I get if I do?

Peggy   Get off now, George.

George   I want to give you a nice welcome home.

Peggy   George . . .

Morley *covers his head with the pillow.* **George** *whispers in* **Peggy**'s *ear.*

Peggy   Honestly. Go on.

George *exits.*

Peggy *laughs.*

Peggy These pyjamas need airing.

Morley *does not respond.*

Peggy So this is the picture.

Morley Yes.

Peggy Mmmm.

Pause.

At grammar school you'll have lots of friends. Friends your own age.

Andy *enters, and is standing in the doorway with just a towel round him.*

Peggy *exits.*

Andy *takes off his towel.* **Morley** *watches.* **Andy** *puts on his underpants and then his jeans. 'Venus in Blue Jeans' is playing in* **Rob***'s bedroom.* **Andy** *sits and rubs his hair.*

Morley I brought you this.

Andy *does not respond.*

Morley It's the rabbit's foot. It will bring you luck. (*He lays it on the bed.*)

Andy *picks it up and puts it around his neck. Then he looks at the picture.*

Andy We never finished the picture.

Morley *shakes his head.* **Andy** *straps up his rucksack. He picks up his cowboy hat.*

Andy Ye keeping this?

Morley *does not answer.*

Andy Are ye?

Morley *nods.* **Andy** *throws it on the bed. He looks at* **Morley***. He sits on the bed.*

Andy Well, pardner, this looks like the end.

Morley *does not respond.* **Andy** *lies on the bed with* **Morley***.*

Andy   It was great waking up in this bed in the morning. I used tae lie here looking at the ceiling.

Morley *looks up*.

Andy   You see where the water comes in and there's all them brown marks?

Morley *nods*.

Andy   See that one there?

Morley   Which one?

Andy   The one that looks like a giraffe.

Morley   Yes.

They look at the ceiling.

That's a lady's arm.

Andy   What – the giraffe?

Morley   It's not a giraffe. She's got a long glove on.

Andy   What, the neck is her arm?

Morley   Yes. She's got her hand like that. (*He puts his arm up*.)

Andy   Ay, so she has.

Morley   She's wearing a dress like a Spanish lady.

Andy   Och yes. And there was me thinking that was a bush in the front of the giraffe.

Morley *giggles*.

Andy   Well, Matt, I guess I gotta go. Gotta head back into town and hand myself over to the sheriff and his men.

Morley   I don't want you to go. (*He curls up beside* **Andy**.)

Andy *puts his arm round him.* **Morley** *looks at* **Andy**. *He kisses* **Andy**.

Peggy *enters with the pyjamas.*

Andy *and* **Morley** *separate.*

Peggy   Here you are, Morley.

Andy *puts on his socks and shoes.*

Catherine *enters.*

Catherine   Ready?

Andy   Nearly.

Catherine   Hope you enjoy your new school, Morley. (*She gives him her ear-rings.*) A keepsake.

Peggy   Don't forget your hat.

Morley   That's mine.

Peggy *puts the hat on the bed.*

Andy   Bye, then.

Catherine *hugs* **Morley**. *He holds on to her.*

Catherine   We've got to go.

Peggy   Morley, let her go. Morley!

Catherine *disengages herself.*

Frank *enters.*

The Beatles' 'She Loves You' plays through to the final curtain.

Frank (*calling to* **Robert**)   I haven't played that yet. You be careful with it.

Catherine   I knew I'd convert you.

Frank   Ready, then?

Peggy   He'll wave from the window, won't you, Morley?

Morley *nods.*

Catherine, **Andy** *and* **Frank** *exit.*

Peggy   Aren't you going to wave them goodbye?

Morley *shakes his head.*

Peggy   Shall I bring you up some hot milk?

Morley   I don't drink hot milk any more.

Peggy   What do you drink?

Morley   Cocoa.

Peggy   Shall I make you that?

Morley   If you like.

Peggy *exits.*

Morley *lies listening. A car starts. Sounds of goodbyes.* **Morley** *puts the cowboy hat on and holds the ear-rings up.*

Robert *enters.*

The car drives off. **Robert** *looks out the window and then sits on the bed.*

Eileen *enters.*

Eileen   They've gone. (*She goes to touch* **Robert**.)

Robert   Get off.

Peggy (*off*)   Go down and get me some water from the well. That's what you can do.

Eileen *looks at the ring.*

Peggy (*off*)   There's no water coming from that tap. Here, turn it on. Now, is there, or isn't there? No, there isn't.

Morley   One day I'm leaving here.

Eileen   Yes?

Morley   Yes.

Peggy (*off*)   This is how things always are on this farm. The electric doesn't work. The roof leaks. The bloomin' water doesn't work. Nothing works.

Eileen *looks out the window. She holds out her hand.*

Eileen   It's starting to rain. (*She closes the window, then looks at* **Robert**.)

Morley *holds the ear-rings up to the light. The cowboy looks down from the picture.*

'She Loves You' comes to an end. Curtain.

Flesh and Blood

Characters

Rose
William
Charles
Shirley

Setting: a farm in Devon

The action takes place over a thirty-year period.

Flesh and Blood was first performed at the Northcott Theatre, Exeter, on 10 April 1996. The production subsequently toured to Poole Arts Centre, Warwick Arts Centre, Oxford Playhouse and London's Lyric Theatre, Hammersmith. The cast was as follows:

Rose	Geraldine Alexander
Charles	Martin Marquez
William	Simon Robson
Shirley	Abigail Thaw

Directed by Mike Alfreds
Designed by Paul Dart

Part One

Scene One

Rose *enters. She is dressed in mourning clothes. She hums a funeral hymn to herself. She goes to her father's photo on the wall and looks at it.*

William *enters. He is also dressed in mourning. He looks lost.*

Rose   You going to get changed?

William   Yeah.

He doesn't move.

Rose (*sings under her breath*)   Father in Thy gracious keeping
   Leave we now Thy servant sleeping.

Charles *comes to the door also in mourning. He stands looking at them.*

Rose   Aunty Cissie looked old.

William   She is old.

Rose   She said to me, 'We're the only ones left now, Rose.'

William   Mmmmm.

Rose *takes off her hat.*

Rose   She was in a lot of pain with her arthritis. She said, 'I'm just waiting for my deliverance.'

William   Sad to end up like that. She hasn't got any money. Uncle Ted left her penniless. He spent money like water. Dad always said he'd end up bankrupt.

Rose   Remember when he wanted dad to buy that new milking parlour?

William   Yeah.

Rose   'Trouble with you, Teddy, your pockets aren't deep enough...'

Rose/William   '...and your arms are too long.'

They laugh.

Charles And the trouble with dad was he was a mean old bugger.

Rose Charlie!

Charles It's true.

He starts to go.

William That sow's about to farrow.

Charles Tonight?

William Looks like it.

Charles Oh.

He looks at **Rose**.

Rose I'll keep an eye on her.

William It's his job.

Charles I'm going out.

Rose Tonight?

Charles Yes, tonight.

Rose Don't you want your tea?

Charles No.

He goes.

William Where's he going?

Rose I don't know.

She calls up the stairs.

Your new shirt is on the bed.

William What new shirt?

Rose The one he bought himself for his birthday.

William *shakes his head. Pause.*

Rose Your other trousers are down here. You want me to press them for you?

Charles (*off*)   You wannoo wipe my arse for me as well?

Rose *looks at* **William**. *She goes to the kitchen and comes back with the teapot and two teacups. She is humming the hymn again. She waits for the tea to brew.*

Rose   Nice of Mr Luscombe to come to the funeral.

William   Well, he's a neighbour.

Rose   There wasn't much love lost between dad and him. Remember when they nearly had a fight about who the hedge belonged to?

William   Yeah.

Rose   Dad threatened to set the dogs on him.

They both laugh.

William   And now dad's dead. Old Luscombe's won that battle.

Charles *returns in his shirt and long johns.*

Rose   When did you last change them?

Charles   They're clean.

Rose   You sure?

William   He idn going to be showing his pants to anyone tonight I hope. Are you, Charlie?

Rose (*handing him his trousers*)   Here. You sure you don't want me to press them?

Charles   No.

Rose   Won't take a minute.

Charles   Haven't got time.

William   What's the rush?

Charles   Mind your own business.

William   Your father's hardly been in his grave for two hours.

Charles   So?

William You didn't ought to be going out tonight, boy.

Charles You mind your own bloody business. You never want anybody to go out anywhere. Scared they're going to spend some money.

Rose Charles.

Charles I can do what I bloody well like.

Rose Don't, Charles!

Charles Am I suppose to sit at home being miserable with you two? Idn going to bring him back, is it?

They don't respond.

Makes me sick the way you two been going on all day. Bloody hypocrites. I'm not going to pretend that I loved that mean old bugger. I was glad to see him go. Maybe we can get on with our bloody lives now.

Rose I wish you wouldn swear.

Charles I'll bloody well swear as much as I bloody well like. I'm not going to ask no other bugger if I can bloody well swear. We can't all be as refined as you two. I didn't get sent to no private school, remember. Not like you and him.

Rose You shouldn swear.

Charles Arsehole, buggery, dick.

He goes.

William *shakes his head.*

Rose *pours* **William** *some tea.*

Rose So cold in that churchyard.

William He didn ought to be talking about dad like that.

He starts to cry.

Rose Come on, now, Bill, that's not going to help anybody.

William So few people at the funeral, Rose.

Rose Don't be soft.

William   Not much to show for a life.

Rose   He wouldn't want us to be sitting here like this.

William   So few people to mourn his passing.

A faint knocking.

Rose   What was that?

William   Your bloody cat drinking the milk, I expect.

Rose   Snowy! Are you in that dairy again?

She goes.

William *crosses to the piano and tinkles the tune of 'The Ash Grove'.*

Rose (*in the kitchen*)   Oh, hello, my dear, come in.

Shirley   Mum sent me up with this.

Rose   Oh, thank you. We're through here.

They enter the parlour.

Look what Shirley's brought, Bill.

She holds up a pie.

Shirley   It's squab pie. Mother thought you might not have time to do any cooking what with the funeral and everything.

William   That's very kind of you, Shirley.

Rose *makes a face at* **William** *behind* **Shirley**'s *back as if to express her incomprehension at* **Shirley**'s *mother's action.*

William   Get another cup, Rose.

Rose   Have that one. I'll get myself another.

Rose *goes with the pie.*

Awkward pause.

Shirley   We just wanted to say how sorry we were.

William   Yes. Yes.

Pause. In the kitchen **Rose** *is prising the pastry off the pie to look underneath.*

How are things down at the Red Lion?

Shirley   All right.

William   Mr Webber's not working your mother too hard.

Shirley   She likes it.

William   You've been here quite a while now.

Shirley   Nearly three years. Mr Webber's talking about moving on though.

William   Is he?

Pause.

You and your mother going to come up and help us out turkey picking this year?

Shirley   Oh yes.

William   You were one of our best workers last year.

Shirley   I enjoyed it. It was the atmosphere. You know, everyone's excited about Christmas coming and they're earning a bit of extra money. And they're all laughing and joking. It's a real occasion. You know what I mean, Mr Thorne?

William   Yes, I do.

Shirley   I want to buy mum a blouse she was looking at in town so the money will come in handy. I love going out and getting the presents, wrapping them up. It's more fun giving the presents than getting them sometimes, idn it?

William (*entranced by her enthusiasm*)   Yes, I suppose it is.

Shirley   And I love decorating the tree. Do you have a tree?

William   We don't tend to go in for all that.

Shirley   Oh dear.

Rose *enters with another cup and pours herself some tea.*

Shirley   I've got to go home and get ready for the dance.

Rose   Dance tonight? Where?

Shirley   Village hall.

Rose   Not working behind the bar tonight, then?

Shirley   No. Not tonight.

Charles *enters.*

Charles   Rose!

Rose   What?

Charles (*changing his tone*)   Oh. Evening.

Shirley   Hello.

Rose   What do you want?

Charles   Nothing.

Rose   Shirley's mum has made us a lovely pie.

Charles   Oh.

Shirley   Right, well . . .

William   See you at the turkey picking.

Rose   Oh, yes.

Shirley   Thanks for the tea.

Rose *exits.* **Shirley** *follows. At the door she turns back.*

Shirley (*mouthed at* **Charles** *behind* **William**'s *back*)   See you later.

Charles *looks at* **William** *who hasn't seen.*

Shirley *goes.*

Pause. **Charles** *combs his hair.*

William   You get the tractor going?

Charles   Not yet.

William   Need to get the manure out.

Pause. They have nothing to say to each other.

Rose *returns with the pie.*

Rose   Here, look at this.

Charles   What?

Rose Got hardly any meat in it. Bit of fatty mutton.

William Very kind thought.

Charles (*quietly to* **Rose**) You got any money?

Rose How much you want?

William Don't you go giving him money.

Charles I only want ten bob.

William You can't go out spending money all the time.

Charles You mean bugger. You're just like the old man.

Rose I saved a bit on the housekeeping this week.

William (*firmly*) He's not having it and that's final.

Charles *stamps his foot.*

William Now get on.

Charles *starts to go.* **Rose** *has taken a ten-shilling note out of her bag and slips it to him without* **William** *noticing.* **Charles** *goes.*

Rose I'm going to give this to the dog.

William Why?

Rose Don't fancy it.

William Why not?

Rose You ever been in that kitchen down the pub?

He doesn't reply.

And you never know what might be in it.

William What you mean?

Rose You know who her family is?

William Whose family?

Rose Shirley's mother's brother is Curtis the gypsy. And their aunt's husband was that gyppo dad threw off our lower field that time.

William You know I never follow it when you go on about who's related to who.

Rose Well, anyway, Curtis is Shirley's uncle. Shirley's mother married a farm labourer from Tiverton way. But they got divorced. So then Mr Curtis got her the job housekeeping at the Red Lion. You know, after Mr Webber's wife ran off.

William (*not really interested*) Oh.

Rose Course you know what they say.

William What about?

Rose About Shirley's mother.

William What?

Rose That she's more than just a housekeeper to Webber.

William You don't know that, Rose.

Rose The lipstick she wears.

Charles (*off*) Bye.

Rose Don't be late.

William He's meant to be looking after those pigs.

Rose All work and no play idn good for anybody.

William He shouldn be going out tonight.

Rose Won't do any harm.

William This is just the start.

Rose You leave him to me.

William You encourage him.

Rose I don't.

William You always have.

Rose You know what dad said to me before he died?

William What?

Rose 'Keep the peace, Rose. Keep the peace.'

William *returns to tinkling on the piano.*

Rose Dad loved that.

William Mmmm.

William *plays the tune of 'The Ash Grove'.* **Rose** *hums along.*

Scene Two

The Ash Grove. Moonlight.

In the background **Rose** *and* **William** *can be heard singing.*

Charles Come on.

Shirley I'll ruin these shoes.

He laughs.

Shhh.

They listen.

Charles That's Rose and William.

Shirley They don't sound too sad.

Charles Always playing music. Drives me mad. They think they're so much cleverer and better than everybody else. (*He mocks their singing by making the sound a dog will make at music.*) Haooo hao hao haoooooh.

Shirley Don't.

They giggle. The music stops.

Rose (*off*) Scamp!

Shirley *and* **Charles** *giggle.*

Rose (*off*) Scamp! Quiet!

Charles She's gone.

Shirley It's a bit spooky here.

Charles This is where you came picking bluebells that time. Remember?

Shirley Yes. That was in broad daylight.

Charles   I was chopping down a tree and I saw you standing there. Like a fairy.

Shirley   We'd only just moved here. I wanted something to brighten up our bedroom.

Charles   Always been my job to keep this wood clear. It's where the logs you use down at the pub come from. Good wood for burning, ash.

Shirley *shivers.*

Charles   You cold?

Shirley   Bit.

Charles   I've got a little hidey-hole over there.

Shirley   Oh yes?

Charles   Yes. It's a hollow tree trunk. I go in there when it rains sometimes. Nice and cosy.

Shirley   Mum says we need another load of logs.

Charles   I'll bring them down.

Pause.

Shirley   What was that?

Charles   Just the rooks.

Shirley   Give me a fright.

He impersonates the rooks.

Charles   Got a rookery over in them elms. Every winter all the crows and rooks from miles around come to roost there. Bloody pests really. Still, you mustn't get rid of a rookery.

Shirley   Why not?

Charles   Bad luck. If rooks desert the rookery it means the heir of the house is going to die. They can foretell doom, rooks.

Shirley   Don't!

He laughs.

Charles   I'll have to come out and just shoot a few of em.

Shirley You superstitious?

Charles No.

Shirley Mum's always going on about things like that. She saw a wren on the window-sill last week and said, 'He's come to tell us somebody's going to die.'

Charles And somebody did die.

Shirley Oh yes!

Charles Ooooohooooo.

Shirley Don't, Charles.

Charles Are you there, Dad?

Shirley Stop it!

Charles She was reading palms last night in the pub, your mum.

Shirley I know.

Charles Can you do it?

Shirley *shrugs.*

Charles (*holding his hand out*) Read mine. Tell me what our future's gonna be like.

Shirley I don't believe in all that.

She kisses his hand.

Charles Yesterday I was standing in my little hidey-hole watching the rain. And I closed me eyes and imagined that you were in there with me.

Shirley Did you now?

Charles Yes. Just you and me in the root of a tree! Safe, see. That's what it'll be like when we get our own place.

Shirley Yes?

Charles Yes. No Rose or William coming knocking on the bedroom door telling me to get up. We'll be able to spend our whole day in bed if we want to.

Shirley *laughs.*

Charles   We'll have a great big brass bed.

Shirley   Oh!

Charles   And loads of kids.

Shirley   You ever brought anybody else here? Like Mary Quick?

Charles   No.

Shirley   Not even Gwen Luscombe?

Charles   Can't remember.

Shirley   What did she used to be called?

Charles   Gwen Small.

Shirley   Mr Webber said she used to be sweet on you.

Charles   Don't know about that.

Shirley   You're much more handsome than Eddie Luscombe.

Charles   What about Tommy Youings?

Shirley   What about him?

Charles   Am I more handsome than him too?

Shirley   Course you are.

She kisses him.

Charles   Sometimes I used to go out with Gwen and I'd only have sixpence in my pocket. Dad never let us have any money if he could help it. (*To the air.*) You won't stop me this time, will you, old man? You bloody bastard.

Shirley   Charles!

Charles   What?

Shirley   He's only just died.

Charles   I wadn sorry to see him go.

Shirley   That's terrible.

Charles   The way he treated us. Like his slaves. We could never have anything when we were kids. Not even a bloody pet. I had a puppy once. He drowned it. I had hamsters, he sold them. He killed mother with overwork. No one knew what he was really like. Vicious bugger. I hated him.

Pause.

Shirley   I miss my dad.

They listen to the music.

Didn they ever want to get married?

Charles   Who?

Shirley   Rose and William.

Charles   Who'd have em?

They laugh.

They wouldn know what to do.

They laugh more.

Shirley   Your brother.

Charles   What about him?

Shirley   The way he stares.

Charles   Perhaps he's sweet on you.

They laugh.

Shirley   He's a lot older than you, isn't he?

Charles *impersonates* **William***'s stare.*

Shirley   Charles.

He carries on staring.

Isn't he?

He is still staring at her.

What are you doing? Stop it.

He carries on staring.

Don't. You're frightening me.

He moves towards her and puts his hands around her neck as if to strangle her. She screams. He holds her.

Shirley He's a good piano player.

Charles Should be. He had lessons at that school he got sent to.

Shirley Why didn't you get sent away to school?

Charles The old man didn wanna fork out the money.

Shirley But he paid for William and Rose to go.

Charles Mother made him. She was dead when it came to my turn.

Shirley How old were you when she died?

Charles Ten.

Shirley Young.

Charles Yeah. She had cancer.

Shirley Oh.

Charles You don't really understand at that age. I asked God if he'd let her live if I stopped having sweets or sugar in me tea.

Shirley Awhhh.

She holds him maternally.

Good job you had Rose.

Charles What you mean?

Shirley Everyone says she dotes on you.

Charles *laughs dismissively.*

Charles Can't wait to see their faces when I tell them. (*To the air.*) Shirley and me are getting married, Dad! What do you think of that?

Shirley Shhhh.

Charles They got to know sometime. There's a farm for sale over Weardon way.

Shirley   Yes?

Charles   Lower Kerscott.

Shirley   You do mean it, don't you, Charles?

Charles   Mean what?

Shirley   You're not just making it up.

Charles   Course I'm not.

Shirley   Sometimes . . .

Charles   What?

Shirley   It's like you live in a dream.

Charles   You sound like Rose. Nobody ever thinks I can do anything.

Shirley   I didn't mean that.

Charles   I'll bloody go and tell them now.

Shirley   No.

Charles   Why not?

Shirley   I don't want you to.

Charles   You don't want to be scared of them.

Shirley   No.

Charles   I'm going to get you a ring.

Shirley   Yes?

Charles   Yes.

He kisses her.

You want to see my hidey-hole?

Shirley   All right.

Charles   Will you show me your hidey-hole?

Shirley   Charles!

He kisses her.

Come on, then.

William *is playing 'Early One Morning'*.

Rose (*off*)   Oh, don't deceive me. Oh, never leave me.
How could you treat a poor maiden so?

Scene Three

Early morning. The yard. **Rose** *is feeding the hens.*

Rose (*calling the hens to be fed*)   Here, cubby, cubby, cubby.
Chick, chick, chick!

Charles *enters with his gun. He has two dead crows on strings.*

Rose   You going to see if you can get us a rabbit?

Charles   Could do.

Rose   I hope you're not going to hang those from any of the
apple trees this time. They stink the orchard out. Cubby,
cubby, cubby.

Charles   You going to town Thursday?

Rose   I wadn planning to.

Charles   Oh.

Rose   Why?

Charles   Wanted your help choosing a ring in Dobbs.

Rose   A ring?

Charles   Yes.

Rose   What sort of ring?

Charles   An engagement ring.

Rose   An engagement ring.

Charles   Yes.

Rose   This is a bit sudden. Who's it for?

Charles   Shirley Stephens.

Rose   Oh!

Charles What?

Rose I thought she was going out with the boy Youings.

Charles Not any more.

Rose You don't want to go rushing into anything, Charles.

Charles I knew you'd be like this.

Rose We've only just got the funeral over with.

Charles So?

Rose It's a big decision. I'm only thinking about what's best for you.

Charles This is best for me. Shirley's best for me. I love her, Rose.

Rose (*to the hens*) Come on, cubby, cubby, cubby.

Charles I always thought this didn happen to us. That twadn something we were capable of. Mother and father never showed each other any affection, did they? Didn even sleep in the same room.

Rose Don't know how you can talk about such things.

Charles Did you ever see them touch each other?

Rose They were brought up to be like that.

Charles Don't know how they managed to do what they had to do to get us.

Rose That's enough, Charles.

Charles Just cause you never wanted to get married.

Rose You don't know what you're talking about.

Charles Well, why didn you marry that bloke from Seale Hayne College?

Rose How could I? With mum just dead? What would dad have done? What would you and Bill have done? Somebody had to look after you. That's your trouble, you only think of yourself.

Charles Is this enough for you, then?

Rose Is what enough?

Charles Living here with us?

Rose You're my brothers.

Charles Brothers, yeah. But there's some things you can't do with brothers, Rose.

Rose You've got a filthy mind, you know that? You're not natural.

Charles You're the one that's not natural.

Rose You can just stop it. How dare you!

Pause.

Charles Rosie, I want this more than anything I've ever wanted in my whole life.

Rose That hen's lame.

Charles I don't want to just live and die and never have any joy like the old man.

Rose The others'll start picking on it.

Charles Rose.

Rose What?

Charles Come to Dobbs with me.

Rose How are you going to afford to buy a ring?

Charles I've got that little bit of money mother left me.

Rose You're not supposed to touch that.

Charles Money's for spending.

Rose It'll be enough to buy a ring but it won't be enough to keep a wife.

Pause.

We ought to talk to Bill about it.

Charles Why?

Rose He ought to know.

Charles Bill can go hang himself.

Rose What are you going to do, Charlie, if you do get married? It's all very fine getting engaged.

Charles I thought you two could buy me out. Lower Kerscott's for sale.

Rose Charlie, you haven't thought this out. Bill would have to agree.

Charles You could talk him round.

Rose Don't know about that.

Charles Look, I'm going to get that ring. Once we're engaged he'll have to like it or lump it.

Rose Just give me a bit of time.

Charles What for?

Rose To bring him round.

Charles I'm not going to keep her hanging on.

Rose You could at least wait till after Christmas.

Charles You come and help me choose the ring, I'll wait till Christmas.

Rose I'll think about it.

He goes to touch her.

Now get off, Charles.

Charles She's a lovely girl.

Rose Mmmm.

Charles You'll get on with her when you get to know her better.

Rose Go and get that rabbit.

He goes.

Cubby, cubby, cubby.

Scene Four

The kitchen. **Charles** *is polishing his shoes and whistling just outside the door.*

William   Don't forget to ask in the butchers if they want some of our geese for Christmas.

Rose   I've got it down on my list.

William   And don't let them beat you down in price.

Rose   All right, all right.

William   I ought to come with you.

Rose   One of us'll have to stay home for the milking.

William   Charlie can do the milking.

Rose   He wants to go to town.

William   Don't know why.

Rose   I said he could.

William   Yes, well . . .

Rose   I didn't know you'd want to go.

William   I don't mind.

Rose (*whispers*)   He wants a little trip.

William   Don't let him go spending all his money.

Rose   We'll have to go again with the geese.

William   I know.

Rose   You and me could go then.

William   I told you, I don't mind.

Pause.

Don't know what's got into him lately.

Rose   What do you mean?

William   Listen to him.

They listen.

There's something going on.

Rose   I'll see what I can find out on our way into town. Probably just as well, you see?

William   What?

Rose   Might be easier for him to talk away from the farm.

William   Don't forget those nails.

Rose   They're on my list.

William   Have to make a bigger pen for those piglets.

Charles *enters.*

Charles   Us'll miss that bus if us dudn get going.

William   Don't forget to call in Curtis the gyppo's and see if he's got a dynamo for the tractor. He owes us for that scrap metal you let him take off us.

Charles   I'm not doing that.

William   Why not?

Charles   He dudn think he owes us anything. He thought if he came and collected it then he'd get it for nothing.

William   That wasn't what I arranged with him.

Charles   Well, I'm not doing it.

William   He knows he owes it to us.

Charles   We can buy a new dynamo. I'm not climbing around scrap-yards getting oil all over me best clothes.

William   Well, don't wear your best clothes.

Charles   I'll wear what I bloody well like.

Rose   Charlie!

Charles   He always has to interfere, dudn he?

William   What are you getting so mad about? Not scared of old Curtis, are you?

Charles   Don't be bloody stupid.

William   You shouldn't have let him take that metal without getting the money off him.

Charles   I told you he dudn think he owes us anything.

William   We won't be able to use the tractor.

Charles   Whenever you wanna go anywhere, there's always some errand he wants to send you on. Do your own bloody errands.

William   See how you like taking the manure out in the wheelbarrow.

Charles   It's my day off.

William   I never get a day off. I haven't had a day off for twenty years.

Charles   Oh, here we go. Tidn my fault you could never stick up to the old man. You should have told him to bugger off. But you were too much of a coward. Let him walk all over you.

William   If dad and me hadn't worked like we did we wouldn't have no farm. Then where would you be? You wouldn be going off to town dressed like a tailor's dummy for a start. You'd be working in some factory down Exeter.

Charles   Yeah and I'd have been a lot better off.

William   Well, there's the door.

Rose   Stop it.

William   Won't even go and take a dynamo off a tractor down Curtis's and then talks about working in a factory.

Charles   I'm not gettin it.

Rose   I'll go down Curtis's and see if he's got a dynamo.

William   Don't let him charge you.

Charles   That's all you think about.

William   Someone has to.

Charles   Come on, Rose.

William I'll get the old one so you don't come back with the wrong model.

He goes.

Charles I'll bloody swing for him one day.

Rose It wouldn have hurt you.

Charles What would he think?

Rose Who?

Charles Curtis.

Rose What do you mean?

Charles I told him he could have the scrap for free.

Rose Why did you do that?

Charles He had to come all the way out here.

Rose Cause of her?

Charles Who?

Rose Shirley.

Charles No.

Rose Just because she's Curtis's niece you don't have to let him walk all over you. Give em an inch and they'll take a mile.

Charles I want to ask Shirley over at Christmas.

Rose Oh.

Charles That all right?

Rose I suppose.

Charles You spoken to him yet?

Rose Patience, Charles.

Charles Come on then.

Rose I'm nearly ready.

Charles The jeweller's closes one till two, you know.

Rose Just check I've got everything.

He goes. **Rose** *checks her list.*

William *returns with the dynamo wrapped up in paper.*

William   What's wrong with him?

Rose   Nothing.

William   He doesn't know how easy he's had it. He never had the thrashings I had as a kid.

Rose   Come on.

She holds out her bag. He puts it in.

Rose *goes.*

Scene Five

Christmas night. The parlour.

Rose, **William** *and* **Charles** *are playing Sevens.*

Rose *burps.*

Rose   Pardon. That's that Christmas pudding. Always gives me indigestion.

They continue playing.

Did you think that goose was a bit tough?

William   What you mean?

Rose   I thought it was.

William   It wadn tough.

Rose   What did you think, Charlie?

Charles   Eh?

Rose   Bout the goose.

Charles   What about it?

Rose   You think it was tough?

Charles   Bit.

William   Come on, play your cards.

Charles *plays a card.* **Rose** *plays.* **William** *plays.*

Rose (*to* **William**)   I wondered who had that. You've been holding that back, haven't you? Charles!

Charles   What?

Rose   Your turn.

Charles   Oh.

He plays a card.

Rose *plays a card.*

William *plays a card.*

Rose   That's another king he's got rid of.

Charles *plays a card.*

Rose   That's a diamond.

Charles   Eh?

Rose   You've put it on the hearts pile.

Charles   Oh.

He takes the card back and plays another.

Rose   Lovely service in church this morning.

She plays. **William** *plays.*

You should have come, Charles.

Charles   Won't get me in there.

Rose   Bill played the organ beautifully.

William   Mmmm.

Charles   Waste a time. Bloody church.

William   Don't be disrespectful now.

Charles *has played.*

Rose   I can't go.

William *plays.*

Charles I can't go either.

William   You sure?

Charles Course I'm bloody sure.

Rose *plays*. **William** *plays*.

Charles I still can't go.

Rose Neither can I.

William   One of you can.

Rose It's not me.

Charles Don't look at me. You always think it's me.

Rose Have you got the eight of clubs?

Charles No.

Rose You sure?

Charles Yes.

Rose Might be behind one of your other cards.

William   He hadn got it.

Rose So you're holding that back as well.

William   Somebody's got the jack of diamonds.

Rose Tidn me.

They look at **Charles**.

Charles The ten's not down, is it?

William   I put it down ages ago.

Charles Oh.

He lays the jack of diamonds. The other two smile at each other.

I didn see you put it down.

Rose You're not concentrating, Charlie.

William   You didn want to put it down, did you?

Charles What you mean?

William   Only teasing.

Charles I wadn bloody cheating.

Rose He didn't say you were.

Charles Bloody stupid game anyway.

William Don't start sulking.

Charles You can bloody well play by yourselves.

Charles *throws his cards down.*

Rose *and* **William** *look at each other.*

Charles Callin me a cheat! I wadn cheating. I hadn't seen the bloody ten.

William All right! All right! It's only a game.

Rose Come on, I'll redeal.

Charles No!

William Don't be childish, Charlie.

Charles I'm not bloody childish. Just shut up!

Rose Shhh.

William What?

Rose Dog's barking.

Charles *and* **Rose** *look at each other.* **Charles** *gets up.*

William Don't go out there kicking him.

Charles *mimes pouring drinks to* **Rose**. *She nods.* **Charles** *goes.*

William *sighs.*

William He's enough to try the patience of a saint.

Rose You going to give us a tune?

William Not feeling like it, Rosie.

Pause.

Has he fed the pigs?

Rose Don't think so?

William Better go and do it.

Rose   Do you want a drink of port?

William   Port?

Rose   Yes.

William   Where did that come from?

Rose   Charlie bought it.

She gets out some glasses.

Charles *returns with* **Shirley**.

Charles   Look who's here.

Rose   Oh. Come in, my dear. Let her get near the fire, Bill.
You walked all the way up the lane? Must be freezing. There
you are. Sit down there.

Shirley   Thank you.

Rose   What a lovely dress.

Shirley   Christmas present.

Rose   From your mum.

Shirley   Sort of. Mr Webber really.

Rose   I see.

Charles   Want some port?

Shirley   Lovely.

He starts pouring the drinks.

Rose   I hear he's thinking of emigrating.

William   Who?

Rose   Mr Webber down the pub.

Charles   I didn't know that.

Shirley   Yes.

Charles   Here we are then.

He hands out the drinks.

Shirley   Happy Christmas.

Will/Charles/Rose   Happy Christmas.

Shirley   I've brought you these.

Rose   Oh, thank you. Look, Bill.

William   Very nice.

Shirley   And I thought you might like this, Mr Thorne.

William   Oh.

She hands him a parcel.

Charles   Aren't you going to open it?

Rose   You shouldn't have gone to all this trouble, Shirley.

Shirley   Twadn any trouble. Here.

She gives **Charles** *a present.*

Rose   Chocolates. Mmm. What have you got, Bill?

William (*holding up a songbook*)   Popular songs.

Rose   Oh, very nice.

William *laughs.*

William   Well I never.

Charles *has opened his present. It is a tie.*

Charles   Thank you.

Rose   Very nice. It will go with your new shirt.

Charles   Hang on.

He goes.

Rose   It's like Father Christmas coming, idn it, Bill?

William   Yes it is. (*He laughs.*) Goodness!

Rose   You want a chocolate?

William   Oh.

Rose   Don't take all day.

William *takes a chocolate.*

Rose   Shirley.

Shirley   They're for you.

Rose   Go on.

Shirley *takes one.*

All   Mmmm.

Silence, apart from the chewing.

Rose   Your mother all right?

Shirley   Yes, thank you. She said the goose was lovely.

Rose   That's good. Didn't see you at church this morning.

Shirley   We had a late night in the pub last night.

Rose   Lovely service. Saw Mrs Youings.

Shirley   Oh yes.

Rose   She hadn heard from Tommy.

Shirley   No?

Rose   Funny him just going off like that, isn't it?

Shirley   Yes.

William   Where's he gone?

Rose   Looking for work up the country, I think.

Pause.

Nice chocolates.

Pause.

Charles *returns. He has put on his new shirt and the tie.*

Charles   There.

Rose   Very smart.

William *is looking at the songbook.*

Charles   Going to give us a tune, Bill?

William   All right then.

Rose *goes to the piano.*

Rose   We usually have carols Christmas night. Here, Bill.

She gets out a music book.

Our mother used to sing this one, Shirley. 'The Cherry Tree', do you know it?

Charles (*sings*)   Mary got cherries
By one two and three.

William   That's the last verse.

Rose   It's the wrong key as well. He's tone deaf, Shirley.

William *starts playing.*

William   Come on, Rose.

Rose   Joseph was an old man
An old man was he,
He married with Mary
The Queen of Glory.

William   Joseph took Mary
Into the orchard wood
Where there was apples, plums, cherries
As red as any blood.

Rose   Then bespoke Mary
So meek and so mild:
Get me some cherries, Joseph
For my body's bound with child.

William   Then bespoke Joseph
These words so unkind:
Let them get you cherries, Mary
That did your body bind.

Charles   Mean old bugger.

William   Then bespake Jesus
All in his mother's womb:
The highest bough of the cherry tree
Shall bow down to Mary's knee.

William/Rose   Mary got cherries
By one, two and three,

Charles *joins in.*

Mary got cherries
For her young son and she.

Shirley *claps.*

Shirley   You're a very musical family.

Rose   William's the musician. He could have gone to music college, Shirley.

Shirley   Really?

Rose   Had a scholarship and everything.

William   I didn have a scholarship.

Rose   You did.

William   The teacher said I stood a good chance of getting one.

Rose   There you are then.

Shirley   Mum used to send me to dance classes when I was small.

Rose   Oh yes?

Shirley   I always said I was going to be a dancer.

Rose   Oh.

Pause.

Shirley   What a lovely brooch.

Charles   Ahhhhhh.

Shirley   What?

Charles   She only ever puts that on at Christmas.

Shirley   It's beautiful.

Charles (*whispers*)   Her fiancé gave it to her.

Rose *laughs.*

Rose   Honestly, Charles.

Charles   Oh, she's going red. Didn know you still blushed, Rosie.

Rose   Don't listen to him, Shirley.

Shirley   I won't.

Rose   Someone I knew at Seale Hayne Agricultural College gave it me.

Charles   Oh Danny Boy, the pipes, the pipes are calling . . .

Rose   He was called Daniel.

Shirley   What happened to him?

Rose   He went to Canada.

Shirley   Wouldn't want to go there. Too cold.

Rose   I like places like that. Remember reading all about the tundra in geography.

Charles   What's the tundra?

Rose   It's the region inside the Arctic Circle.

Charles   Tell I never listened at school, can't you?

Rose   And the Himalayas, that's another place I'd like to go.

William   She followed all that stuff about whatshisname, Hillary, in the papers. Think she wanted to go up Everest with him.

Rose   I did.

Pause.

Charles   Aren't you going to play us one of Shirley's songs, Bill?

William   I could have a go I spose.

Shirley   Play that one.

He starts to play 'How Much is that Doggy in the Window?'.

Charles   That's more like it.

Rose   Don't know it.

Shirley *sings the chorus of 'How Much is that Doggy in the Window?'* and **Charles** *barks at the end of each line.*

Charles   Come on, Rose.

They all sing the verse again.

Shirley *does a tap dance to the tune.*

Rose   Oh, very good.

They all clap.

Rose   Time for a sandwich I think. We always have cold meat sandwich Christmas night, Shirley.

Shirley   I'll come and help you.

Charles   No, you won't. I'll help you, Mum.

Rose   Eh?

Charles   What?

William *laughs.*

Rose   You called me mum.

Charles   I didn.

He is embarrassed.

Rose   Well, come on, then. They're all done. You can carry em through.

He goes with **Rose**.

William *plays the last line of the song and* **Shirley** *joins in, singing it.*

Charles (*off*)   Woof woof.

They laugh again.

William   I'm going to enjoy playing these.

Shirley   So why didn't you go to music college then, Mr Thorne?

William   Oh, you know how it is, dear.

Shirley   What?

William   Dad wanted me on the farm.

Shirley   Yes.

William   Probably for the best, you know.

Shirley   Mrs Youings says you play the organ like a professional.

William   Don't know about that.

Shirley   She said you've got a magic touch.

William (*laughs*)   Oh.

Shirley   It's hard for people with artistic temperaments.

William   What?

Shirley   To fit in.

William   Maybe.

Shirley   I mean, I'm not like you. You've got a special gift. But sometimes when I dance I feel like it's not me dancing, it's like I'm being danced. Do you know what I mean?

William   I do. It's a form of possession you see. It takes you into another world.

Shirley *shivers*.

William   You cold?

Shirley   No.

William   Come and get warm.

He takes her hand.

Freezing.

She blushes.

Shirley (*looking at his palm*)   Let me see.

William   What can you see?

Shirley (*laughing*)   A long life.

William   You look very pretty in your new dress.

Shirley   Thank you.

Charles *returns with the sandwiches.*

Charles   You two are quiet. It's Christmas, you know.

Rose *enters with the teacups.*

Rose   Hand them round.

Charles *hands out the sandwiches.*

Charles   Ummm.

Rose   What?

Charles   I haven't bought you a Christmas present,
Shirley. But there is something I'd like to give you.

Rose *shakes her head at him furiously behind everyone else's back.*

Charles   And I reckon now's as good a time as any.

He takes a small box from his pocket.

Here.

Shirley   What's this?

Charles   Open it.

Shirley   Maybe I should save it for later.

Charles   Go on.

She opens the box.

Put it on then.

He takes it from her and puts it on her.

There. You like it?

Shirley   It's lovely.

Charles   Rose helped me choose it.

William *looks at* **Rose**.

Charles   We wondered about getting the diamond. But we
decided on the sapphire in the end, didn't we, Rose?

Rose   Yes.

Shirley   Thank you.

William   Very pretty.

Rose   It is.

Pause.

Want a sandwich, Bill?

William   No thanks.

Rose   You sure?

William   I'll have one later. The pigs still have to be fed.
You'll have to excuse me.

Charles   There's plenty of time for that.

William   Don't want to leave it too late.

Rose   You want me to come?

William   No. You stay here. Thanks again for the
songbook. I'm going to get a lot of enjoyment out of that.

He goes.

Charles   Well, let's have some more port. Celebrate.
Shirley?

Shirley   Um . . .

Charles (*pouring more port into her glass*)   Here. Don't I get a
kiss?

Shirley   Of course.

She kisses him.

Charles   Rose?

Rose   Not for the moment. I'll just make sure he's found the
torch.

She goes. **Charles** *looks at* **Shirley**.

Shirley   It's a beautiful ring.

Charles   Yeah.

Shirley *looks towards where the other two have gone.*

Scene Six

William *is mixing food for the pigs. He has a tilley lamp.*

William   Get out! Get out.

Rose *enters with a torch.*

Rose   Thought you might need this.

William *doesn't answer.*

Rose   Luscombe's have got mains electric now, you know.
In the buildings as well as in the house apparently.

No response.

Mrs Luscombe told me in church this morning.

No response.

Might be worth looking into how much it would cost.

No response.

They're fattening up. Have to get the boars done.

No response.

You gonna get the vet to do it?

No response.

I'll ring him after Christmas.

No response.

Shall I?

No response.

Bill?

William   What?

Rose   Shall we get the vet to castrate the pigs?

William   Are you going to pay him if we do?

Rose   You're not going to do it, are you? Thought you
didn't like that job.

Pause.

I didn't know he was going to give her the ring tonight.

William   What are you talking about?

Rose   Charles and Shirley.

William   Doesn't bother me what he does.

Rose   Thought if I let him buy the ring it would keep him quiet for a while. Anyway he promised he'd wait till I'd talked to you.

William   Wanted to choose your moment, did you?

Rose   I thought it might all blow over.

William   Trying to handle me, were you, Rose?

Rose   No.

William   You and him think you can pull the wool over my eyes, don't you? I don't trust you, Rose.

Rose   What you mean?

William   You're sly. Always have been.

Rose   Thought you'd be pleased anyway.

William   Eh?

Rose   You're always defending her. Thought you'd like having her in the family.

Charles *appears out of the darkness.* **Rose** *shines the torch in his face.*

Rose   Nearly finished.

William *pours the food into the trough.*

Rose   You left her on her own?

Charles   She's washing up.

Rose   Charles!

Charles   I want you two to come back in there.

Rose   We're coming.

Charles   I'm going to marry her. We got to sort it out.

Rose Not now, Charlie.

Charles That's your solution to everything, idn it? Not now, Charlie.

Rose It's Christmas.

Charles Bugger Christmas. I want you two to buy me out.

Pause.

Did you hear? I want my share of the farm so I can go and get somewhere of my own. I've thought it all out. There's two ways we can do it. Either we sell off some of the land –

Rose Charlie!

Charles Or we get a mortgage on the farm.

Pause.

What do you say?

Rose You want us to run up debts, Charlie?

Charles A mortgage idn a debt. It's more like a loan.

Rose We couldn do that.

Charles Why not?

Rose What would father say?

Charles He idn here. He's dead.

Rose He wouldn want us running into debt.

Charles It wouldn be getting into bloody debt.

Rose Don't start swearing.

Charles It'd just be a way of getting another farm.

Rose Father didn leave us this place so we could end up giving the money to the bank.

Charles Then we'll have to sell some of the land. Luscombe has always wanted those fields down by the river.

Rose *looks at* **William**.

Charles Don't look to him. What do you think?

Rose   Twoudn feel right.

Charles   Does this feel right?

William   This is our birthright. I'd rather see us dead than sell one acre of it.

He goes.

Rose   Oh, Charlie!

Charles   What?

Rose   How could you do this to us?

Charles   Do what?

Rose   We were happy. We were living together, gettin on fine. Then you have to upset it all.

Charles   Me?

Rose   Rushing into things.

Charles   You promised you'd speak to him.

Rose   You can't wait. You want things now, today. You don't really know anything about the girl.

Charles   I know all I need to know.

Rose   Hasten slowly, that's what dad would have said.

Charles   Most blokes my age have been married for years.

Rose   I'd've brought him round in the end.

Charles   I'm marrying her. He'll have to agree in the end. It'll be two against one.

Rose   Mmmm.

Charles   He'll be outvoted.

Rose   I suppose.

Charles   Perhaps we should get some advice from Prout.

Rose   What do you want to go running off to the solicitor for?

Charles   He'll know what to do.

Rose Hope it won't come to that.

Charles If it does. It does. Bill can like it or lump it.

Shirley *has entered and heard this last line.*

Shirley Mum'll be wondering where I've got to.

Charles I'll walk you home.

Shirley Night.

Rose Night.

They go. **Rose** *shines her torch on the pigs.*

Scene Seven

The yard.

Sound of pigs squealing — high-pitched disturbing screams. **Rose** *is watching from the distance.*

William *enters.*

Rose Persuaded Charlie to do them boars while you were in town.

William Hope he's doing it properly.

Rose He did it with dad often enough. I thought you'd be pleased.

William Is he using disinfectant?

Rose I don't know.

William The Dettol for it is in the barn.

Rose Did you tell him that?

William He hadn spoken to me for three weeks now. Since Christmas. Haven had the chance to tell him anything.

More screams.

Rose You go and see Mr Prout?

William Yes.

Rose   What did he say?

William   The way the will is, Charlie can't make us buy him out.

Rose   Hmmm.

William   He said it would be better to go for a mortgage rather than sell any of the land.

Rose   You don't want to do either though.

William   No.

Pause.

You think he's set on it?

Rose   He thinks he is.

William   Has he said anything to you lately?

Rose   You know Charlie. Changes with the weather.

Pause.

I don't trust Prout.

William   Why not?

Rose   He's very friendly with the bank manager.

William   Yeah.

Pause.

Those fields down by the river are boggy, mind.

Rose   So?

William   If Luscombe give us a good price.

Rose   Dad spent fifty years fighting with old Luscombe.

William   Mmmm.

Pause.

Rose   How much would the interest on the mortgage be?

William   Dunno.

Rose   Lot, I expect.

William   Yeah.

Pause.

Rose   Do you think us should speak to Luscombe about it?

William   Maybe.

Rose   Better to sell some land than get a mortgage really.

Pause.

William   Do you want to?

Rose   What?

William   Speak to Luscombe.

Rose   Do you?

William   Dunno.

Rose   Or should us go and have a chat to the bank manager?

William   What about?

Rose   A mortgage.

William   Could do.

Pause.

If you think we should give him what he wants.

Rose   You've changed your tune.

William   Who are we doing it all for?

Rose   You never wanted to be a farmer, did you?

William   Don't know what you're talking about.

Rose   Dad dedicated his life to this land.

William   I know.

Rose   Charlie can't go off on his own.

William   No?

Rose   He'd go bankrupt in no time.

William   You think?

Rose Don't you?

William Don't know.

Rose Course he would. I don't know how you can consider such a thing.

William I just thought maybe us should let him go.

Rose And let him ruin his life? He'll soon go off her when he finds out what sort of girl she is.

William What you mean?

Rose Things I've heard about her. Like mother like daughter.

William Can't always believe gossip.

Rose You going to start defending her again, are you?

William Don't be daft.

Rose We should sit it out.

William Yeah?

Rose That's what dad would do. You know what he'd want.

William What?

Rose Keep the farm together. Keep the family together.

More screams from the pigs.

The screams subside.

Charles *enters.*

William You use disinfectant?

Charles *ignores him.*

William Charles!

Charles *carries on walking.*

William *stops him.*

Charles Get your hand off me.

William I just want to know if you used Dettol. Don't want em dying of some infection.

Charles *shakes his hand off and carries on again.*

William For Christ's sake! How much longer is this going to go on? I'm fed up with this. Bloody well ignoring me like a bloody child.

He throws his hat on the ground and stamps on it.

Charles You start treatin me like a grown-up and I'll start behaving like one.

William Don't be stupid.

Charles You're gonna have to agree in the end. Rose and me have already talked about it.

William *looks at* **Rose**.

Charles We can outvote you. Two to one.

William Two to one. I see.

Charles If you don't agree then I'm going to go and see Prout. Get him to send you a letter. Me and Rose want to sell the land down by the river to Luscombe. It's a majority decision.

William Rose?

Charles No use tryin to persuade her otherwise. We've agreed.

Rose Wait, Charlie.

Charles I'm buggered if I'm going to do any more waiting. This has gone on since Christmas. He'll have to face up to it sometime. Might as well be today.

William So? Rose? This true?

Rose You know it idn.

Charles What you mean?

Rose This is no way to settle things.

William Whose side you on, Rose?

Rose   I'm not on anybody's side.

Charles   She knows what's fair.

William   Tell him, Rose.

Charles   Tell me what?

William   Rose.

Pause.

Rose dudn want to sell the land.

Charles   What?

William   We talked about it.

Charles   You been putting pressure on her?

William   No.

Charles   She wants to see me settled.

William   Tell him.

Rose   Stop it.

William   She wants to keep it all together.

Charles   No.

William   Ask her.

Charles   Rose?

Rose   Father wouldn want it. Twoudn be right, Charlie.

Charles   You let him persuade you? You know why he's doin this? He's bloody jealous. The way he looks at her. Me and Shirley had a good laugh about it. Filthy bugger.

William   I didn persuade Rose. She persuaded me.

Charles   Don't believe you.

William   You're beaten, Charlie boy.

Rose   It's for the best, Charlie.

Charles *goes.*

Rose   Now look what you've done.

William   Eh?

Rose   That was no way to tell him.

William   You have a better way?

Rose   You should have let me do it in my own time.

William   Couldn go on like that forever. He had to know.

Charles *returns with the gun.*

Charles   (*to* **William**)   I'll bloody kill you.

Rose   Charles!

William   Don't be daft.

Charles   Think I won't? You're not going to stop me marryin her. I love her.

William   Marry her. Go and work down the egg factory.

Rose   William! Charles, she idn worth it.

Charles   Don't you start.

Rose   She used to go and spend the night with Tommy Youings in the Nissan hut on the aerodrome. People saw them there together.

Charles   Bloody gossipmongers.

Rose   Mrs Luscombe's no gossipmonger. Why do you think Tommy Youings left so sudden? He skidaddled before she could get him up the altar.

Charles   Don't talk about her like that.

Rose   Nobody else would have her.

He points the gun at her.

Go on. Shoot me if you don't believe me.

Charles   Jealous, are you, Rose? Never had anything between your legs, have you? Nobody would want you.

Rose   And who'd have you? You really think any decent girl would be interested in you?

William   Rose!

Rose   You'll never amount to anything. You wouldn't survive on your own for one minute. You haven't got the staying power. You're just like Uncle Ted. And you've got his temper too. Look at you standing there pointing a gun at your own sister. Everybody in the village knows about that temper of yours. That's why Mary Quick wouldn have you. And that's why Gwen Small married the Luscombe boy. They were scared of you. You're unstable. You're nothing. You're nobody.

Charles *goes because he is about to cry.*

Rose   Don't you look at me like that.

William *goes to the pigs.*

Rose *looks after him. Pigs start screaming again.*

Scene Eight

The Ash Grove.

Charles *and* **Shirley** *are sheltering from the rain.*

Charles   We can't keep arguing about it.

Shirley   I know.

Charles   Come here.

He kisses her.

Shirley   Aowhh.

Charles   I'm sorry.

He tries to undo her clothes.

Shirley   Charles!

Charles   What?

Shirley   Don't.

Charles   What's wrong?

Shirley   Nothing.

Charles   Why don't we just get married. It'll sort itself out.

She doesn't reply.

We could go and see the vicar.

Shirley   Yes.

Charles   What about tomorrow night?

Shirley   I'm working behind the bar.

Charles   The next night then.

Shirley   I'll have to see if I'm free.

Charles   We didn't ought to wait too long.

Pause.

You been to the doctor?

Shirley   No.

Charles   But you're sure?

Shirley   Never been this late before.

He puts his arm around her.

Charles   What'll we call it?

Shirley   What?

Charles   The baby.

Shirley   I don't know.

Charles   Frances.

Shirley   Get shortened to Frank.

Charles   Not if it's a girl. That was my mother's name.

Shirley   Oh, I see.

Charles   This'll shake that old house up. Show those buggers.

Shirley   Who?

Charles   Them two. The two barreners.

Shirley Mmmm.

He buries his head in her breasts.

Charles.

Charles What?

Shirley I can't live in that house.

Charles Don't start again.

Shirley But I can't.

Charles We haven't got any choice.

Shirley I don't even want to stay in this village.

Charles Why not?

Shirley Because of the way people look at me. The way they look down on mum.

Charles You don't want to listen to drunks gossiping in the Red Lion.

Shirley It's not just them though, is it?

Charles What you mean?

Shirley It's Rose and William.

Charles What about them.

Shirley I can't live with them.

Pause.

We don't have to stay here, do we?

Charles (*violently*) This is what they want!

Shirley What?

Charles They want me to move out. Then they can have the farm to themselves. Do what they like with it.

Shirley Let them.

Charles Why should they get it their way? It's mine as much as theirs.

Shirley You'll get your share one day.

Charles   Yes. And in the meantime I have to go and slave my guts out for somebody else! They're not getting rid of me that easy. I'm not going to be somebody else's wage slave just to suit them.

Shirley   But I can't live in that house with them.

Charles   They'll soon get used to it.

Shirley   But I won't. It wouldn't work out, Charles. We could go to Australia with mum and Mr Webber. There's all sorts of opportunities out there.

He takes her face in his hands and speaks into it.

Charles   Now listen to me! We're getting married and we're living here. There's no argument. That's what's going to happen.

He releases her.

She takes the ring off.

Shirley   Here.

Charles   Don't be bloody daft!

Shirley   Take it!

Charles   Put it back on.

She looks at him. He kisses her.

You have to be kept on a tight lead I can see that.

Shirley   What you mean?

Charles   You're too wilful. I'll have to break you in.

He tries to undo her clothes.

Come on.

Shirley   You're hurting me.

Charles   Come on!

Shirley   (*violently*)   No!

He looks at her.

I'm not a bloody pony you bought at Bampton Fair you know.

Charles I'm sorry.

She puts her head in her hands.

Shirley.

Shirley It'll never work, Charles.

Charles We'll make it work.

Shirley When I was a kid I used to lie in bed listening to my mum and dad rowing in the next room. We lived with my dad's parents. My gran always looked down on my mum. So then mum used to go and complain to dad about her and they'd end up rowing. Mum always says if they'd had a house of their own they'd still be together now. That'll happen to us, Charles.

Charles Bit late for second thoughts now, idn it?

Shirley What you mean?

Charles You're carrying my kid.

Pause.

Shirley And what if it idn yours?

Charles Eh?

Silence.

Shirley What if the baby looks like Tommy Youings when it's born?

Charles Will he?

Shirley I don't know. But all the old hens in the village will be clucking over it and nudging each other. (*She mimics them sounding like a hen.*) 'Awwwhhhh, dudn look much like Charlie Thorne to me.'

Charles Bugger them.

Shirley I can't say that. Mr Webber will find you a job in Australia, you know. He's got relations over there.

No response.

Charles?

Charles   What?

Shirley   I do love you.

She holds up the ring.

It's up to you.

Charles *looks at her.*

Suddenly he grabs the ring and goes.

Shirley *cries.*

Scene Nine

William *is playing the piano.*

Sound of knocking.

Rose (*off*)   Charlie! Charlie!

Pause.

(*Off.*)   Charlie, come on, you've got to eat.

William *stops playing and listens.*

Rose (*off*)   Charlie, please. It's dumplings.

Pause.

Rose *enters with a tray.*

William   Has he eaten anything?

Rose   Don't think he's touched it.

William   He'll have to eat it in the end.

Rose   You eat that chutney in the larder?

William   What chutney?

Rose   The chutney we had with the pie yesterday.

William   No.

Rose   He must have been down in the night and had it.

William   Why?

Rose   Because it's all gone.

William   Whole jar of chutney?

Rose   Yes.

Pause.

It's been going on for nearly a month now.

William   Mmmm.

Rose   You think we ought to get the doctor for him?

William   What can the doctor do?

Rose   I'm worried, Bill.

William   No point being worried.

Rose   I'd hate to see him . . .

William   What?

Rose   Always remember when they took Mrs Warren's sister down Digby.

William   Charlie won't end up in no lunatic asylum.

He plays. She listens.

Rose   We'll be all right, won't we, the three of us?

William   Course we will.

Rose *starts humming the tune.*

Rose   They're leaving next week.

William   Who?

Rose   Mr Webber, Mrs Stephens, Shirley.

William   Oh.

Rose   They're going to Sydney. That's where his folks are.

William *plays 'Linden Lea' on the piano.*

William (*sings*)   Within the woodlands, flowry gladed
    By the oak trees' mossy moot
    The singing grass blades, timber-shaded,
    Now do quiver underfoot;
    And birds do whistle overhead
    And water's bubbling in its bed

Rose *joins in.*

Both   And there, for me, the apple tree
    Do lean down low in Linden Lea.

William *starts the next verse with* **Rose** *accompanying him with her humming.*

William   When leaves that lately were aspringing,
    Now do fade within the copse
    And painted birds do hush their singing
    Up upon the timber tops;

Both   And brown-leaved fruit's aturning red
    In cloudless sunshine overhead,
    With fruit for me, the apple tree
    Do lean down low . . .

They notice **Charles** *standing in the doorway. He has just a pair of long johns on.*

Rose   You'll catch your death.

William   Get his night-shirt.

Rose *goes.*

Charles (*sings tunelessly*)   Three German officers crossed
    the line
    Parlez-vous
    Three German officers crossed the line
    Parlez-vous

William   Stop that, Charlie.

Charles   Three German officers crossed the line
    Kissing the girls and shagging the wives

William   Stop it.

Rose *returns with the night-shirt.*

Rose Here you are, Charlie.

He continues singing and runs away from her.

Charles Inky pinky parlez-vous.

Rose Stop mucking around, Charlie.

Charles They came across in a Panzer tank
Parlez-vous
They came across in a Panzer tank
Parlez-vous.

William Give it to me.

Charles They came across in a Panzer tank
Two to steer and one to wank
Inky pinky parlez-vous.

William *approaches* **Charles**. **Charles** *runs away again.*

William Don't be so bloody daft.

Charles *turns round and moons at them.*

They chase him round the room. Every time he escapes he cocks a snoop at them.

Charles The landlord's daughter she was there
Parlez-vous.

Eventually they corner him. **William** *tackles him and pins him to the ground.*

William Give me the shirt.

Rose *and* **William** *struggle to get the shirt on him.*

William Pull it down.

Even though he is trapped **Charles** *continues singing.*

Charles The landlord's daughter she was there
Parlez-vous.

William Stop singing that.

Charles The landlord's daughter she was there.

William Stop it. You should be ashamed of yourself singing that in front of your sister.

Charles Bloody great knockers and long blonde hair.

William *covers* **Charles**'s *mouth.* **Charles** *moves his head aside and carries on.*

Charles Inky pinky . . .

William You want me to get dad's horsewhip?

Rose Bill, don't.

Charles Parlez-vous.

William *gets a horsewhip.*

William You want this?

Charles *stops singing.*

William You want it?

Charles (*sings mock sweetly, mimicking* **Rose**) Oh, don't
    deceive me,
  Oh, never leave me.
  How could you treat a poor maiden so?

They look at each other as the lights fade.

Part Two

Scene Ten

It is thirty years later. An exposed field in winter.

William *has been pulling mangolds. He carries a sack and puts it down. Coughs. Blows into his hands. Coughs again. He is an old man and frail.*

Rose *enters. She is arthritic.*

Rose   Wondered where you'd got to.

William   Getting some mangolds pulled.

Rose   Go back home, Snowy. Go on, my lovely. She's followed me all the way up here.

William   Bloody cat thinks it's a dog.

He coughs.

Rose   You shouldn't be out in this wind.

William   Had to be done.

Rose   You taken your medicine this morning?

William   Forgot.

Rose   Brought your gloves.

She hands them to him.

William   Ground's frozen solid.

Rose   Snowed last night on the moors.

They stand looking into the distance. Two forlorn figures on a frozen landscape.

In the distance a tractor can be heard. They look in that direction.

Rose   Walter Luscombe's out on his new tractor.

William   Where?

Rose *points. They watch.*

Rose   Got his little boy with him.

She sings quietly to herself.

We plough the fields and scatter the good seed on the
land . . .

William   Dunno how they afford all that machinery.

Rose   Letter came this morning from the bank.

William *doesn't respond.*

Rose   You want to read it?

William   Haven't got my glasses.

Rose   You ask the bank manager if he could wait for the
interest payment?

William   Yes.

Rose   What will we do if he won't?

William   Mmm. Here! Charlie! Charlie! Bag em up!

Rose (*sings*)   He sends the snow in winter
The warmth to swell the grain . . .

He's building his parents a bungalow.

William   Who?

Rose   Walter Luscombe.

William   Look at him! What's he doing?

Rose   We could sell some land.

William   Still have to farm the rest.

Rose   Charlie will have to do more of the heavy work.

William   Charlie! What can he do? Any job I give him I
have to stand over him.

Rose   He's not that bad.

William   He can't be relied on.

Rose   So what should we do?

William We'll have to think of something.

He coughs.

Rose He's going to put central heating in.

William What?

Rose Walter Luscombe. In this bungalow.

William Ohhh.

Rose Mornacott Cottage is coming up for sale.

No response.

If we sold the farm we could easy afford that even after paying off the bank.

Still no response.

It'd be big enough for the three of us. And it's got a field, we could keep a few hens and pigs. Charlie would be pleased. He hates the work.

William I'm not living in a bloody cottage in the village.

Rose (*sings*) All good gifts around us
Are sent from Heaven above
Then thank the Lord
Oh, thank the Lord
For –

William You read the letter?

Rose No. You want me to?

William (*calling to* **Charles**) Come on, get on with it!

Rose If they won't let us have any more we'll have to do something.

William *coughs.*

Rose Look at you! Out pulling mangolds with that cough.

William We can't afford to buy cow cake.

Rose And we can't carry on like this. I need some money for the baker.

William   Haven't got any.

Rose   He comes today.

William   Have to pay him out your egg money.

Rose (*sings*)   Much more to us, His children
He gives our daily bread.
All good gifts around us
Are sent from Heaven above . . .

William *opens the letter.*

Rose   I was going to use the egg money for my trip.

William   What trip?

Rose   With the church. To Oberammergau.

William   Have to pay the interest to the bank.

Rose   That heifer will be calving soon. You can sell the calf
to do that.

William   Won't be worth selling till spring.

William *is trying to read the letter.*

Charles *enters with a sack of mangolds and some of the green tops in
his hand.*

William   You need to take them down and give them to the
bullocks.

Charles *stands looking at Walter Luscombe on his tractor.*

William   What you looking at?

Rose   That's Walter Luscombe.

Charles   Big tractor.

Rose   Yes, it's new.

Charles   Bout time we had a new tractor.

William   Get those bullocks fed.

Charles (*quietly*)   Bugger off.

Rose   Charles!

William   What did you say? What did he say?

They don't answer.

What you doing with those greens?

Charles   Feed my rabbits.

William   Bloody rabbits. We're supposed to be farmers.

Rose   Leave him.

William   Dad must be turning in his grave. Waste of bloody time.

Charles (*mimicking their father*)   'We're not bloody townies, we don't have bloody pets.'

Rose   Charles.

Charles   'If you want to keep a pet go and live in a rabbit hutch in Exeter.'

Rose *starts to giggle.*

William   Don't encourage him.

Charles   'And you should have got these mangolds pulled out before Christmas. Not wait till they get frozen in.' Look, there he is over there behind the hedge. He's watching you, Billy.

Rose *find this hysterically funny and tries to stifle her giggles.*

William   You'll end up back in that hospital if you say things like that.

Rose   Shut up, Bill. Take the mangolds down and feed the cows, Charlie.

Charles *picks up the sack and goes.*

They stand watching him.

Rose   Sometimes I think I see mum. I was looking out the kitchen window the other day and it was like I saw her in the lane out the corner of my eye. In that blue dress of hers. Funny.

William   You're both mad.

He is trying to read the letter.

Rose   Here.

She reads it.

William   Well?

Rose   Dear Mr Thorne, as you are aware, the interest payments on your loan are now over a year in arrears. I'm afraid we are unable to offer you any further extension and would ask you to pay the outstanding amount as promptly as possible. Yours faithfully, D.W. Lambert.

They stand watching Walter Luscombe on his tractor.

Look at Snowy. She's waiting for me to walk home with her. I'm coming, my lovely. You want your dinner, don't you?

William   Take some mangolds down with you.

Rose (*sings*)   All good gifts around us
    Are sent from Heaven above . . .

What are we going to do?

William   I don't know.

He goes to pull some more mangolds.

Rose *picks up the sack.*

Scene Eleven

The yard.

Charles *is standing with a fork looking at the sky. The rooks are gathering in the elms.*

Charles   Caw, caw, caw.

Rose *enters.*

Rose (*sings*)   Blessed assurance, Jesus is mine:
    Oh what a foretaste of glory divine!

She starts chopping wood.

What you doing, Charlie?

Charles *doesn't respond.*

Rose   I thought you were going to muck out the pigs.

He still doesn't respond.

Don't let Bill catch you standing around.

Charles   There was rooks in the wood down Digby.

Rose   Yeah?

He goes.

(*Calling after him.*) Bring me some milk for the house.
You want a drink, don't you, Snowy? I'll get you some in a
minute.

(*Sings.*) Heir of salvation, purchase of God;
   Born of his spirit, washed in his blood,
   This is my story, this is my song
   Praising my Saviour, all the day long . . .

Keep out the way, Snowy.

(*Sings.*) This is my story, this is my song,
   Praising my Saviour all the day long.

William *enters.*

Rose   You get back indoors. You shouldn't be up. Doctor
said you had to stay in bed.

William   Has Charlie mended that gap in the hedge?

Rose   I don't know. Look at you. If you don't shift that
cough off your chest you'll get pneumonia.

(*Sings.*) Perfect submission, perfect delight.
   Visions of rapture burst on my sight . . .

William   Cows'll be gettin into Luscombe's winter kale
again.

Rose (*sings*)   Angels descending, bring from above
   Echoes of mercy, whispers of love.

William   I'll go and have a look at that heifer later.

Rose   No you won't. I'll do that.

(*Sings.*) This is my story, this is my song.
  Praising my Saviour all the day long.

William   Letter came from the solicitor.

Rose   What?

William   Forms to sign.

Rose   What forms?

William   For the auctioneer.

Rose   Oh.

William   What?

Rose   Didn know you'd already asked him to do that.

William   I hubm asked him to do anything.

Rose (*sings*)   This is my story, this is my song,
  Praising my Saviour, all the day long.

William   He just said he'd send me the forms in case we
decided to sell up.

Rose   All right, all right. No need to start shouting about it.

William   We don't have to sign em if we don't want to.

Rose (*sings*)   Perfect submission, all is at rest,
  I and my Saviour am happy and blest.

William   Anybody'd think I was going behind your back.

Rose (*sings*)   Watching and waiting, looking above,
  Filled with his goodness . . .

William   You're the one who wants to go and live in the
village.

Rose   Just said it might be easier.

William   You want to go off gallivanting with the church
group. Spending all the egg money on a ticket to bloody
Austria. But you don't want to give up anything.

Rose   That egg money's mine. I don't sit in the pannier market all day Thursdays just to end up spending that money on you two.

William   You eat the bread too.

Rose   I've sacrificed everything all my life and the one time I want to do anything, go somewhere, you tell me I can't. I could have grandchildren by now if it wadn for you two.

William   Why didn you marry bloody Danny Marks then?

Rose   Because I couldn leave you and Charlie. That's why.

William   We've all made sacrifices.

Rose   You going to start talking about music college again? I didn't stop you going to music college. All our lives you've talked about how dad stopped you going to music college. It's a tune you've played for the last fifty years. I'd've thought you'd've got tired of it by now. I am.

William   And I'm sick and tired of hearing you talk about spending money we haven't got.

Rose   Whose fault's that?

William   What you mean?

Rose   We wouldn't be in debt if you hadn borrowed that money from the bank.

William   You bloody old fool. I only did it because of you. Going on about how we needed a new milking parlour.

Rose   You can't have my egg money.

William   We'll sell the bloody farm then.

Rose   Sell it for all I care. I don't want to stay living here with a nincompoop and an old miser.

Charles *is standing watching them, holding a milk jug.*

William   You mended that gap in the hedge?

Charles   I'm cleaning out the pigs.

Rose *takes the jug from him.*

Rose Here you are Snowy. My pretty little darling.

William Have a look at that heifer.

Charles *goes.*

Rose Nice drink of milk. There you are my lovely. He'll have to agree, you know.

William He'll bloody well do what we tell him.

Rose I'll have a word with him.

William He won't bloody care.

Rose Do you like that, my darling? Lap, lap, lap. My pretty little Snowy.

William *goes in disgust.*

Rose (*returning to the chopping*) This is my story, this is my song . . .

A car drives up.

Rose *looks.*

Sound of car door slamming.

Shirley *enters. She is tanned and looks young for a woman in her early fifties.*

Rose You lost?

Shirley No.

Rose Thought you might be looking for Luscombe's.

Shirley No, Rose. I was looking for you.

Rose Sorry, my dear, do I know you?

Shirley Don't you recognise me, Rose?

Rose Now you do look familiar. You're the old vicar's daughter, aren't you?

Shirley No.

Rose Well, let me see . . .

Shirley It's me, Rose.

Rose Yes.

Shirley *laughs*.

Rose I know the face.

Shirley Shirley.

Rose Shirley? Oh my . . . No! Oh, so it is! Who'd have thought! Oh, I knew I recognised the face. But I just didn . . .

Shirley Haven't got that old, have I?

Rose Old? No. You don't look old. You don't look old at all. It's just, well . . . look at you!

She laughs.

Shirley Stephens. Well I never.

Shirley Thought it was about time to come back and visit the old country.

Rose Yes.

Shirley When I arrived in London everything seemed to have changed so much. But the closer I got to here the more familiar it all started looking.

Rose You driven all the way?

Shirley From Australia?

Rose No, from London. From Australia! That's a good one!

Shirley Be a long drive.

Rose Yes. That's right. It would.

Shirley I got a train to Exeter and hired a car.

Rose Oh yes. Goodness. So have you been here long?

Shirley You remember my uncle, Mr Curtis? He used to be a car breaker.

Rose Oh yes, he moved up to Essex, didn he?

Shirley That's right. I've been staying with him for a couple of weeks.

Rose He's still alive then?

Shirley Oh yes. And Mr Thorne?

Rose What?

Shirley Is he well?

Rose Bill?

Shirley Yes.

Rose Well, we're all getting older.

Shirley Yes.

Rose Where are you staying?

Shirley I was going to try the Red Lion.

Rose The Inn Place it's called now.

Shirley Yes?

Rose You can't stay there.

Shirley Why not?

Rose It's a terrible place. The police are always getting called there.

Shirley Oh dear. I'll need to find somewhere.

Rose Yes.

William *comes to see who has driven up.*

Rose Look who it is, Bill.

Shirley Hello, Mr Thorne.

William How do.

Shirley I knew you'd recognise me.

William Oh yes.

Rose Who is it, then?

William Ummmm.

Rose See, I knew he didn't. It's Shirley.

William Ahhhh.

Rose   Shirley Stephens.

William   Oh!

Rose   Come all the way from Australia.

William   I knew I knew you.

Rose   That's what I said.

Shirley   How are you, Mr Thorne?

William   I can't complain.

Rose   Got a terrible chest.

Shirley   Oh dear.

William   We're all getting older.

Shirley   Yes. Thirty years, you know.

Rose   No.

Shirley   It is.

Rose   Never believe it. Hear that, Bill? Thirty years since she was here.

William   Your mother well?

Shirley   She died.

William   Oh, I'm sorry.

Shirley   In seventy-eight. And Mr Webber, you remember him?

William   Course we do.

Shirley   He died last year. He never got over mum's death.

Rose   Sad.

Shirley   They had some good years. They ran a roadhouse up near Alice Springs.

Rose   Fancy.

Shirley   That building wasn't here before, was it?

Rose   No. We built that a few years after you went to Australia. It's a milking parlour.

Shirley   Thought I didn't recognise it.

Pause.

Rose   She's looking for somewhere to stay, Bill.

William   The Luscombe's do bed and breakfast.

Rose   Oh, I don't think . . .

Shirley   No.

Rose   There's a new place at Haddon Cross. It's a motel.

Shirley   Is it expensive?

Rose   I don't know.

Shirley   Perhaps I could phone them.

Rose   We're not on the phone, dear.

Shirley   Oh.

Rose   We're backward.

She laughs.

Shirley   Don't expect you miss it.

Rose   Don't have telly either.

William   Nearest phone is down at the crossroads.

Shirley   Right.

William   You over here on your own then?

Shirley   My son came with me.

William   Oh.

Shirley   He's stayed in Essex with my uncle.

William   Doesn't he want to see where you used to live?

Shirley   I might bring him down here later. We're here for a month.

Rose   And your husband?

Shirley   Pardon?

Rose   He not with you?

Shirley   No. I uhh, I'm not married.

Pause.

I've got some photos in the car of mum and Mr Webber and places we lived.

William   We'd like to see them, wouldn we, Rose?

Rose   Yes.

William   Kettle on?

Rose   She doesn't want to be too late getting to the motel. They say it's going to snow.

Shirley   Oh dear.

Rose   I've got their number written down cause they buy their eggs off us sometimes. I'll just go and see if I can find it.

She goes.

Shirley *gets out a cigarette.*

Shirley   Would you like one?

William   No thanks. Never smoked.

Shirley   Of course. It's probably these things that killed mum. But I need one after that drive. I learnt to drive in the outback where you can see anything come for miles. Not used to those hedges.

The rooks caw. They look up.

I'd forgotten about the rooks.

William   Oh yes.

Shirley   Your brother . . . Charles . . . used to shoot them.

William   They can be pests.

Shirley   Yes. Is he . . . ?

William   Don't know where he is. Might be down over mending a hedge.

Shirley   Oh. Is he well?

William   Oh, he's all right, yes. He's very well. We're still going down the same old track. Just the ruts have got deeper.

They laugh.

Shirley   Just the three of you?

William   Eh?

Shirley   I just wondered if . . .

William   No, we all stayed single.

Pause.

Shirley   I often used to think about you.

William   Ahhh.

Rose *returns.*

Rose   There you are.

She hands **Shirley** *a piece of paper.*

Shirley   Thank you.

William   Sure you haven't got time for a cup of tea?

Shirley   Rose is right, I'd better check in.

William   But you'll come back?

Shirley   All right.

Rose   Tonight?

Shirley   Or tomorrow.

Rose   Roads will be treacherous.

Shirley *looks at her watch.*

Shirley   I expect you go to bed early.

William   No, no. You come back later. We want to see your photos.

Rose   She'll have to drive all the way back in the dark.

Shirley   I don't want to put you out.

William   We'll save you some food.

Shirley   Thank you.

Charles *enters. He stops.*

Shirley   Good evening.

Charles   Yes.

Rose   Do your trousers up. How many times do I have to tell you?

She goes and pulls up his zip.

Shirley (*she still hasn't recognised* **Charles**)   So where is this motel?

William   Don't you remember Haddon Cross?

Shirley   Ummm . . .

William   Other side of the old aerodrome.

Shirley   Oh, yes.

Charles   That heifer looks like calvin.

William   Shouldn be due yet.

Charles   Her's springin. Got her tail in the air.

Rose   Why haven't you started the engine?

He doesn't answer. They all look at him.

Charles.

Shirley *gasps.*

Rose   It's getting dark. I need some light in the kitchen.

Charles *goes.*

Shirley *looks at them.*

Shirley   I didn't recognise him.

William   No.

Rose   Is there diesel in the engine?

Shirley   Is he . . . he seemed so . . .

Sound of engine starting.

Rose   That's our generator. Got electric now.

Shirley   Yes.

Rose   Tidn mains. But it's good enough for us. Better get that supper on.

William   We're having stew. You like stew, Shirley?

Shirley   Maybe I should leave it for tonight.

William   No, my dear, you come back. Us'll have a good chinwag.

Shirley   I see. Right. Well. I'll see you later.

William   See you later.

Shirley   Bye.

She goes.

Rose   Drive careful.

Shirley (*off*)   I will.

She goes.

The car starts. **William** *and* **Rose** *wave. Headlights cross them.*

William   Bye.

They stop waving.

Rose   What do you think she wants?

William   Eh?

Rose   Must be after something.

William   Don't be daft.

Rose   Coming back here after all these years.

William   Spec she wants to show her son where she was brought up.

Rose   He's not with her though, is he?

Charles *crosses.*

William   He didn't even recognise her.

Rose   Don't you believe it.

Pause.

Don't stay out here getting cold.

She follows **Charles**.

Scene Twelve

The parlour.

Shirley, **William** *and* **Rose** *are laughing. They have been drinking* **Shirley**'s *duty-free Baileys.*

Shirley   And do you remember old Bert who used to come round the village with the baker's van?

William   Oh, yes, Bert Gibson. Come from Crediton way.

Shirley   He only had one arm.

Rose   That was from the Great War.

Shirley   'Want any cakes today, missus?'

Rose/Shirley   'Fresh out the oven.'

They laugh.

Rose   He was our mother's fourth cousin, twice removed.

Shirley   Really?

Rose   Yes, I found that out when I was looking into our family history.

Shirley   Oh.

William   Don't start going on about that.

Rose   Why not?

William   Get her started on family history and you'll never stop her.

Shirley   I used to be scared of him.

Rose   He was harmless.

Shirley   Oh, Rose!

She laughs.

Rose What?

Shirley Can you hear what you just said?

William Ah, that's right. That's right.

Rose What did I say?

William *and* **Shirley** *are laughing.*

Shirley You said he was armless.

Rose Eh? Oh, that's terrible. Oh no! Oh!

She laughs.

That's a good one, Bill. Armless! Oh!

They all laugh.

She was only a baker's daughter but how she kneaded the dough!

William Yeah.

Shirley What?

Rose That was one of dad's jokes.

Shirley Oh, yeah. Here, have some more.

Rose Oh, no. I mustn't, dear. You'll get me drunk.

Shirley *pours some more Baileys in her glass.* **Rose** *gets some papers.*

Rose Here, what do you think of this, Shirley?

Shirley What is it?

William Oh my God!

Rose You be quiet. She'll be interested in this. It's our family tree. I've traced dad's family back to the sixteenth century and mum's back even further.

William The hours she spends on it.

Rose I went through all the church records.

William Spent a fortune writing off to Somerset House in London.

Shirley   It's amazing.

Rose   See this is Bert Gibson's family over here.

William   He's dead now, you know.

Rose   Went out delivering in the rain on the Wednesday. Got pneumonia. Died on the Friday.

Shirley   Oh dear.

Rose   Yes.

Shirley *starts laughing.*

Rose   You're terrible.

They all laugh.

Twadn the cough that carried him off, twas the coffin they carried him off in.

Shirley   Yes, yes.

Rose   That was another of dad's.

The laughter subsides.

Shirley   You still play the organ at church, Mr Thorne?

Rose   No, he doesn't. He doesn't go to church any more.

Shirley   Oh.

Rose   Says he's an atheist.

Shirley   Don't you play at all?

William   No, my dear.

Shirley   That's a shame.

William   I've forgotten.

Rose   Course you haven.

William   What do you know about it?

Rose   All right. All right. See what he gets like, Shirley? Number of times I ask him. He never will.

Shirley   Not even for me, Mr Thorne?

William   I'm too rusty my dear.

Shirley This will oil you up.

She pours some more drink in his glass.

Rose That's a good one.

Shirley We won't mind if you play a few wrong notes.

William Oh, I don't know.

Shirley Just for me?

William *hesitates.*

Rose Go on.

They clear the piano.

William What shall I play?

Rose I don't know.

He starts playing 'Waltzing Matilda'.

William (*sings*) Once a jolly swagman camped by a billabong
Under the shade of a . . .

Shirley Koolaba tree.

Shirley/William And he sang as he watched and waited while his billy boiled
You'll come a-waltzing Matilda with me.
Waltzing Matilda, waltzing Matilda *etc.*

They laugh.

Rose Oh, look at Snowy. She wants to join in. Go on, nosy parker, you know you're not allowed in here.

Shirley Hello, there, puss.

Rose Go on.

She giggles.

That's my little baby.

Shirley She's lovely.

Rose Yes.

William Give us a song then, Rose.

Rose I'm not singing.

William Come on, give us 'The Ash Grove'. You know that one, Shirley?

Shirley I can't remember.

William There, she can't remember it. So you gotta sing it to her.

Rose I can't.

Shirley I remember you having a lovely voice.

Rose Not any more.

William *starts to play.*

William (*sings*) Down yonder green valley
Where streamlets meander . . .

How does it go?

He begins playing the song from the beginning.

Rose *sings.*

Shirley *is thoughtful.*

Charles *enters. He and* **Shirley** *look at one another. Suddenly the others notice him standing at the doorway with his hot water bottle in his hand.* **Rose** *stops singing.*

Rose There you are. Thought you were going to stay out there all night with those rabbits.

Charles Want to fill my bottle.

Rose Put the kettle on and I'll come and do it.

Charles Snowing.

Rose Is it?

Charles Settling too.

Shirley Would you like some of this, Charles?

Charles No thank you.

He goes.

Rose He's been out feeding his rabbits.

William Where's these photos you were going to show us?

Shirley Oh yes.

Rose You won't be able to see anything without your glasses.

William I can see.

Rose What's the point of having them if you never wear them? He's vain, that's what it is, Shirley.

Shirley *gets the photos.*

Shirley That's mum and Mr Webber outside the roadhouse.

Rose It's like a hotel, is it?

Shirley Yes. Right out in the bush. Our nearest neighbour was forty miles away.

Rose Goodness me. Look, Bill.

Shirley That was a party we had for mum's seventieth birthday.

Rose Lot of people.

Shirley And that was a holiday we went on to the Snowy Mountains in Victoria.

Rose Fancy that. Never think of Australia having snow.

Shirley Oh yes.

Rose They very high mountains?

Shirley Only about four thousand feet.

William Thinking of going over there and doing a bit of skiing, are you, Rose?

Shirley People do.

William Imagine Rose trying to walk up there with her arthritis.

He laughs.

Rose   He never thinks I can do anything, Shirley.

William   Tidn true.

Rose   I wanted to go to Austria next year but he won't let me.

William   I'm not stopping you.

Rose   Says we can't afford it. Never afford anything.

William   Wants to go and see the Passion Play with the church.

Shirley   Oh.

Rose   What's wrong with that?

William   Nothing.

Rose   Just because you've stopped believing.

William   What good's going to church ever done you?

Rose   Hear that, Shirley? If mum could hear you running down the church.

William   Pah.

Rose   And dad wouldn't like it.

William   He didn go from one year to the next.

Rose   He believed in God.

Shirley   These are some of Francis. My son. This was one Christmas on the beach when he was ten.

William   Oh yes.

Rose   Let me see.

He hands it to her.

Rose *gasps.*

William   What?

Rose   Nothing. Come on, show me the rest.

Shirley This is him when he was fifteen with some friends of mine.

Rose Where was that taken?

Shirley In a hotel in Sydney. I was working there as a dancer. Those are other women in the troupe.

Rose You kept up your dancing then.

Shirley Yes. That's Frank in his car. He'd just got it. And this is one of me and him and his girlfriend, Laura.

Rose Yes.

Shirley They're getting engaged when we get back.

William You look more like sisters.

Shirley Oh, Mr Thorne, you're such a gentleman.

William You do.

Shirley She's a lovely girl.

William You both are.

Charles *enters.*

Charles Kettle's nearly boiling.

Rose All right.

Charles *goes.* **Rose** *follows him.*

William *is looking at the photo of Francis.*

Shirley *looks at the picture of their father on the wall.*

Shirley He was a handsome man.

William Yeah.

Shirley How old was he there?

William Late twenties?

Shirley Same age as Frank.

William He had a temper mind.

Shirley Yes?

William   When I was a boy I climbed the apple tree in me best trousers and tore em. He took me out in the barn and whipped me with the horsewhip.

Shirley   That's terrible.

William   That's what parents were like in those days.

Shirley   How old were you?

William   Eight or nine.

Shirley   It's barbaric.

William   I deserved it I expect.

Shirley   Well . . .

William   He was preparing us for a hard life.

Shirley   Farming?

William   Yes.

Shirley   But you wanted to go to music college, didn't you?

William   You get daft ideas when you're young.

Shirley   You don't regret not going?

William   No point regretting anything, is it?

Shirley   No.

William   You can't escape your fate.

Shirley   What?

William   That's what I've come to believe, Shirley. Some people are born to happiness. Some aren't.

Shirley   Maybe.

William   You was one that was born to happiness.

Shirley   Was I?

William   Bet you haven't got many regrets.

Shirley   It's not all been plain sailing, Mr Thorne.

William   No?

Shirley It was hard work. Specially when Frank was small. It was just me and him. We were on the road a lot. But there were compensations.

William Yeah?

Shirley The girls, all the other dancers, got on well. It was like being in a family really. Frank had lots of aunties.

William Ahhhhh.

Rose *enters.*

Rose He says that heifer's not looking too good.

William What's wrong with it?

Rose Just lying there, he says.

William Better get out and have a look.

Rose You wrap up, it's snowing.

Shirley I should be going.

William You stay there. We won't be a minute.

Rose *and* **William** *go.*

Shirley *walks to the photo of the father on the wall. She has a photo of Frank. She covers the bottom half of the face and compares the eyes on the two photos.*

Charles *appears in the doorway.*

Charles I knew you as soon as I saw ee.

Shirley Did you?

Charles Yeah. Never forget a face.

Shirley It's a long time.

Charles They say you been living in Australia all this time.

Shirley That's right.

Charles I know a bloke who went to Australia.

Shirley Really?

Charles Archie.

Shirley Oh yes.

Charles Archie Blackmore. He lives near Perth.

Shirley That's Western Australia.

Charles Went out there sheep-shearing.

Shirley I see.

Charles Tall bloke. Bit cross-eyed.

Shirley Ah.

Charles You never come across him?

Shirley Uh, it's a big country.

Charles Might be dead by now. Fair few years ago.

Pause.

Shirley You sure you wouldn't like some of this?

Charles What is it?

Shirley It's whiskey and cream.

Charles Whiskey and cream in a bottle?

Shirley Yes.

Charles Caw!

Shirley Would you like some?

Charles Don't know.

Shirley Here.

She pours him a glass.

He smells it.

Tastes nice. Honestly.

He tastes it tentatively.

Well?

Charles Yeah.

She smiles.

They tell you about me rabbits?

Shirley   Your rabbits?

Charles   Yeah, I breed em.

Shirley   Oh.

Charles   Won a prize at the Flower Show with me chinchilla.

Shirley   That's good.

Charles   I got quite few rosettes.

Shirley   Great.

Charles   Thing about showing rabbits is you gotta look after em. Keep em clean.

Shirley   I'm sure.

Charles   Then you have to shampoo em before the show.

Shirley   Really?

Charles   Yeah, it's quite an art mind.

Pause.

What's the photos?

Shirley   Pictures of Australia. My mum.

Charles   Can I have some more of that drink?

Shirley   Help yourself.

Charles   Funny stuff, idn it?

Shirley   Would you like to see them?

Charles   What?

Shirley   The photos.

Charles   I'm not one for looking at photos.

Shirley   This is my son. Francis.

She hands him a photo.

Charles *looks at it.*

Charles   Yeah, I won second prize for me chinchilla and got a special commendation for me New Zealand white.

Shirley   Great.

Rose *enters.*

Rose   Thought you'd gone to bed.

Charles   I'm on me way.

Rose   How many of those have you had?

Charles   This is my first.

Rose   Did you ask?

Charles   Course I bloody asked. You bloody fool.

Rose   That's enough of that.

He finishes his drink and leaves the room.

Tidn good for him to get drunk.

Shirley   Oh, I don't think –

Rose   He started going down the pub a few years ago. I had to put a stop to it.

Shirley   I see.

Rose   It's his temperament you see.

Shirley   Yes?

Rose   Always been highly strung. They had to give him that electric shock treatment when he was in the hospital. Depressed, you see, so they had to shake him out of it.

Shirley   When was that?

Rose   Back in fifty-five.

Shirley   I see.

Pause.

Rose   Good job he didn't have children, isn't it?

Shirley   How do you mean?

Rose   Might have passed it on.

William *returns. He has snow in his hair.*

Rose   Look at you, I told you to put your hat on.

William *doesn't respond.*

Rose   Well?

William   Don't know.

Rose   Gonna be all right though, idn it?

William (*snaps*)   I don't know.

Pause.

Shirley   I ought to be going.

William   Hope you can get through to Haddon Cross.

Rose   The grit lorry will have been out.

William   Not on the road down to the village.

Shirley   I'll be all right.

William   We could light a fire in the back bedroom, put you up for the night.

Shirley   It's OK.

Rose   I'll show you out. Where did you leave the torch, Bill?

William   Kitchen table.

Shirley   It's OK.

Rose   It's dark out in that yard. Don't want you slipping up. Anyway I gotta come and switch off the generator.

She goes.

Shirley   Well . . .

William   Yes.

Shirley   It's been lovely to see you again, Mr Thorne.

William   And you, my dear. And you.

Shirley   I'm going to take a look round the village tomorrow.

William   Come up and see us.

Shirley   All right. Night, then.

He plays the piano.

William   Good night, Irene, good night, Irene.
  I'll see you in my dreams.

She kisses him on the cheek.

Rose *enters with an unlit candle and the torch.*

Rose   Here's your candle.

Shirley *and* **Rose** *go.*

William *plays the piano – something classical he learnt as a boy.*

The lights go off. (**Rose** *has turned off the generator.)*

William *continues playing.*

Rose *returns with her own candle.*

Rose   Haven't you lit it?

She lights **William**'s *candle.*

She goes and gets **William**'s *medicine and pours it out in a spoon.*

Rose   Here.

He opens his mouth and she gives it to him.

Get the vet in the morning for that heifer.

William *doesn't respond.*

Rose   Come on.

She hands him his candle.

William *stops playing, closes the piano and takes the candle.*

William   She's left one of her photos.

He picks up the photo of Frank. He starts to get his glasses out.

Suddenly **Rose** *snatches the photo from him.*

Rose   No.

William   What?

Rose   I know what you're thinking.

William   I'm not thinking anything.

Rose   Nice little trap she's laid and you're falling straight in it.

William   Don't be daft.

Rose   I'm not the one that's daft. He could be anybody's kid.

William   You can see the likeness then, can you?

Rose   You never saw her for what she was.

William   What you mean?

Rose   She's a scheming bitch.

William   Rose.

Rose   I've got a long memory, William Thorne. I remember how you looked at her that Christmas Charles brought her here. And I saw the very same look in your eyes tonight. When was the last time you played the piano for anybody? 'Irene, good night, Irene.' I heard you. And I saw your eye wandering all over her body.

William   You're bloody mad.

Rose   She's pulled the wool over your eyes good and proper.

William   There's no wool over my eyes.

Rose   Well, if there idn, let's get that paper signed and this farm sold so we don't get into any more debt. Then we can go and live in a bit of comfort in our last few years.

William   I don't mind signing the forms.

Rose   So why haven't you? And now you're going to have second thoughts, aren't you? Think you might be able to leave it to your nephew, do you? Just cause that tramp can wind you round her little finger. It's disgusting. An old man like you!

William *goes and gets the papers.*

William   Get me the pen!

Rose *hesitates.*

William   Go on! What you waiting for?

Rose *still doesn't move.*

William   There's usually one in here on the mantelpiece. Where's the bloody pen, woman?

Rose   Keep your voice down.

William   You're telling me I'm wavering about selling this place. Just give me the pen and I'll sign it.

Rose   That one doesn't write.

William   Well, find me one that does. Go on! Where do you keep your pen? In here? No. In here? Ahhhh, here we are. Now hold the candle so I can see.

Rose   William, you'll tear it.

William   Hold it!

He takes her wrist and brings it close in order to illuminate the paper.

Rose   You're hurting me.

He signs the paper.

William   Now you.

Rose   What's the point?

William   Eh?

Rose   We've still got to get Charles's signature.

William   Soon do that. Come on! Sign!

She hesitates.

Ahhhhh! Scared, are you? Take the pen!

Rose   I'm not doing it tonight like this.

William *throws the paper at her.*

Knock at the door.

Shirley (*off*)   Hello? Haven't gone to bed, have you?

Rose *goes through to the kitchen.*

Shirley *enters the kitchen.*

Shirley   Got stuck in the lane.

Rose   Oh dear.

Shirley   I don't think I'll be able to get out tonight.

William (*from the parlour*)   Get that fire lit in the back bedroom, Rose.

Rose *smiles at* **Shirley**.

Scene Thirteen

The kitchen.

The Baileys has been put on the mantelpiece together with the paper from the auctioneers. **Charles** *enters and helps himself to the Baileys. He sees the papers and reads them. He hears someone coming and hides with the Baileys.*

Rose *enters. Sits. She is crying and wipes her eyes.*

William *enters with a half-plucked white chicken.* **Rose** *blows her nose.*

Rose   It's old, this one. Be tough.

She starts plucking the chicken.

How long do you think it had been dead?

William   The calf?

Rose   Yes.

William   Week or so.

Rose   Least we've got it out now.

William   Ahhh.

Rose   Will the heifer be all right?

William *doesn't answer.*

Rose   She doesn't look too good. Better call the vet.

William *stares into space.*

Rose (*sings*)　Breathe on me breath of God,
　Fill me with life anew –

William　Where's Shirley?

Rose　How do I know?

William　All right.

Rose　Shirley this. Shirley that. I'm fed up with it. Going
and pulling the neck of one of my best layers just so Shirley can
have chicken for dinner. You should be thinking about how
we're going to pay the interest at the bank now we've lost that
calf.

William　Thought you wanted to sell up. All you gotta do,
Rose, is sign that bit of paper.

Rose *doesn't answer.*

William　It's there.

No response.

You know what dad would want.

Rose　What?

William　If there was someone to pass it on to.

Rose *says nothing.*

William　If dad thought he had a grandson to carry on
farming the place then he'd want him to have it.

No response.

Wouldn't he?

Rose　He's a gyppo.

William　Then sign that bit of paper if that's what you feel.
You want to cut your nose off to spite your face then do it,
Rose.

He goes.

Rose *wipes her eyes.*

Rose (*sings*)　Breathe on me breath of God.
　Until my heart is pure.

Until with Thee I will one will
To do and to endure.

Shirley *enters.*

Rose Just picking this hen. William's pulled its neck in your honour. Said we ought to have something special for dinner.

Shirley You don't have to worry about me.

Beat.

How's the calf?

Rose Dead.

Shirley Oh no.

Rose Been dead a week, Bill reckons. He's worried about the heifer. Thinks it might not survive.

Shirley You called the vet?

Rose Not yet.

Pause.

Shirley The car won't start.

Rose No?

Shirley I went down to the phone box.

Rose Oh yes?

Shirley To talk to the car hire people. I have to phone them back tomorrow morning. They can't get out here until the roads are cleared.

Pause.

Always remember plucking the geese and turkeys for Christmas.

Rose Yes.

Shirley You used to have about ten women doing it, didn't you? Everyone laughing and joking.

Rose We haven't done that for years. Can't compete. All factory farming now. We been left behind.

Rose *cries.*

Shirley You all right?

Rose This hen's old. Have to boil it.

Shirley You all right, Rose?

Rose We were banking on that calf. We got interest to pay at the bank.

Shirley Did you borrow money?

Rose We had a run of bad luck. The milk marketing people wouldn't take our milk because we weren't on mains. So we borrowed some money from the bank to get mains laid on and build a new milking parlour. Then the very next year we had an outbreak of foot and mouth. All the cattle had to be slaughtered and burnt. We never recovered our losses. So we still owe the bank and we could never afford to build up the herd again. Hasn't been used for years that milking parlour. Just sits there. Don't know what dad would say.

Shirley You did your best.

Rose It wadn good enough.

She cries.

Shirley Rose. Rose.

Rose It's all we know, this place. It's all we know.

Rose *sobs.* **Shirley** *holds her.*

William *enters.*

William (*not unkindly*) Look at you, you silly old thing.

Rose Leave me alone.

She goes.

Shirley *gets up to follow her.*

William You'd better leave her.

Pause.

Shirley   I'm sorry about the calf.

William   It's the heifer I'm worried about.

Shirley *nods*.

Shirley   What are you going to do?

William   Rose had some daft idea about us moving into Mornacott Cottage. We'd spend the rest of our lives looking out the window at the churchyard waiting for the day when they take us in there and bury us.

Shirley   Is it a lot of money you owe?

William   Well, no, it idn really.

Pause.

I went up the attic this morning.

Shirley   Oh yes?

William   Found this.

Shirley   What is it?

He gives her the ring.

William   It's been up there in an old tea box for years. Sort of thing you come across when you're looking for a collar-stud or a button. Thought you should have it.

Shirley   But it's his.

William   He hasn't looked at it for years. Probably thinks it's lost. Your son could give it to his girlfriend. As an engagement ring.

Shirley   I couldn't.

William   He won't miss it.

She holds the ring.

Shirley   You know, don't you?

William   What?

Shirley   About Frank. Who his father is.

William   Yes.

Rose *hears this as she enters. They look at her.*

William   You all right?

Rose   Course I am.

Pause.

William   He looks like our dad.

Shirley   I thought that.

William   What does he do?

Shirley   He works night shift in a car factory.

William   Ahhh.

Shirley   But he doesn't like it. He wants a change.

William   I see.

Shirley   But he hasn't got any qualifications. That's my fault. We travelled around so much. So his schoolwork suffered. I can't help him out. I was never one for saving money. And I can't dance any more.

William   So you thought you'd come and look us up?

Shirley   Well I . . .

William   You think he'd make a farmer?

Shirley   He's a good boy. Hardworking.

Rose *is listening. Picking the hen.*

William   We haven't got anybody else to leave the farm to. Our branch of the tree hadn got any more shoots on it has it, Rose?

Rose   This chicken's gone cold. I can't get the feathers out.

William   Why don't you bring him down to see us?

Shirley (*looking at* **Rose**)   Well, I don't want to . . .

William   Rose?

Rose   Yes. Bring him down.

William *and* **Shirley** *smile at her.*

William   You could scald it. Then the feathers'll come out.

Rose   Mmm.

He goes to try and help her.

Rose   Get off, Bill.

She throws some feathers at him by mistake. He laughs.

William   Get off yourself.

He picks some out and throws them back.

Rose   Stop it. Honestly!

Shirley *picks up a handful of feathers from the floor.*

Shirley (*threatening*)   Leave her alone, Mr Thorne.

Rose   Go on, Shirley.

Shirley *throws the feathers at* **William**. *They all laugh.*

Rose   Go and get the bucket.

He goes whistling 'Waltzing Matilda'. **Shirley** *and* **Rose** *look at each other. They laugh at* **William**'s *whistling.*

William (*off*)   Come on then.

Rose *and* **Shirley** *go to the scullery.*

William (*off*)   Just dip it in the water.

(*Sings.*) And he sang as he watched and waited while his billy boiled.

Rose/William/Shirley (*sing*)   You'll come a-waltzing, Matilda, with me.

They all laugh. **Charles** *has emerged from his hiding place and listens.*

Scene Fourteen

The rabbit shed. Rosettes are pinned up.

Charles *is looking into his rabbit hutch and stroking the rabbit inside.*

Rose *enters.*

Rose   The dinner's nearly ready.

No answer.

Charles.

No response.

Aren't you coming in for your dinner?

Still no response.

I gave them some cabbage leaves this afternoon.

No response.

Is that the one that won the rosette at the show?

Charles   This is Esau.

Rose   Is he the one?

Charles   What?

Rose   The one that got the prize?

Charles   That was his father, Isaac.

Rose   Don't know what the vicar would say about you giving them names from the Bible.

Charles   He's got more fur, that's why.

Rose   That's why what?

Charles   That's why he's called Esau.

Rose   What you mean?

Charles   Esau was a hairy man.

Rose   That's right, he was.

Pause.

Got to talk to you, Charlie.

Charles   I'm feeding me rabbits.

Rose   It's important though.

Charles   How much longer is she staying?

Rose   Who?

Charles Her.

Rose Shirley?

Charles Yes.

Rose She's waiting for them to bring her another car from Exeter.

Charles Mmm.

Rose Charles, we been talking.

Charles Who?

Rose Me and Bill.

Charles What about?

Rose Bout the farm. Bout how it's too much for us. If something doesn't happen soon we're going to lose the place.

Pause.

Need someone young to help us.

Charles Stephen Warren.

Rose Eh?

Charles He's young. He used to work for Luscombes but they don't need him no more because Michael Luscombe's left school.

Rose We can't afford to pay wages. We need someone young to pass the farm onto.

Charles We haven't got anybody.

William *enters.*

William You give that heifer any water?

Rose I haven't.

William (*to* **Charles**) Have you?

Charles *picks up the rabbit's bowl and goes.*

William Hasn't touched any of the cake we gave her.

Pause.

Sittin out here with the rabbits when we got a heifer that might die.

Rose I was trying to get him to come in for his dinner.

William Let him starve if he wants to.

He sees the photo in her hands.

What's that?

Rose I thought I'd try and talk to him.

William What about?

Rose This boy. Frank, whatever his name is.

William No point talking to him about it.

Rose He'd have to want it.

William Don't be so bloody daft. What's the point of talking to him? You drive me bloody mad.

Rose We couldn't just go ahead without getting Charles to agree.

William Course he's going to agree. It's his son, isn't it?

Charles *returns with water for the rabbits.*

William Here, Charlie.

Charles *ignores him.*

William We got some news for you.

No response.

Now listen. You got a son. In Australia.

Rose Bill!

William He's going to come over here and help us run this place, see.

Rose Stop it, Bill. Let me talk to him.

They look at **Charles** *who is still busy with his rabbits.*

Charles.

No response.

Charles. He's a nice-looking boy.

William *grabs the photo from* **Rose***'s hand.*

William   Here, Charlie. Look at this.

Charles   I don't want to see it.

William   Don't be so bloody daft. See, this is what you get for trying to talk to him.

Shirley (*off*)   Hello! Where are you?

They look at each other.

(*Off.*) Hello? Rose? Mr Thorne?

William   Here we are, Shirley.

Charles   I haven't got a son.

William   You have. Shut up!

Shirley *enters.*

Shirley   The potatoes are done.

Rose   We're coming.

Shirley   Oh, are these your rabbits?

Charles *doesn't answer.*

Shirley   Isn't he magnificent?

Rose   That's Esau because he's hairy.

Rose *laughs.*

Shirley   Pardon?

Rose   Don't you remember the story of Jacob and Esau?

Shirley   Oh yes.

Charles   I want my ring back.

Rose   What ring? What are you talking about?

Charles   He gave her my ring.

Rose   What's he talking about, Bill?

Charles   Give it back to me.

William   You shut your mouth.

Charles   Come on.

Shirley   It's indoors.

Charles   I want it back.

William   You watch yourself. We'll get you committed. The doctor will send you back to that mental hospital.

Charles   Give me back my ring. I know what you're up to. All of you. You didn't want it thirty years ago so you can't have it now. Give it back.

William (*to* **Rose**)   This is your bloody fault. Coming out here talking to him as if he was normal. He's your son, you daft bugger.

Charles   I haven got a son.

William   Course you have.

Charles   Her's lying.

Shirley   Charles?

Charles   What?

Shirley   Please.

Charles   Please? Please what? Please yourself. That's what you did. With whoever you wanted. Except me. We never did it. So he can't be mine. He's Tommy Youings' son. That's who's son he is. Not mine. Everybody knew she was a bloody whore.

William *struggles with him.*

Rose   Bill.

Charles *throws him off.*

Shirley   He's your son, Charles.

Charles   Give me back my ring.

Shirley *goes.*

Charles   He idn my son.

William   He's doing this to spite us.

Charles   You'll never know, will you?

He goes.

William   There's tests they can do.

Rose   We can't force him to make the farm over.

William   We can get the doctor to say he idn fit though.

Rose   No.

William   What?

Rose   I'm not going to make him do anything.

Pause.

Perhaps this is our retribution.

William   What's that supposed to mean?

Rose   For what we did to him.

William   We didn't do anything to him.

Rose   Don't get yourself worked up.

William   You're enough to try the patience of a bloody saint.

Rose   It wouldn be right to do anything against his wishes.

She goes. **William** *throws his hat on the floor and stamps on it.*

Scene Fifteen

The Ash Grove.

Shirley *is standing, looking.*

William *enters.*

William   Ahhhh.

Shirley   You shouldn't come out here with your cough.

William   I'm all right.

Shirley   Why aren't you with the vet?

William   I know what he's going to say.

Rooks. They look up.

They always gather here before they go and roost over in the rookery.

Pause.

Look . . .

Shirley   Yes.

William   Bring him here.

Shirley   No.

William   They'd have to come round in the end.

Pause.

Shirley   This is where it happened, you know. What he said didn't happen.

William   Covered in bluebells in the spring.

Shirley   I remember.

William   The Venus of the Woods.

Shirley   Pardon.

William   That's what they call the ash.

Shirley   Oh.

William   Very useful wood, ash.

Shirley   Yes.

William   Used to make all the implements out of ash.

Shirley   Really?

William   Not any more.

Pause.

Wouldn't he like to be given the chance?

Shirley   What?

William   Your boy. To run this place.

Shirley   No, Mr Thorne.

William   Why not?

Shirley   This is no life for him. He's an Australian. He belongs in the sun. I don't want him to – I think it would be hard for him.

William   With Charlie?

Shirley   Yes.

Pause.

He'll be all right. He'll find his way.

William   Dad used to keep the Ash Grove immaculate. Every year we used to come out and harvest a few trees. You had to thin em out see. They can't grow properly if they're too close.

Rose (*off*)   William!

Shirley *goes to move.* **William** *puts his finger over his lips.*

Rose   William!

William   You think you'll ever come back?

Shirley   No, probably not. I shouldn't have come this time. You can't go back.

William   That was your fate, you see, to leave.

Shirley   Maybe.

William   And this farm was ours. Now it's draggin us back into the earth.

Shirley   You mustn't give up.

William   I sit out here sometimes. Think about the world. How it's changed in my lifetime. But things don't get better, do they?

Shirley   Don't they?

William   Bombs. Wars. Just gets worse.

Shirley   Maybe.

William   Only comfort I can find is that it's probably all happened before and will happen again. Endless circles going round and round. A world comes into being. People evolve. Civilisation. Then we destroy it all, blow it all up. And it all starts up again.

Shirley *says nothing.*

William   Stands to reason.

Shirley   You don't have to think like that, you know.

William   People invent reasons for carrying on, like Rose with her family tree and her church and her God. But they're just deluding themselves.

Shirley   There's always hope.

William   Hope?

Shirley   Anything could be round the corner.

William (*holding up his palm*)   What does it say here?

She smiles.

Too late for me to turn any corners.

Shirley   My mum always said it's never too late to start again.

Pause.

William   I'll see him all right, your son. Once we get this place sold. He can expect a little windfall.

Shirley   You don't have to.

William   I want to.

Rose *enters with the gun.*

Rose   There you are.

William   What do you want?

Rose   The vet was going to put that heifer down but I said we'd see to that. Are you going to do it or shall I?

William I'll do it.

William *goes*.

Rose You see the man from the car hire?

Shirley Yes.

Rose He says the plugs are damp. He's trying to fix it.

Shirley I'm ready when he is.

Rose You be careful on those roads. They're still icy.

Shirley I will.

Rose You going back to Essex?

Shirley Yes.

Rose To your uncle.

Shirley Yes. He's going to come to Australia for the wedding.

Rose Old Mr Curtis?

Shirley Yes.

Rose Fancy him going all that way at his age.

Gunshot.

Oh dear.

Shirley It's a shame.

Charles *enters*.

Rose Go on, Charles.

Charles *starts to go*.

Shirley Here.

She takes out the ring.

Take it. He shouldn't have given it to me. It's yours.

Charles Thank you.

Shirley I'm leaving, Charles. I won't be back again.

Pause.

William *returns.*

William   That bloke's got your car going.

Shirley   Right, well.

Rose   Mind that black ice.

Shirley   I will.

She goes to kiss **Rose**. **Rose** *puts her hand out.*

Charles   Thank you.

William *and* **Shirley** *go.*

Charles *looks at the ring.*

Sound of car starting.

Rose   It's started this time.

Sound of car departing.

She has the auctioneer's papers in her pocket.

Charlie?

Charles   What?

Rose   We got these papers from the auctioneer's.

Charles   Oh yes?

Rose   It's to let him put the farm up for sale.

Charles   I see.

William *returns.*

Rose   We'll all have to sign it.

Charles   Then what'll us do?

Rose   We can go and live in Mornacott Cottage. Look, I've signed it.

Charles   I'm not signing anything.

Rose   Charles.

Charles   You didn't want to sell it thirty years ago. I don't want to sell it now.

Rose   We'll end up losing everything.

Charles   You can't make me. This is our home.

Rose *looks at* **William**.

Rooks.

Charles   You got any money?

Rose   What for?

Charles   I want to go to Hatherleigh. There's a rabbit breeder going to be at the market.

Rose   You should save your money.

Charles   I don't get paid.

Rose   I haven't got any.

Charles   Can't you let me have some of the egg money?

Rose   We need that.

Charles   Just a couple of quid.

Rose   This is the last time mind.

She gets her purse.

William *aims at the sky and shoots at the rooks. He reloads.*

Charles   Look at him. Begrudge it to me, do you, you old miser?

Rose   Charles!

Charles   He thought he'd found somebody to hand it all on to. You hadn't though, had you, you daft old bugger!

Rose   Here take it.

Charles *looks at* **William** *in triumph.*

Rooks. They look up.

Rose   There's Snowy. Hello, my darling. I'm coming.

Suddenly **William** *aims the gun at* **Charles**.

Blackout.

Two gunshots.

Sound of birds flying away. **William** *reloads.*

A third gunshot.

Lights up on the bodies lying on the ground like bundles of old rags.

It is snowing.

The lights fade.

For a Complete Catalogue of Methuen Drama titles
write to:

Methuen Drama
Michelin House
81 Fulham Road
London SW3 6RB